"Robin S. Brown, the editor of this important, eru[...] pare the contributions of Freud and Jung, including [...] some relational thinkers along the way, hoping thro[...] come the rift between these two protagonists and their respective theories. Brown, as do I, believes that this is an auspicious time for more openness between these two camps, evidenced by Jungians and contemporary psychoanalysts appearing more often on each other's respective conference panels. Undoubtedly, movement from the hegemony of the classical model to a pluralism of models within contemporary psychoanalysis, as well as the opening of Jungians to these contemporary trends, has made this détente possible. I find this volume to be unusually informative and highly recommend it to all levels of mental health professionals and to lay persons interested in this subject matter."

James L. Fosshage, Ph.D., Co-founder, Board Director and Faculty Member of the National Institute for the Psychotherapies and Clinical Professor of Psychology for the New York University Postdoctoral Program in Psychotherapy and Psychoanalysis, USA

"For over a century the schools of depth psychology that developed out of the break between Freud and Jung have been characterized by mutual suspicion, while at the same time often consciously or unconsciously adopting principles and practices from one another. The essays collected by Robin Brown in this volume have set as their objective an assessment of the break between Freud and Jung, the implications of their theories for the mutual development of depth psychology and the variety of hitherto obscured connections that already exist. This is a long overdue project, but one that is admirably fulfilled by this group of psychoanalysts and analytical psychologists. The essays range from the impact of the organizational structures of Freud's Wednesday Group and the Burghölzli Hospital on the origins of psychoanalysis to Lacan's *object a* and Jung's anima, covering a host of issues central to understanding what happened to depth psychology at its beginning, and providing essential insights into how the project originally envisioned at that time may yet go forward. This collection of thought-provoking, deeply researched papers is highly recommended."

George B. Hogenson, Ph.D., Vice President of the International Association for Analytical Psychology, and author of *Jung's Struggle with Freud*, USA

"I have always felt that the tragic theoretical split between Freud and Jung left a dissociative gap from which our field of psychoanalysis has been struggling to recover ever since. The stimulating essays in Robin Brown's *Re-Encountering Jung* are a significant contribution toward the healing of that rift. What's more, they are exciting to read, and contribute to the hope that a united psychoanalysis will be a stronger and more integrated voice on behalf of the human soul. I highly recommend this book!"

Donald E. Kalsched, Ph.D., author of *The Inner World of Trauma* and *Trauma and the Soul* (both Routledge), USA

"The acrimonious separation of Freud and Jung in early 1913 fostered divisions between psychoanalysis and analytical psychology that persist to this day, and which, until recently, have largely prevented a mutually beneficial dialogue between these disciplines. This collection of stimulating essays is a timely and significant contribution that explores the fertile common ground and creative differences between a number of approaches to the psychology of the unconscious, carefully illuminating historical points of division and issues of contemporary relevance, both theoretical and therapeutic. Readers will come away from this book enriched and energized by the ideas under discussion, and inspired by the contributors' endeavors to bring forth a more integral understanding of the field."

Keiron Le Grice, Ph.D., Chair of the Jungian and Archetypal Studies specialization, Pacifica Graduate Institute, USA

"This collection of divergent essays is a most welcome and timely contribution to a long overdue dialogue among various schools of depth psychology. Comparative studies are not easy, and the care taken by the authors here is exemplary. Robin Brown is to be applauded for initiating this important step in the further development of the field of psychoanalysis."

Murray Stein, Ph.D., past President of the International Association for Analytical Psychology, and author of *Jung's Map of the Soul*, Switzerland

RE-ENCOUNTERING JUNG

Since the split between Freud and Jung, psychoanalysis and analytical psychology have largely developed in an atmosphere of mutual disregard. Only in recent years have both discourses shown signs of an increasing willingness to engage. *Re-Encountering Jung: Analytical Psychology and Contemporary Psychoanalysis* is the first edited volume devoted to a reconciliation between these two fields. The contributors explore how Jungian thinking influences, challenges and is challenged by recent developments in the psychoanalytic mainstream. In examining the nature of the split, figures from both sides of the conversation seek to establish lines of contrast and commonality so as to reflect an underlying belief in the value of reciprocal engagement.

Each of the chapters in this collection engages the relationship between Jungian and psychoanalytic thinking with the intention of showing how both lines of discourse might have something to gain from attending more to the voice of the other. While several of the contributing authors offer new perceptions on historical concerns, the main thrust of the collection is in exploring contemporary debates.

Re-Encountering Jung reflects a unique undertaking to address one of the longest-standing and most significant rifts in the history of depth psychology. It will be of great interest to all academics, students and clinicians working within the fields of psychoanalysis and analytical psychology.

Robin S. Brown, PhD, LP, NCPsyA, is a psychoanalyst in private practice and a member of adjunct faculty for the Counseling and Clinical Psychology Department at Teachers College, Columbia University, USA. He is the author of *Psychoanalysis Beyond the End of Metaphysics: Thinking Towards the Post-Relational* (Routledge).

RE-ENCOUNTERING JUNG

Analytical Psychology and Contemporary Psychoanalysis

Edited by Robin S. Brown

Routledge
Taylor & Francis Group

LONDON AND NEW YORK

First published 2018
by Routledge
2 Park Square, Milton Park, Abingdon, Oxon OX14 4RN

and by Routledge
711 Third Avenue, New York, NY 10017

Routledge is an imprint of the Taylor & Francis Group, an informa business

British Library Cataloguing in Publication Data
A catalogue record for this book is available from the British Library

Library of Congress Cataloging-in-Publication Data
Names: Brown, Robin S.
Title: Re-encountering Jung : analytical psychology and contemporary psychoanalysis / Robin S. Brown.
Description: New York : Routledge, 2017. | Includes index.
Identifiers: LCCN 2017016968| ISBN 9781138225336 (hardback) | ISBN 9781138225343 (pbk.) | ISBN 9781315400181 (ebk)
Subjects: LCSH: Psychoanalysis.
Classification: LCC BF173 .B836 2017 | DDC 150.19/54—dc23
LC record available at https://lccn.loc.gov/2017016968

ISBN: 978-1-138-22533-6 (hbk)
ISBN: 978-1-138-22534-3 (pbk)
ISBN: 978-1-315-40018-1 (ebk)

Typeset in Bembo
by Deanta Global Publishing Services, Chennai, India
Printed and bound by CPI Group (UK) Ltd, Croydon, CR0 4YY

CONTENTS

LIST OF CONTRIBUTORS

Barnaby B. Barratt, PhD, DHS, is a Radical Psychoanalyst, Somatic Psychologist, Sexuality Consultant and Practitioner of Tantric Meditation. Formerly Professor of Family Medicine, Psychiatry and Behavioral Sciences at Wayne State University (Detroit), he is now Senior Research Associate at the Wits Institute for Social and Economic Research, University of Witwatersrand in Johannesburg. Among his more recent books are *Liberating Eros* (Xlibris, 2009), *The Emergence of Somatic Psychology and Bodymind Therapy* (Palgrave Macmillan, 2010), *What Is Psychoanalysis?* (Routledge, 2013) and *Radical Psychoanalysis* (Routledge, 2016).

Paul Bishop is William Jacks Chair in Modern Languages at the University of Glasgow. He has worked on different aspects of Jung's analytical psychology from varying intellectual historical perspectives, publishing articles, book contributions and monographs on this area. His most recent book is *On the Blissful Islands: Nietzsche and Jung in the Shadow of the Superman* (Routledge).

Robin S. Brown, PhD, LP, NCPsyA, is a Psychoanalyst and a Member of Adjunct Faculty for the Counseling and Clinical Psychology Department at Teachers College, Columbia University. He is a Member of the Editorial Board for *Psychoanalysis, Culture, and Society*. His academic work has been published widely and spans the disciplines of psychoanalysis, Jungian psychology and transpersonal theory. His first book, *Psychoanalysis Beyond the End of Metaphysics: Thinking Towards the Post-Relational*, was published by Routledge in 2016.

Warren Colman is a Training and Supervising Analyst for the Society of Analytical Psychology and Consultant Editor of the *Journal of Analytical Psychology*. He teaches, lectures and supervises internationally and has published many papers on diverse topics, including couple interaction, sexuality, the self, symbolic imagination, synchronicity and the therapeutic process. His book *Act and Image: The Emergence of Symbolic Imagination* was published in 2016.

Angela Connolly, MD, is a Psychiatrist and Jungian Analyst in private practice in Rome, Italy. She is an Analyst of CIPA with training and supervisory functions, a member of the training commission and a faculty member. She lived and worked as an Analyst in Russia for five years from 1996 to 2001. Previously Deputy Editor (Europe) of the *Journal of Analytical Psychology*, she is currently a Member of the Editorial Advisory Board. She was a Member of the Executive Committee of the International Association for Analytical Psychology from 2004 to 2010 and at present is the Honorary Secretary. She has published widely in English, Italian and Russian.

Marcia D.-S. Dobson, PhD, is a Professor of Classics and Psychoanalysis at Colorado College, located in Colorado Springs, where she maintains a private practice in psychoanalytic and relationally oriented self psychology. She is presently the Co-Chair of the American Psychoanalytic Association Committee on Undergraduate Education and is a Contributing and Associate Editor of *Psychoanalysis, Self and Context*.

David Henderson, PhD, is Senior Lecturer in Psychoanalysis at the Centre for Psychoanalysis, Middlesex University. He is a Member of the Association of Independent Psychotherapists. He is a Convener of the Jung/Lacan Research Network and a regular discussant at the Jung/Lacan Dialogues. His research interests include the conditions for comparing psychoanalytic theories; the Freud/Jung relationship; and psychoanalysis and religion.

R.D. Hinshelwood is Professor in the Centre for Psychoanalytic Studies, University of Essex, and previously Clinical Director for the Cassel Hospital, London. He is a fellow of the British Psychoanalytical Society and a Fellow of the Royal College of Psychiatrists. He is the author of *A Dictionary of Kleinian Thought*, and in 2013 he published *Research on the Couch: Single Case Studies, Subjectivity and Psychoanalytic Knowledge*, which developed out of his interest in the divergent nature of psychoanalytic theorizing.

David Sedgwick, PhD, is a Jungian Analyst in private practice in Charlottesville, Virginia. He is the author of numerous papers and books on analytical psychology, including *Jung and Searles: A Comparative Study* (1993), *The Wounded Healer: Countertransference from a Jungian Perspective* (1994), *Introduction to Jungian Psychotherapy: The Therapeutic Relationship* (2002) and *Jungian Analysis and Relational Psychoanalysis: A Selective Integration* (forthcoming). He is currently Co-Editor in Chief of the *Journal of Analytical Psychology*.

Mary Tennes, PhD, is a graduate of the Psychoanalytic Institute of Northern California in San Francisco and is in private practice in Berkeley, California. She is currently a Supervisor and Faculty Member at The Psychotherapy Institute in Berkeley and has taught extensively at graduate programs in the Bay Area. Her writing and teaching have focused on the challenges of integrating, within a psychoanalytic framework, the often uncanny, mysterious and disruptive dimensions of psychoanalytic work that are not yet clearly conceptualized within its language and theory.

Marcus West is a Training Analyst of the Society of Analytical Psychology. He is the author of three books, *Feeling, Being and the Sense of Self, Understanding Dreams in Clinical Practice* and *Into the Darkest Places—Early Relational Trauma and Border-line States of Mind*, and a number of papers, one of which was joint winner of the Michael Fordham Prize in 2004. He sits on the editorial board of the Journal of Analytical Psychology and is currently Chair of Psychotherapy Sussex.

Mark Winborn, PhD, NCPsyA, is a Jungian Psychoanalyst and Clinical Psychologist. He is a Training/Supervising Analyst of the Inter-Regional Society of Jungian Analysts and the C.G. Jung Institute of Zurich, as well as serving on the American Board for Accreditation in Psychoanalysis. His publications include *Deep Blues: Human Soundscapes for the Archetypal Journey* (2011) and *Shared Realities: Participation Mystique and Beyond* (2014), both with Fisher King Press. His third book, *Interpretation in Jungian Analysis: Art and Technique*, is scheduled for publication by Routledge in 2018.

ACKNOWLEDGEMENTS

Earlier versions of the papers constituting Chapters 1 and 9 were published under the same titles in the *Journal of Analytical Psychology*.

INTRODUCTION

Robin S. Brown

So severe was the break between Freud and Jung that, over the course of the last century, Jungian psychology has developed in virtual isolation from the wider psychoanalytic community. But while psychoanalysts have conventionally dismissed Jung's work as mystical and by definition unworthy of consideration, this is largely how the medical mainstream now perceives psychoanalysis. With this in mind, perhaps it might be hoped that the field at present is growing moderately less prone to dismiss the theoretical contributions of perceived outliers merely on the basis of hearsay. To better understand our own profession, analysts of all persuasions might seek to reconnect with those elements of psychoanalytic discourse they hitherto rejected. In North America, the relational turn of the last 30 years has reflected a striking movement in this direction. Although relational psychoanalysis has paid only scant concern to Jungian thinking, the implications of this shift are significant—not only because Jung's psychology might itself be characterized to a considerable extent as relational, but also in the degree to which the relational emphasis on dialogue has succeeded in fostering an atmosphere of genuine open-mindedness. In the year 2000, the decision of the editorial board for the leading relational journal *Psychoanalytic Dialogues* to dedicate an issue to the work of Jungian practitioners (vol. 10.3) was particularly noteworthy in this respect. Yet with the relative lack of interaction that has followed this endeavor, the question remains as to how such an engagement might be sustained. While professional narcissism has no doubt played a significant role historically,[1] it may be that the biggest obstacle at the present time is in fact pedagogical—the diversity of thinking reflected within the psychodynamic tradition is so extensive that aspirations of inclusivity inevitably give rise to the conundrum of breadth versus depth. In attempting to negotiate this challenge there will always be a temptation to invoke the "narcissism of small differences" (Freud, 1918), yet doing so clearly fails to acknowledge the very real existence of *fundamental* differences. Efforts to synthesize different schools of thinking always run the risk of perpetrating some measure of violence towards the intellectual traditions concerned. Nor are these questions of a merely academic nature—insofar as divergent theoretical assumptions might be taken to reflect different experiences of being human (as opposed to varying degrees of psychopathology), then the field's capacity to tolerate its own theoretical diversity might be considered directly suggestive of the profession's capacity to meet the clinical needs of a culturally diverse society (see Brown, 2017).

Reflecting Freud's own status as an outsider, the guild system of training has enabled the field to remain relatively independent of the academy. The prestige and influence that psychoanalysis once enjoyed allowed it to operate in isolation from the wider intellectual community. This early success, achieved in relationship to mainstream medicine, also afforded the luxury of a dissociation from any perspective regarded as diverging too far from accepted dogma. Psychoanalysis refused to manage the question of contradiction in its own discourse. This basic intolerance is witnessed in the recurrent and damaging trend towards splitting and a lack of intellectual containment that has seen the field undermine its own strength and creative vitality by repeatedly disavowing new ideas. While the relational shift of the last 30 years has made considerable progress in stimulating engagement between schools, recovery from the ruptures of the past remains a work in progress. Young-Eisendrath (2009) suggests that the problem of theoretical splitting might start to be ameliorated by fostering a system of education that emphasizes a spirit of shared inquiry between students and teachers alike. Similarly, Blechner (2009) argues for the necessity of developing psychoanalytic curricula that are inclusive of material from a range of disciplines outside the typical psychoanalytic milieu. Perhaps the most central concern for any question of a reform in psychoanalytic education, however, needn't be to focus on what needs explicitly to be imparted to students, so much as to simply avoid creating power structures that actively suppress curiosity and originality. While struggles of this nature are perhaps to some extent inevitable (see Benjamin, 1997), promoting a theoretical breadth of influence in training is an inherently egalitarian gesture that might be expected to go some way towards disarming authority. In this spirit, the present volume seeks to continue fostering conversation between analytical psychology and contemporary psychoanalysis.

Note

1   It should be stressed that this tendency has hardly been one-sided. More than 30 years ago, Mario Jacoby (1981) argued that the Jungian movement couldn't afford to minimize Freud as a figure of only historical interest while largely ignoring psychoanalytic developments since that time unless only to confirm the apparent validity of Jung's ideas (p. 31). Yet, as Andrew Samuels (1998) argues, analytical psychology has, by way of the developmental school, nevertheless shown a good deal more willingness to meaningfully engage psychoanalysis than the reverse.

References

Benjamin, J. (1997). Psychoanalysis as a vocation. *Psychoanalytic Dialogues*, 7, 781–802.

Blechner, M. J. (2009). Research, curriculum, and diversity. *Contemporary Psychoanalysis*, 45, 306–310.

Brown, R. S. (2017). *Psychoanalysis beyond the end of metaphysics: Thinking towards the post-relational.* London and New York: Routledge.

Freud, S. (1918). The taboo of virginity (contributions to the psychology of love III). In *The standard edition of the complete psychological works of Sigmund Freud* (Vol. 11, pp. 191–208). London: The Hogarth Press.

Jacoby, M. (1981). Reflections on Heinz Kohut's concept of narcissism. *Journal of Analytical Psychology*, 26(1), 19–32.

Samuels, A. (1998). Will the post-Jungians survive? In A. Casement (Ed.), *Post-Jungians today: Key papers in contemporary analytical psychology* (pp. 15–32). London: Routledge.

Young-Eisendrath, P. (2009). Psychoanalysis as inquiry and discovery, not suspicion. *Contemporary Psychoanalysis*, 45, 363–369.

PART I

Negotiating theoretical differences

1

ON INTEGRATING JUNGIAN AND OTHER THEORIES[1]

David Sedgwick

We are always integrating other theories, whether we know it or not. In a broad sense, a process of mutual theoretical integration occurs whenever patient and analyst meet: the patient's theory—that is, their understanding—of themselves is affected by the analyst's theory, or theories, of them. From this perspective, analysis is a theoretical dialogue on a personal level and a creative theoretical discussion.

Such dialogues exist, of course, on a larger scale, and the integration, or not, of theories is crucial to Jungian analytic practice. The paradoxical goal of this chapter is to theorize in a general way about some of the minutiae and subtleties involved. At the same time, I loosely speculate on some of the psychology of the process: the intrapersonal and interpersonal *eros* involved, the intimate bond analysts bring to their theories, and the challenges inherent in integrating new perspectives with old ones.

Why integrate theories?

The late Stephen Mitchell, pioneering voice of relational psychoanalysis and an expert at comparative psychoanalysis, put it this way: "Current traditions of psychoanalytic thought are not isolated conceptual islands but are, in principle, often integratable, and … it is interesting, clinically useful, and fun to integrate them" (1988, p. 12). Mitchell sounds almost offhand here—"fun," "interesting"—and his understated tone does capture a playful aspect that, if achieved, can accompany integrative work. Synthesizing theories is a creative process, although it might seem like a merely academic one, since it initially focuses on preexisting theories. Aside from the "fun" aspects of putting things together (or taking them apart and rebuilding them), "clinical usefulness" is the driving force. New theories are necessary, because old ones do not work forever; all theories require supplement or correction. Integrating other theories provides the corrective.

Integrating anything is a complex operation, whether "integration" is referring to psychoanalysis, theory, or social justice. The root of the word is informative and fits with the idea of repair: it comes from the Latin *integrare*, which can be translated not only as "to make whole" but as "to renew" or "to refresh." Etymology does not prove anything—words are in constant motion—but it does open up imaginative possibilities, and the idea of "refreshing" theories is ... refreshing (and undoubtedly worthy and necessary). Synthesizing theories is an attempt at renewal. Synthesizing theories also means changing theories, which resembles Jung's chemical or alchemical descriptions of the analytic encounter: "For two personalities to meet is like mixing two different chemical substances ... both are transformed" (Jung, 1929, p. 71). Both theories are transformed. You can't go home again. Any theoretical integration, or attempt at integration, is an act of "individuation"—meaning individuation in the traditional Jungian sense of coming to one's true self (which is also embodied in one's theoretical position) and individuation in the different sense of separating from what is called in non-Jungian parlance "separation-individuation." However, almost all acts of individuation are resisted, by self or others.

C. G. Jung, Sigmund Freud, Michael Fordham

The first great integration in analytical psychology was Jung's integration of Freud's theories, which ultimately ended in dis-integration, theoretically and personally. It could be called a failure, although on the other hand it did help each man sharpen his own viewpoint. Sharpening viewpoints is an understatement. Jung, especially, came to himself and his theories in this process of differentiation from Freud; he was individuating personally as well as theoretically. Freud, perhaps to a lesser extent personally, formed his crucial definition of psychoanalysis—transference and resistance—in the wake of his clash with Jung. In fact, Freud, analyzing wildly, felt those very things were the psychic sources of Jung's theories, or at least of Jung's differences from him. Jung likewise analyzed Freud according to his (Jung's) own theories.

Thus, the first Jungian effort (by Jung himself) to integrate another theory (Freud's) was ultimately a failure at integration by Jung and Freud both—sometimes theories cannot be synthesized. Segregation of Jungian analysis and psychoanalysis ensued. Jung (1931) suggested that he did make use of Freudian and Adlerian notions in analytical practice, but the evidence of his highly creative, even visionary (and vision-based) theories suggests otherwise. His work, like Freud's, was *sui generis*, and although they each had forebears—including to some degree each other during their time of creative collaboration—the twain did not meet.

A subsequent, and radical, synthesis of analytical psychology and psychoanalysis did occur during Jung's lifetime, however. This was the development of a so-called Jung-Klein hybrid by, mainly, Michael Fordham and the Society of Analytical Psychology (SAP) in Britain. Jung, though his original theories and focus seem to me to be considerably different from Fordham's, gave de facto approval to this, as seen in his positive responses to both Fordham's work and his formation of a training institute. However, in a deeper sense it is unclear whether there was fundamental agreement. As is often the case, some of Jung's first followers were explicit, and adamant, in their rejection of these "New Developments in Analytical Psychology" (Fordham, 1957)—of this apostasy—and later splits across Jungian societies worldwide evidenced this type of thing. This resistance to radical change is ironic, in that Jung himself was the original defector from a traditional program, in his case psychoanalysis.

Efforts besides Fordham's have been part and parcel of Jungian development ever since, and there may be considerable truth in Alfred North Whitehead's (1916) oft-quoted statement that "a science which hesitates to forget its founders is lost" (p. 413). Analytical psychology and psychoanalysis are not science (not hard science, anyway), and Whitehead's statement is probably extreme. But Jung's development of analytical psychology epitomizes it. He had to go his way, contra Freud, at considerable professional and internal risk. He often spoke of daimons and vocation. Freud, also called and chosen, saw himself early on as by nature a "conquistador" (Masson, 1985, p. 398), and later, "Moses" (McGuire, 1974, p. 196). It is as if Jung and Freud were heeding the call of God.[2]

As mentioned, Fordham's was the first radical revisioning of Jungian psychology. First, he pays tribute: "C. G. Jung has opened so many new paths to knowledge, has revealed so many new facts and has given meaning to these and so many old ones as well, that it is tempting to live comfortably on the capital provided by him" (Fordham, 1955, p. 3). The metaphor is literally rich. Jung is pictured here as a kind of *bank*, and his words as money (capital). Jung is a virtual *estate* his heirs could live off of, as Fordham says, quite "comfortably."

But Fordham suggests we resist the temptation to live off this Jungian inheritance: "The truly gigantic and fundamental nature of Jung's labours, however, could never blind us to our own capacity to work out in more detail, or to apply in new spheres, those concepts which can and need to be subjected to scrutiny, constructive criticism, and elaboration" (ibid., p. 4). Critique is possible; change is possible.

Jung's example

Jung's personal example and his theories both suggest he would have approved. In fact, we know he did. As he acknowledged toward the end of his life to Ernest Harms regarding the fate of analytical psychology, "To complete this psychology would take more than a lifetime" (Harms, 1962, p. 732). If further encouragement is needed, Jung also said, as quoted, with variants, by Fordham among others, "There's only one Jungian, and that's me" (Fordham, 1988, p. 34). And if, as Jung wrote in a letter in 1945, "I can only hope and wish that no one becomes 'Jungian' [...] I abhor 'blind adherents'" (Jung, 1973, p. 405), then he has given us a new charge: Go forth and multiply ... but don't be a Jungian.

This kind of statement has a certain complicated charm. It emphasizes individuation and being yourself, and as such is really Jungian-style advice. But in another sense, as Stefano Carta (2012) has noted, there may be some abdication of paternal and institutional responsibility here. This may be for the best, because when Jung did get involved in institutions, from the International Psychoanalytic Association to the International General Medical Society for Psychotherapy, things tended to go awry. Organizational development was probably not his forte.

Nevertheless, before he became the world's only "Jungian," Jung wrestled with being a Freudian. Alongside his *Transformations and Symbols of the Libido* (1911–12), Jung's 1912 lectures on "The Theory of Psychoanalysis" (that is, *his* theory of psychoanalysis) were a rite of sortie. In a foreword to the latter, Jung wrote:

> When, some ten years ago [in 1902, when he was 27] it came home to me what a vast distance Freud had already travelled beyond the bounds of contemporary knowledge of psychopathological phenomena, especially the psychology of complex mental processes, I did not feel in a position to exercise any real criticism. I did not possess the courage.
>
> *(Jung, 1912, p. 85)*

An honest statement. He goes on, quoting the American philosopher-psychologist William James to the effect that theories are "*instruments, not answers to enigmas, in which we can rest.* We don't lie back upon them, we move forward" (p. 86, italics James's). Then, returning to his own words, Jung politely drives home the message: "I know that my own experience in no wise approaches Freud's quite extraordinary experience and insight, but nonetheless it seems to me that certain of my formulations do express the observed facts more suitably than Freud's version of them."

Jung, polite, is not exactly throwing down the gauntlet here, but he is declaring, "Here *I* am." It is time; he is now 37, not 27. He is much more himself and is being himself—being, as D. W. Winnicott put it, "the man he had it in him to be, and then was" (Winnicott, 1964, p. 450). *Jungian* psychology starts here, with this tactful yet bold announcement. This represents Jung's personal individuation and the individuation of his theoretical perspective, now truly his own. This is his *credo*.

By the time of this 1912 introduction, Jung had synthesized all he could of what was then newly emerging psychoanalytic theory. He also tries to anticipate criticism of his own criticism, insisting that he is not a schismatic:

> It has wrongly been suggested that my attitude signifies a "split" in the psychoanalytic movement. Such schisms can only exist in matters of faith […] I am far indeed from regarding a modest and temperate criticism as a "falling away" or a schism; on the contrary, I hope thereby to promote the continued flowering and fructification of the psychoanalytic movement.
>
> *(Jung, 1912, p. 86)*

But psychoanalysis *was* a matter of faith, and Jung, who had indeed been baptized by Freud, was a lapsed Freudian. Ultimately, in terms of the psychoanalytic movement he wished to promote, Jung was banished to what Stephen Mitchell once referred to as the "psychoanalytic Gulag" (Mitchell, 1997, p. 15). But the feeling was mutual, and Jung left voluntarily: if he had wanted to be or could have been a Freudian psychoanalyst, then he would have been.

But Jung couldn't do it. He had to be a Jung, not a Freud. To paraphrase the movie *Bulworth*, he had to be a spirit, not a ghost. Whatever the personal meanings and sense of loss for Jung and Freud, which were significant, it had to be like this. Without the split, there would have been no analytical psychology and a different kind of psychoanalysis. Freud couldn't take Jung in. Jung helped Freud define psychoanalysis and define what it was not. Likewise, his brief years with Freud helped Jung define what analytical psychology was and was not about.

Jung had to leave the house of his father, and what a painful process this was. Some suggest that Jungian analysts, and perhaps other types of analysts, have been suffering from this ever since. I think not; it was a dynamic conflict and, apparently, a necessary divorce. However, this failed marriage gave birth to two theories. Were they twin theories? Not exactly (not identical twins, anyway). Fraternal twins? Maybe.

Freud, Jung, Hamlet, and love

There was no brotherly love lost between Jung and Freud when they split up. While their break-up was possibly a tragedy on the theoretical level, it was without doubt a painful personal tragedy. One cannot help but feel this when reading *The Freud/Jung Letters*: their incredible intimacy, Jung yearning for a father, Freud yearning for a son; their—this is not too strong a word for it—*love* for each other (see Carta, 2012; Solomon, 2003; Trilling, 1974; and others).

We all fall in love with our theories—for good reason, because they are life-giving to us ("As the hart panteth after the water brooks, so panteth my soul after thee"). And naturally we fall in love with people who create them. Their "subjective confession," to use Jung's brave, felicitous phrase, matches our own. A separation, a break-up, then, can be painful beyond words. Yet, as in analysis or therapy, it seems crucial to find words for such tragedy.

Jung's famous last words to Freud? "The rest is silence" (McGuire, 1974, p. 540)—from, of course, *Hamlet*, the greatest tragedy of them all. Hamlet speaks these dying words directly to Horatio, his steadfast friend, whom he loves like a brother. In fact, some time earlier, Hamlet tells his soul-brother Horatio, beautifully, "Give me that man who is not passion's slave, and I will wear him in my heart's core, ay, in my heart of heart. As I do thee." There was much between Jung and Freud that, while undoubtedly a father-and-son dynamic, was simultaneously, if not as successfully, this kind of brotherly love. Love—whatever it is—is not any one thing, nor is it based on any one object-relationship or archetype.

What Hamlet says of Horatio, long before the final "silence," might be applied to Jung and Freud too. Jung and Freud were passionate about each other, one way or the other, though Freud was less passion's slave, being older and also, compared to Jung, simply a less passionate man. Jung tended to burn a little hot. It also seems significant in this context that Freud, reportedly, was celibate for various reasons by the time he was only 41 (though lately this has come into question; see Macie-jewski, 2006). Jung, meanwhile, was all over the place erotically when he was in his 30s (and beyond), not just with Freud, however platonically; there were also Sabina Spielrein, Toni Wolff, his wife Emma Jung, and maybe others. In my view, it was not just his break-up with Freud but these tumultuous relationships, along with whatever had been boiling up spontaneously in him for years, that contributed to the breakdown—or breakout—that came to be called Jung's confrontation with the unconscious.[3]

Indeed, the main theoretical differences between Jung and Freud are mirrored in the play's famous first act by the reactions of Hamlet and Horatio. When the ghost of Hamlet's dead father appears on the battlements, as if in a dream, Horatio, though rarely passion's slave, is more than a little spooked: "Oh day and night, but this is wondrous strange!" To which Hamlet responds—in probably the first and best description ever of active imagination—"And therefore as a stranger give it welcome." Then, outlining what is basically the core difference between Freud and Jung, Hamlet is bold to say, "There are more things in heaven and earth, Horatio, than are dreamt of in your philosophy."

In changing theories, or in trying to protect and preserve them, people tend to become passion's slaves, and sometimes passion's betrayers. Comparing theories, and trying to integrate them, requires *eros*, a passion like Hamlet's passion and Jung's and Freud's, but also a steady dose of Horatio's calm heart. But then again, in this merry-go-round, a capacity to be disloyal to first love may be called upon.

The Freud-Jung love letters

Of course, it all began so beautifully ... those halcyon days ... when Jung and Freud first fell in love—analogous perhaps to when we first found analysis and/or a life-giving theory or person that helped us, finally, to understand ourselves. Here's Freud to Jung after Jung had defended Freud's theories at a meeting in Amsterdam in 1907:

> Now of all times, *I wish I were with you*, taking pleasure in no longer being alone and, if you are in need of encouragement, telling you about my long years of honourable but painful solitude, which began after I cast my first glance into the new world, about the terrifying moments when I myself thought I had gone astray and was wondering how I might still make my misled life useful to my family, ... and [telling you] about the serene certainty which finally took possession of me and bade me wait until a voice from the unknown multitude should answer mine. *That voice was yours.*
> *(McGuire, 1974, p. 82, italics added)*

I was all alone, "Till There Was You." Jung, with his hunger for a father, must have found this irresistible. This is an irresistible force (Freud) meeting a movable object

(Jung). Indeed, just two weeks before Freud's voice-in-the-wilderness letter, Jung had declared to Freud not only his "unconditional *devotion* to the defense and propagation of your ideas" but also "my equally unconditional *veneration* of your personality" (ibid., p. 78, italics added). Jung, in deep feeling, is down on his knees, ready to venerate, ready to worship. And Freud, as we know, was ready to knight him.

Fittingly, in this same devoted-to-you letter, Jung also confesses that he is "jealous" of Karl Abraham because, Jung says to Freud, "he corresponds with you." Sigmund has been writing to another Karl (Abraham, not Jung) too. Sharing intimate letters – *what?!*

So, ten days after Freud's passionate "that voice was yours" letter, Jung asks Freud to please, please send him a picture:

> Perhaps I may take this opportunity to express a long cherished and constantly repressed wish: I would dearly like to have a photograph of you, not as you used to look but as you did when I first got to know you [...] Would you have the great kindness to grant me this wish sometime? I would be ever so grateful because again and again I feel the want of your picture.
>
> *(Ibid., p. 86)*

I want you. I want your picture. I want the *image* of you. So I can wear you in my heart. And Freud sent one and asked for one back.

This is all very frank, very romantic really, between these two men. Jung is so sweet, so open—which was a dangerous place to be, for both of them. Dangerous for Jung, because Freud could be a hard man: he loved his theory more than he loved Jung. But Jung was tough too, or got to be (after all, it was Freud who fainted). And Jung, eventually, found he loved his way of seeing things more than he loved Freud or loved being loved by Freud.

Integration now

For a long time, Jung was a follower of Freud, and then he was not; now, many of us are followers of Jung. We are "followers" in the literal sense that we come after Jung; we are all post-Jungians. He died in 1961, so very few people alive today knew him personally. As I have noted before, Jung exists and only ever existed for us in the form of words on a page (plus a few precious films in which he is a lively presence). However, many of us are also followers of Jung in the sense of being "designated Jungians," those who represent Jungian psychology: analysts, devotees, patients, teachers, and so on. But if there's only one Jungian, who was Jung himself, then we're faced with a Hamlet-like dilemma: to be a Jungian means to not be a Jungian.

What the always compelling Jung-Freud story suggests in terms of synthesizing theories is that sometimes theories can be integrated, and sometimes they cannot. Things may open up for a while: the Freudian perspective was not Jung's starting point, but it made sense to him for several years. Things change in relation to one's original standpoints, and theories that were sufficient become insufficient. In other words, one may have learned all that one can learn from a theory. Certainly one measure of a theory's viability is how much ongoing clinical utility it has, and another measure is how much it allows one to branch out creatively, if necessary, to renew that clinical usefulness. Does the theory constrict, or does it set one free?

The need to integrate new theories arises, obviously, where there is a need to grow. Integrating newer perspectives, or additional perspectives, in whole or part, begins right there, where a predecessor theory no longer works. It no longer has that "cash value" that William James was speaking about in his book on *Pragmatism* (1907), which Jung made use of, both in his Fordham-lecture introduction and later in *Psychological Types* (1921).

Sometimes it seems as if there is something in a theory itself that wants to change, as if the theory took the lead. To personify things—and Jung's theories encouraged patients and practitioners to personify everything and to imagine any-thing—theories, like words, are living things, and sometimes it is as if *they*, the theories, will not sit still. A theory wants to go somewhere. It is like a child (or a complex) with a mind of its own, which sometimes requires freedom and some-times needs some management.

Clinicians dialogue with their theories all the time, implicitly or explicitly, and are guided but also limited by their metaphors and theories of choice. The way one thinks and the possibilities a theory dictates completely shape experience. Most theories are themselves metaphorical, in the traditional Jungian case composed of complexes, archetypes, and other personifications of experience that are thought to live in an imaginary psychogeographic place (the psyche, the unconscious, or somewhere in the body, possibly not even in the brain). Or, in other systems, persons may be similarly inhabited by ids, egos, superegos, baby selves, part selves, internal objects, part objects, introjects, representations or replicas of desires and relationships, instincts, others, even things.[4] Every theory has a particular language, and a particular culture of analysis and technique grows up around it.

But sometimes, for various reasons, we, like Hamlet, welcome the stranger, one that was never dreamt of in our previous philosophy. (Or one that *was* dreamt of, as a theoretical addition may have come first in a kind of dream, as if already there, waiting to be discovered.) New perspectives arrive from many sources: analysis, of course, training, experience, patients who really teach us something, or from "the unconscious" or what Jung calls the "not yet" conscious, "the seeds of future conscious contents" (1928, p. 128). It may come from "inside," or it may come from a lecture or, serendipitously or perhaps synchronistically, from an article or a book that gets inside.

A personal example

Perhaps a simple personal example of the latter—a lucky find—is in order, because this chapter so far has presented rather generalized reflections on some interior and interpersonal processes. Detailed study of such personal processes in past and present Jungian assimilations is neither feasible nor possible, as one can only speak of personal processes firsthand.

While in graduate school, I discovered, completely by chance, the work of the psychoanalyst Harold Searles (1918–2015). I had never heard of him, but someone at a job interview mentioned his work, so I picked up a book of his, *Collected Papers on Schizophrenia and Related Subjects* (1965), and turned to the introduction. The first thing I read was Searles's description of his mood when his first paper was published:

> I felt weighed down by a depression for which I could not account. Then I had a fantasy of making gashes in my analyst, tearing out the pages of the paper and stuffing them savagely into the wounds, and thereupon my feeling of depression was instantly gone [...] I noticed later, after I had undergone much change, that I visualized the core of myself as being, none the less, like a steel ball-bearing, with varicoloured sectors on its surface, which of course would not change. This too eventually changed. It dissolved in grief.
>
> *(Searles, 1965, p. 20)*[5]

I was floored by this candor—and this was only the introduction. His words seem slightly overdramatic now, but I had never read anything like this in the analytic literature. In fact, no analyst that I was aware of *had* ever written like this (though certainly analysts from Freud to Jung to Reik had been self-revealing in print).

Thus, I began a long journey with Searles's written work. I found his ideas about countertransference— he was a pioneer in this regard, alongside Racker, Heimann, Little, Winnicott, Fordham, Ferenczi, and, of course, Jung—tremendously liberating, and I eventually wrote a doctoral thesis which became a book on Searles and Jung, an attempt to integrate their theories.

The point is: we make a chance *discovery*, and it's like Keats's "On First Looking into Chapman's Homer." Keats reads a book and a new world opens up. (In his case, it was a translation of Homer, just as for many of us Jung's work comes in translation.) One can substitute "Jung" for "Chapman" here in the last half of the poem:

> Yet did I never breathe its pure serene
> Till I heard Chapman speak out loud and bold:
> Then felt I like some watcher of the skies
> When a new planet swims into his ken;
> Or like stout Cortez when with eagle eyes
> He star'd at the Pacific—and all his men
> Look'd at each other with a wild surmise—
> Silent, upon a peak in Darien.

The inspiration from such a find is undeniable, and indeed, one may initially be struck dumb ("silent").[6] Then the work begins: how to work the epiphany in, give it further words (give it welcome), see if the concepts encouraged by those words fit with the words and ideas that have gone before. Sometimes the match cannot be made: for example, Winnicott, intrigued but not inspired by Jung's terms such as anima and animus, declared, "I cannot be communicated with in this language" (Winnicott, 1960, p. 159). At other times, a full personal synthesis can be made, as in Fordham's Jung-Klein hybrid.

Integration processes

With Freud and Jung, Keats and Cortez in mind, let us turn again to the processes and particulars involved in the integration of theories, or sometimes in their non-integration or dis-integration.

Discovery, resonance, immersion

The work of integration begins with an opening up, usually a striking "ah ha" experience, aptly described in the title of the Keats poem ("On *First* Looking into …"). The resonance overwhelms, then grows. Of course, to have that degree of significance, a need must be there in the first place. A theoretical gap pulls one or opens one in a certain direction. It is hard to know which is the chicken and which is the egg: was a theory, as noted earlier, "there, waiting to be discovered," or was it created "brand new"? Or both, or neither? Discovered or found? Such are the enigmas of creativity, and, incidentally, of theories of the unconscious (i.e., repressed, as in Freud's case, or *in statu nascendi* and "not yet" conscious, as in Jung's).

Once an additional theory is discovered, or found, immersion follows. One has to immerse, and be willing to go there. The initial epiphany may make this easy. So, there has to be a need, and there has to be an interest in, even a drive toward, the thing one seems to need. If there's no interest, then why bother, because a *genuine* attempt at integration is painstaking work, and because it may mean leaving home—individuating. Davies (2008) describes this "immigration" and its motivation well, speaking in the context of relational psychoanalysis:

> I've often thought of the community of early relational writers as a group of intellectual and clinical immigrants. Some were classical Freudians, some Kleinians, some Self psychologists, some Interpersonalists. What they all had in common was some dissatisfaction with the theory and technique that had marked their training and early practice. And so they all arrived on the shores of "the relational turn."
>
> *(n.p.)*

Always synthesizing, always integrating

The love/hate relationship of Jung and Freud is a reminder that attempts at synthesis, successful or otherwise, are an historical constant. As Jung wrote to Freud (several years before—ironically enough—they found they could *not* coordinate their ways of seeing things): "If there is a 'psychoanalysis' there must also be a 'psychosynthesis' " (McGuire, 1974, p. 216, italics added). Synthesis, perhaps more than "analysis" (in the separating-into-components sense), has always been a keynote of the classical Jungian program, with its emphasis on Hegelian dialectics, "the third," the transcendent function, etc. The "tension of opposites" and their differentiation, which is what Jung himself was attempting to negotiate with Freud, has always been a launch point for Jungian projects.

Attempts at integration also seem to be in the larger nature of things; that is, nature and human nature appear to seek some kind of unity, though not necessarily and perhaps not for long (as "love and death," "creation and destruction" seem to be either simultaneous or sequential phenomena). But there does seem to be some tendency toward evolution. To paraphrase the American civil rights leader Martin Luther King, who was paraphrasing an abolitionist, "The arc of the theoretical universe is long, but it bends toward unification." Even Einstein hoped and asserted that "God does not play dice with the universe" (though he was apparently wrong, according to subsequent developments in quantum mechanics). We all yearn for a unified field theory.

Each individual analyst, too, has his/her own interpretation of each theory, her particular understanding and inflection—something like her own "voice." Likewise, as noted earlier, each analysis is a meeting of minds, which is also a meeting of theories, which is also a meeting of private languages. Analyst and patient together create new theories, consisting of new understandings, affectively based, of the patient's experience. From the analyst's point of view, "You're making up theories all the time, called interpretations" (Fordham, 1988, p. 22).

On the other hand, against this "striving for unity" idea is Alfred North Whitehead's aforementioned recommendation about forgetting the "founders." His implication is that, to progress, one may have to give up the original way entirely (the opposite of "forsaking all others"). This is where Freud and Jung went off the rails, but conflict need not necessarily be the only impetus for theoretical synthesis or theory-building. Sometimes, the challenge is to maintain a dynamic tension between tradition and innovation. Evolution can happen, and evolution moves in fits and starts—what Eldredge and Gould (1972) called "punctuated equilibrium"—rather than smoothly.

Passion

Integration or synthesis of other theories can become a mere intellectual exercise, on the order of an exam question ("compare and contrast the theories of …"). But theories are obviously chosen not just because they work but because they fit personally or "feel right." Head and heart, as Thomas Jefferson might say, need to line up. Theories are built on personal conviction, and theoretical passion is as heartfelt as any love affair (again, see Freud and Jung). We love our theories and "believe" in them and what they have done for us. The latter also extends to gratitude to those who in effect taught us "everything we know," whether that be through analysis, training, supervision, books, or whatever form of life-learning.

Part of this passionate conviction may imply an unshakeable loyalty. As Freud protested to Jung on the very day when Jung proclaimed his freedom from Freud's "paternal authority": "I formally adopted you as eldest son and *anointed* you as my successor and crown prince *in partibus infidelium*" (McGuire, 1974, p. 218, italics added). The Latin phrase means "in the lands of the unbelievers"—the infidels. In the realm of analytic theory and practice, sometimes it's the Middle East out there: passions run high, maybe too high. Requiring a loyalty oath is understandable, but these passions can have the unfortunate effect of solidifying entrenched positions or polarizing arguments, such that the theories, like Jung's complexes, "have us" (Jung, 1934, p. 96) rather than we having them.

Two levels of integration, closely bound

The process of integrating theories involves two levels, or two components, of synthesis that are intimately tied and in fact overlapping. The first, just mentioned, is emotional. Bringing in another theory requires an affective commitment to it, of sufficient strength that one has the energy to take the trouble. It also requires a certain degree of trust to open that door. As Michael Polanyi, another philosopher of science, noted regarding conflicting theories:

> Formal operations relying on one framework of interpretation cannot demonstrate a proposition to persons who rely on another framework. Its advocates may not even succeed in getting a hearing from these, since they must first teach them a new language, and *no one can learn a new language unless he first trusts that it means something.* ... Proponents of a new system can convince their audience only by first winning their intellectual sympathy for a doctrine they have not yet grasped.
>
> *(Polanyi, 1958, pp. 150–1, italics in original)*[7]

In other words, the problem is that you are speaking different languages, and who wants to learn a new language or trust it to convey deeper meanings? Such trust may be quite restricted, due to the above-mentioned "subjective confession" aspect of theoretical preference and one's parallel investment in one's professional identity. A considerable amount, to put it mildly, of training, time, and commitment goes into one's theory of choice, and this results in a deep, and deeply desired, professional affiliation, interlaced with personal connections. This home base is vitally important, and one may not wish to endanger it. This in turn contributes to the psychological difficulty of leaving, or even altering, one's theory (or family) of origin. Also, such alterations may involve some de-idealization of the original theory and persons, so one runs the risk of losing one's anchor, one's base camp. Just as there are rewards for leaving home, there are the safe pleasures of staying at home.

The second process element involves negotiating the integration in a nonemotional way. (Nonemotional versus emotional is, of course, a false dichotomy: a cognitive synthesis of various theoretical points of view has an affective component, and, vice versa, an interpretation alone must have an affective reference to carry weight.) But once one has opened up to a new perspective, then a careful process of consideration takes place.

The late Stephen Mitchell, the aforementioned "founder" of relational psychoanalysis, was a past master of comparative psychoanalysis. Mitchell's work was notable for the careful, respectful way he approached other theories: it was not just the sheer number of theories he studied but the way he studied them, whether this led ultimately to their integration into his own evolving theories or not.[8] He looked at them meticulously and openly, raised interesting questions about them, and, when challenged, was not defensive about the challenge. The almost unavoidable mind-set when first approaching other theoretical perspectives is to set them up as straw men or foils for one's theory. For an analyst, it is as difficult to be neutral about a theory as it is to be totally neutral with a patient, but one can strive to be "neutral" in the best sense of that now oft-challenged word—that is, to try to forget everything one knows or to "not know beforehand" (as Jung, Fordham, and Bion counseled) and to be as receptive, within one's inevitable limits, as possible.

One of the fundamental questions Mitchell asked was: "How does one both preserve a theory and introduce into it new concepts at variance with its basic thrust and underlying assumptions?" (Mitchell, 1988, p. 136). This question is both crucial and vexing. The answer is: you can't. It cannot be done because it is a contradiction in terms. If one bends the core theory overmuch—and Jungian theory, for example, has considerable flexibility—its center will not hold. Mitchell, however, offers a more nuanced standard when trying to integrate another theory into a preexisting one: "Do [the two theories] seem to work together in a smooth, consistent fashion that is mutually enhancing? Does the synthesis establish a coherent frame of reference or [is there] a sense of being jolted back and forth between fundamentally different and mutually inconsistent vantage points?" (p. 53).

Answering these questions is a major challenge and requires integrity, but before even digging into the questions, one needs, as just noted, some sense that there's something there to be found—some hope—and some degree of trust. It is the easiest thing in the world to pull a theoretical statement out of context and out of its assumptions or philosophical bases. Theories are embedded in assumptions and contexts, and are developed step by step. To put it another way, paraphrasing Mitchell (2000), we locate a new theory in terms of our own conceptual categories, our preexisting conditions. A great deal of honesty is required to locate a different theory on its own terms—to give it welcome—and then, in a judicious manner, see if and how it fits. Aye, there's the rub.

Conclusions

This chapter has presented a loose collection of reflections on some of the overall as well as underlying processes of integrating theories. A precise method for such integrations has not been provided, because precise formulas for synthesis are individualized and do not exist, though some factors and principles have been suggested. A successful integration, like a successful personal integration in life or analysis, is an organic, slow-growth process.

Comparative psychoanalysis is a relatively recent phenomenon, whether that be within or without analytical psychology. The project for the earliest analytic theories, which were typically the creations of heroic, lonely pioneers (like Freud, until he found Jung), was the consolidation of a unique theoretical stance. This had to be fought for. The theories then found followers and coalesced into "schools." Roy Schafer, in his nicely titled paper "On Becoming a Psychoanalyst of One Persuasion or Another" (1979), points out that "the existence of schools raises the problem of comparative psychoanalysis, which [...] is a virtually undeveloped intellectual pursuit" (p. 346). A generation later, comparative psychoanalysis is no longer undeveloped (and not strictly intellectual, as has been pointed out). In addition, for decades there have been schools within schools as well as intra-school and extra-school combinations; the amount of in-breeding and out-breeding is daunting. Analytical psychology is a case in point, currently consisting of a sort of United Nations of theoretical perspectives which meet, or sometimes do not meet and therefore split off and go away, under one roof.

Members of any theoretical persuasion may make honest claims for the superiority of their particular perspective. However, such truth-claims are not provable, nor do they have to be unless one actually asserts a claim of superiority over other claims. In that case, one has to back it up. However, as Fred Plaut once noted, "In all theoretical discussions we have to remember that we are unable to show with any degree of reliability the superiority of results based on one theory or technique over against another" (Plaut, 1970, p. 89). Indeed, the first and best statistical research on the effectiveness of psychotherapy, a meta-analysis of all 475 outcome studies at the time, indicated 1) that psychotherapy and psychoanalysis (which is a form of psychotherapy) work and 2) that different forms of therapy work equally well (Smith, Glass, and Miller, 1980). That's a fact (or at least, a statistically significant conclusion), a fact that does not necessarily sanction pluralism but does encourage awareness that one's convictions are just that—one's convictions—and thus subject to limitations.

New theory arises when needed and is always arising. Having more theories, or a more comprehensive theory, extends one's range of options for understanding or interpreting. In a sense, a more comprehensive theory increases one's affective options too, because the words allow the emotions to move. However, there is no requirement that one integrate new, old, or any additional theories. If the status quo is fine, then there is no need for anything else. But if the current option does not work as well as it once did, then, as Jung (1939) said, one has "to go on the Quest" (p. 285).

Integrating Jungian and other theories is a complex program. This chapter has been suggesting what may be self-evident: that it is always in some way part of the program. And, to repeat, "Current traditions of psychoanalytic thought are not isolated conceptual islands but are, in principle, often integratable, and [...] it is interesting, clinically useful, and fun to integrate them" (Mitchell, 1988, p.12).

Attempting to integrate them would seem to represent analytical psychology itself trying to individuate.

Notes

1 This paper, in slightly different form, was first published in the *Journal of Analytical Psychology,* 2015, 60.4, 540–58.

2 Jung, as we know, was nominated by Freud to be his Joshua, who "will take possession of the promised land of psychiatry, which I shall only be able to glimpse from afar" (McGuire, 1974, p. 197). As Joseph Cambray (personal communication) first reminded me, Freud wanted Jung named *president for life* of the International Psychoanalytic Association (which is interesting to imagine); see Brabant, Falzeder, and Giampieri-Deutsch (1992, p. 156, note 1). Freud's Moses-Joshua reference is from Deuteronomy, 34:1–4: "Then Moses climbed Mount Nebo [...] There the Lord showed him the whole land [...] Then the Lord said to him, 'This is the land I promised on oath to Abraham, Isaac and Jacob [...] I will let you see it with your eyes, but you will not cross over into it'." Also of note are the Rev. Martin Luther King's chilling precognitive words on the night before he was assassinated: "I have been to the mountaintop.... I just want to do God's will. And He's allowed me to go up to the mountain. And I've looked over. And I have seen the Promised Land. I may not get there with you. But I want you to know tonight, that we, as a people, will get to the Promised Land."

3 Freud had to work through things, too, though he had a different kind of support—"the Committee," or the "paladins," as Ernest Jones, lead knight, had called them. Freud's epigraph for his own version of these events, "On the History of the Psychoanalytic Movement" (1914), was telling: *Fluctuat nec mergitur* ("It is tossed by the waves, but it does not sink"). This is the motto for Paris, the "city of love," or in this case broken love.

4 Harold Searles (1960) was among the first to stress the importance of one's relationship to the "nonhuman" environment. Jung, too, appreciated and to a large extent lived in an animated, alive physical world. One's relationship to the natural world and the "environment" can now be considered a crucial part of one's psychological picture and internal ecology, not simply in a political sense but in a basic sense.

5 In a later version of this tale, Searles (1965) wrote: "I have long since lost any such image of the core of my identity; it became dissolved in grief, and my sense of identity now possesses something of the fluidity of tears" (p. 68).

6 The first analysts were similarly elated by their discovery of the New World—the unconscious—though rarely silent. And it was Balboa, not Cortez, who was the first white man to "discover" the Pacific. Perhaps Keats did not know this, or perhaps the line simply scans better with "Cortez." Freud's greatest discovery, as he saw it, was "the secret of the dream" (Masson, 1985, p. 417), and he wrote of his *Interpretation of Dreams,* "Insight such as this falls to one's lot but once in a lifetime" (Freud, 1900/1932, p. xxxii).

7 I am indebted to my college classmate Paul Stepansky, formerly the managing director of The Analytic Press, for this reference and quote from Polanyi. See Stepansky (1983).

8 By my count, based on a close acquaintanceship with his writings, Mitchell carefully studied Freud, Sullivan, Fairbairn, Klein, Guntrip, Winnicott, Loewald, Kohut, Schafer, Bowlby, Gill, Kernberg, Jacobson, Mahler, Hartmann, Fromm, Thomson, and Jacobs, not to mention the myriad voices within relational psychoanalysis itself.

References

Brabant, E., Falzeder, E., & Giampieri-Deutsch, P. (1992). *The correspondence of Sigmund Freud and Sandor Ferenczi, Vol. 1, 1908–1914.* Cambridge: Belknap Press of Harvard University Press.

Carta, S. (2012). Narcissism, solitude, friendship: notes on the therapeutic alliance in the context of the Freud-Jung relationship. *Journal of Analytical Psychology*, *57*, 483–499.

Davies, J. (2008). The question of technique – the view from relational psychoanalysis. *International Association for Relational Psychoanalysis and Psychotherapy (IARPP) Online Colloquium*, December 2008.

Eldredge, N., & Gould, S. (1972). Punctuated equilibria: an alternative to phyletic gradualism. In *Models in paleobiology*, ed. T. J. Schopf. San Francisco: Freeman, Cooper & Co.

Fordham, M. (1955). Editorial note. *Journal of Analytical Psychology*, 1, 3–5.

Fordham, M. (1957). *New developments in analytical psychology*. London: Routledge and Kegan Paul.

Fordham, M. (1988). Michael Fordham in discussion with Karl Figlio. *Free Associations*, 1, 7–38.

Freud, S. (1900/1932). Preface to the third (revised) English edition. *The interpretation of dreams. Standard edition* 4. London: Hogarth.

Freud, S. (1914). On the history of the psychoanalytic movement. *Standard edition* 14. London: Hogarth.

Harms, E. (1962). Carl Gustav Jung. *American Journal of Psychiatry*, *18*(8), 728–32.

James, W. (1907). *Pragmatism: A new name for some old ways of thinking*. New York: Longmans, Green, & Co.

Jung, C. G. (1912). The theory of psychoanalysis (foreword to the first edition). *Collected works* 4. Princeton: Princeton University Press.

Jung, C. G. (1921). *Psychological types. Collected works* 6. Princeton: Princeton University Press.

Jung, C. G. (1928). The relations between the ego and the unconscious. *Collected works* 7. Princeton: Princeton University Press.

Jung, C. G. (1929). Problems of modern psychotherapy. *Collected works* 16. Princeton: Princeton University Press.

Jung, C. G. (1931). The aims of psychotherapy. *Collected works* 16. Princeton: Princeton University Press.

Jung, C. G. (1934). A review of the complex theory. *Collected works* 8. Princeton: Princeton University Press.

Jung, C. G. (1939). The symbolic life. *Collected works* 18. Princeton: Princeton University Press.

Jung, C. G. (1973). *C.G. Jung, letters. Vol. 1: 1906–1950*. Princeton: Princeton University Press.

McGuire, W. (Ed.) (1974). *The Freud/Jung letters*. Trans. R. Mannheim & R. F. C. Hull. Princeton: Princeton University Press.

Maciejewski, F. (2006), Freud, his wife, and his "wife". *American Imago*, *63*, 497–506.

Masson, J. M. (1985). *The complete letters of Sigmund Freud to Wilhelm Fliess, 1887–1904*. Cambridge, and London: The Belknap Press of Harvard University Press.

Mitchell, S. M. (1988). *Relational concepts in psychoanalysis: An integration*. Cambridge: Harvard University Press.

Mitchell, S. M. (1997). *Influence and autonomy in psychoanalysis*. London: Routledge.

Mitchell, S. M. (2000). Response to Silverman. *Psychoanalytic Psychology*, *17*, 153–9.

Plaut, A. (1970). Comment: on not incarnating the archetype. *Journal of Analytical Psychology*, *15*, 88–94.

Polanyi, M. (1958). *Personal knowledge: Towards a post-critical philosophy*. New York: Harper & Row.

Schafer, R. (1979). On becoming a psychoanalyst of one persuasion or another. *Contemporary Psychoanalysis*, *15*, 345–60.

Searles, H. F. (1960). *The Nonhuman environment in normal development and in schizophrenia.* New York: International Universities Press.

Searles, H. F. (1965). *Collected papers on schizophrenia and related subjects.* New York: International Universities Press.

Smith, M., Glass, G., & Miller, T. (1980). *The benefits of psychotherapy.* Baltimore: John Hopkins University Press.

Solomon, H. M. (2003). Freud and Jung: an incomplete encounter. *Journal of Analytical Psychology*, *48*, 553–569.

Stepansky, P. (1983). Perspectives on dissent: Adler, Kohut, and the idea of a psychoanalytic research tradition. *Annual of Psychoanalysis*, *11*, 51–74.

Trilling, L. (1974). The Freud-Jung Letters. *New York Times*, 21 April 1974.

Whitehead, A. N. (1916). The organization of thought. *Science*, *44*(1134), 409–19.

Winnicott, D. W. (1960). Countertransference. In *The maturational processes and the facilitating environment.* London: Hogarth.

Winnicott, D. W. (1964). Memories, Dreams, Reflections. *International Journal of Psychoanalysis*, *45*, 450–5.

2

FREUD AND/OR JUNG

A group dynamic approach

R.D. Hinshelwood

> We may one day be played off against one another.
>
> *Freud in a letter to Jung (January 1907)*

This chapter will consider the groups that formed around Freud and Jung from about 1902 and examine how their cultures evolved in relation to the work each group did. Ellenberger (1970) characterised the two group cultures as follows:

> In Vienna, men such as Kraft-Ebing, Weininger, and Schnitzler had conditioned the public to accept Freud's sexual theories. In Zurich, another type of *genius loci* caused psychoanalysis to be accepted as a key to religious and educational problems, and to the understanding of myths and psychosis. It was inevitable that clashes should occur between these two diverging perspectives.
>
> *(p. 815)*

Each group had a history, a certain place in the world, specific aims and a characteristic culture. These will be outlined in brief for both groups, with the main points of reference being Gay (1988), McGlynn (1996) and Makari (2008). Reference will also be made to Jones (1955), Hannah (1976) and Bair (2003). The two cultures will be scrutinised for evidence of unconscious conflicts and defensive psychodynamics. My hypothesis is that if each group's culture exhibited defensive characteristics serving to protect its members, then these defences may have been mutually undermined in the course of the two groups coming together.

The groups and their cultures

When Jung first met Freud in 1907, the Wednesday Psychological Society in Vienna and the Burghölzli Hospital in Zurich had already established their own identities. The following table indicates the more notable personalities associated with each group:

Vienna 1907	Burghölzli 1907
Freud	Bleuler
Adler	Jung
Stekel	Eitingon
Federn	Binswanger
Sadger	Abraham
Rank	Ferenczi
Wittels	Brill
	Nunberg
	Trigant Burrow
	Jelliffe

The Vienna group began in 1902 when Freud invited four colleagues – Wilhelm Stekel, Alfred Adler, Max Kahane and Rudolf Rietler – to meet weekly on Wednesday evenings in the waiting room of Freud's clinical suite (Nunberg & Federn, 1962; Mühlleitner & Reichmayr, 1997; Makari, 2008). The four original members were all medically trained and Jewish. They had attended Freud's extramural lectures, which he had been giving at the University of Vienna since the 1880s. Of the five original members, three worked in their own practices and two had established private clinics. Discussions appear to have initially been very congenial. In his colourful style, Stekel describes "complete harmony amongst the five, no dissonances [...] a spark seemed to jump from one mind to another, and every evening was like a revelation" (quoted in Gay, 1988, p. 174). The atmosphere was convivial and even offered safety as a forum for self-disclosure (none of the members had yet received a full psychoanalytic treatment). The laissez-faire attitude that prevailed might be considered reflective of the wider society, with the libidinous Viennese culture being quick to embrace innovations in art and science. Despite the hierarchical influence of a monarch and the Catholic church, transgressive attitudes and behaviours were prevalent. The authoritarian Austrian Empire was on its last legs, and dissenters were demanding a more libertarian set of values. This included a freedom to question sexual mores. Psychoanalysis thus gained early credibility in seeming to lead the revolt against sexual oppression. Notwithstanding the lack of reception for Freud's ideas among the medical community, the permissive affability of the Wednesday Psychological Society seems to have been entirely commensurate with the wider culture. Over time, the group's membership expanded and diversified so that at least a third of its members were not medically trained. Many of the new recruits were political and social reformers, as well as intellectuals of various stripes and libertarian views. Freud's sense that he could not draw sufficient interest from the medical world caused him to look elsewhere. He believed that his theories could speak to all kinds of social, philosophical and historical issues, and he actively attracted people to his Wednesday meetings from the wider intellectual culture – figures such as Max Graf, a musician, Arthur Schnitzler, a writer, and Hugo Heller, a publisher who eventually established the *Internationale Psychoanalytische Verlag*. The content of the meetings included presentations from figures who were critical of Freud's ideas, alongside those who accepted Freud as an established authority and sought to apply his views in other disciplines. Those members more explicitly aligned with Freud's teachings rubbed shoulders with others pursuing their own research.

The culture of the Burghölzli Hospital in Zurich could hardly have been more different. In contrast to the fluid atmosphere of the Viennese group, the Burghölzli was focused and business-like. The hospital had a clear and functional purpose, which was to care for the insane. Founded in 1870 as the hospital of the University of Zurich, the institution only really got into its stride with the 1879 appointment of Auguste Forel as director. Forel was succeeded by Eugen Bleuler in 1898, with Carl Jung being appointed as one of his assistants in 1900. Bleuler introduced Jung to Freud's work, arranging for Jung to present a lecture on dream theory that same year. By this point, the Burghölzli's international reputation had burgeoned to the extent that it could be described as a place of psychiatric pilgrimage – one that attracted young doctors from all over Europe and the United States. It was an establishment that placed strict demands on its staff, including abstinence from alcohol. Work started at 6 a.m. every day, with evening rounds and write-up running as late as 10 p.m. Even by the standards of the conservative Swiss, this was a rigid institutional structure. In contrast to Vienna, there was no question of a relaxed and egalitarian social atmosphere. Quite the reverse – the strictness that prevailed demanded high standards and industry. For those willing to renounce worldly pleasures and abide by this Protestant work ethic, however, a significant opportunity was presented for career development. The hospital was an elite institution which drew the finest students. It seems likely that in such a pressured culture there would be a great deal of rivalry. Personal achievements were closely guarded possessions that could fire off quarrels among members. In fact, at the very first of the international conferences in Salzburg, 1908, a dispute over the provenance of experimental results broke out – Jung (whose results they were) accused Abraham (who was using them) of plagiarism (Mahony, 1997; Kuhn, 2000). Experimental results were at the heart of the Burghölzli contribution, and achievement in this arena was critical to advancement.

Besides the institutional emphasis on psychological experiments, another element of the Burghölzli's particular group culture was given by Bleuler's acceptance of a strong psychogenic component to mental illness. Such a position was at variance with the standard explanation of psychopathology as the consequence of physical degeneration – an outlook that was taken prominently by Charcot (Goertz, Bonduelle, & Gelfland, 1995). Bleuler's emphasis on the psychogenesis of mental illness placed him in the same camp as Freud. A little after the first contacts with Vienna (initiated by Eitingon and Jung), Jung started an informal group calling themselves the "Freud Society" and consisting of some 25 or so members. In an effort to provide scientific support for Freud's work, Bleuler charged Jung and Franz Riklin to conduct the word association test in an effort to demonstrate the impact of unconscious forces on conscious performance. Adopting the latest technology in experimental psychology, the association test was invented by Francis Galton in Britain, and was subsequently developed as a quantitative instrument by Wilhelm Wundt in Germany. By 1906, the Zurich group had been able to produce strong quantitative evidence for the existence of a dynamic unconscious – a notion which Freud had postulated since 1895. Having previously lacked the kind of evidence with which he might impress the demanding experimental psychiatrists of Europe, Freud was delighted that the Zurich contingent were producing results that might support his work. Nevertheless, both Jung and Bleuler were quite open concerning their reservations over the exclusive role of sexuality in psychoanalytic theory, and they sought to make Freud more aware of how his position on this matter made it difficult to defend psychoanalysis.

In the extent to which Bleuler accepted psychoanalysis as a cutting-edge development, the Burghölzli came to reflect a kind of "recruitment centre" for Freudian thinking:

> The first generation of physicians who practised psychoanalysis as a profession came almost exclusively via Jung and Bleuler, amongst them Karl Abraham, Roberto Greco Assagioli, Ludwig Binswanger, Abraham Arden Brill, Trigant Burrow, Imre Désai, Max Eitingon, Sándor Ferenczi, Otto Gros, Johan Jackob Honegger, Smith Ely Jeliffe, Ernest Jones, Alphonse Maeder, Hans Maier, Hermann Nunberg, Johan K. W. von Ophuijsen, Nikolai J. Ossipow, Franz Riklin, Hermann Rorshach, Tatiana Rosenthal, Leonhard Self, Eugénie Sokolnicka, Sabrina Spielrein, Füöp Stein, Wolf Stockmayer, Johannes Irgens Strømme, Jaroslaw Stuchíik, and G. Alexander Young.
>
> *(Haynal & Falzeder, 2011, p. 182)*

Visiting from across Europe and America, these names reflected the cream of psychiatry at the time. This contrasted strikingly with the less prestigious status of Freud's colleagues in Vienna. Freud (1914) would subsequently acknowledge the key role played by Zurich:

> Everywhere psycho-analysis was becoming the object of ever-increasing interest. But in all other places this accession of interest at first produced nothing but a very emphatic repudiation, mostly a quite passionate one; whereas in Zurich, on the contrary, agreement on general lines was the dominant note. Moreover, nowhere else did such a compact little group of adherents exist, or could a public clinic be placed at the service of psycho-analytic researches, or was there a clinical teacher who included psychoanalytic theories as an integral part of his psychiatric course. The Zurich group thus became the nucleus of the small band who were fighting for the recognition of analysis. The only opportunity of learning the new art and working at it in practice lay there.
>
> *(p. 27)*

The cultures clash: Administration and/or liberation

The first contacts between the two groups began with a correspondence initiated by Jung with Freud in April 1906. The mutual admiration evident in their letters and the relief gained from their idealising support of each other pushed reservations into the background. By 1907, the two groups were courting each other. In January of that year, Max Eitingon was the first emissary from Zurich to visit Berggasse 19. He attended the Wednesday meeting in Vienna to discover that a widely diverse set of interests, topics and aims were being explored, with the group presided over by a relatively tolerant authority in Freud. Jung visited in April, and Karl Abraham (also studying at the Burghölzli) in December.

Impact on the Vienna group: Subsequent to the initial letters exchanged between Freud and Jung, a clear shift appears to have taken place in Vienna. Contact with the Zurich group had promoted awareness of the benefits of good administration, and a sharp change in the Vienna group coincides with the impact of Zurich's experimental findings:

- In October 1906, Otto Rank was appointed to be the group's paid secretary. He was not a clinician. By that time, the society had expanded to around 20 members.
- The picture offered by Stekel of the group's early days contrasts strikingly with Rank's official minutes (Nunberg & Federn, 1962). Gay (1988) states: "The meetings grew testy, even acrimonious, as members sparred for position, vaunted their originality, or voiced dislike of their fellows with a brutal hostility, masquerading as analytic frankness [...] Max Graf sadly observed, 'We are no longer the fellowship we once were'" (pp. 176–177).
- In April 1908, the Wednesday Psychological Society changed its name to the more official-sounding Vienna Psychoanalytical Society.
- Significantly, the Viennese did not take the lead in organising the joint Salzburg conference of 1908, where the two groups first gathered. It was the Burghölzli group that had the organisational competency to launch an international conference.
- Rivalry spluttered into existence in Vienna and was finding full expression by 1910 at the second international conference in Nuremberg. According to Jones (1957), members of the Vienna group objected to suggestions of the Swiss being appointed to the highest jobs in the new international organisation. Rivalrous demands had always been endemic in the Zurich culture, but had not until this time been a feature in Vienna.

Impact on the Zurich group: Despite Vienna's "possession" of Freud himself, the attitudes in Zurich towards Vienna were not respectful (Mahony, 1997). Morale at the Burghölzli was high, and an atmosphere of heroic self-idealisation prevailed (Eisold, 2002). For the Zurich group, the challenge from Vienna concerned the influence of libertarianism:

- Both Bleuler and Jung embraced psychoanalysis with enthusiasm, yet not without significant reservations concerning the place of sexuality. While this difference of opinion was at first expressed openly, it became politically expedient to ignore it. This divergence nevertheless remained and was the ultimate cause of Jung, and then Bleuler, distancing themselves from Freud.
- In addition to Jung's favoured position at the Burghölzli as a senior physician, after Salzburg he also became Freud's favoured crown prince for the psychoanalytic movement. This was likely a provocation both to more junior Burghölzli staff and to members of the Viennese group: "beginning in 1907, with visits from Jung and others from Zurich, affinity had ripened into friendship and, in Freud, into great expectations. The Nurnberg congress only hardened the uneasiness of the Viennese into grim certainty" (Gay, 1988, p. 219).
- The Viennese libertarian attitudes and even behaviour, as perceived in Zurich, were considered transgressive. For Jung, however, they were perhaps also seductive and played into his own ambivalence towards the Burghölzli culture. As Graf-Nold (2001) has uncovered, Jung in fact resigned his post in July 1902, only two years after being appointed, although he continued to work off and on at the hospital up until 1910. Furthermore, Jung would also find himself caught between professional stricture and personal intimacy in terms of his relationship with Sabina Spielrein (Carotenuto, 1981). Jung's maverick position in Burghölzli seems to have perfectly represented the potentially undermining impact of the Viennese on the Zurich culture.

In 1910, resulting from the contact between the two groups, the International Psychoanalytic Association (IPA) emerged – mutually created, but based in Vienna. The new organisation inherited the efficiency of the Burghölzli, yet not without the cost of internal friction as the Viennese contingent struggled to match their Swiss partners. While exhibiting the organised nature of the Zurich group, in an effort to support the development of Freud's ideas, the IPA had still to preserve the Viennese group's atmosphere of openness. It might be argued that the IPA's culture – hierarchical, exclusive and rivalrous – failed to provide an effective space for this kind of exchange. The subsequent fissiparous history of the IPA may be interpreted as a continuing legacy of that failure to provide an adequate reflective space for the marriage of administrative conformity (Burghölzli) and libertarian inclusiveness (Vienna).

Social defence system

The idea of a "social defence system" was first described by Elliott Jaques in 1953 (Jaques, 1955). This notion is used to describe an unconscious social formation resulting in specific cultural practices that function to defend against shared anxieties. Such practices are expressed by conscious cultural attitudes that have emerged to substantiate the practices. Isabel Menzies (1959) offers the example of nursing staff, where employees are confronted by the stress of working with the ill and dying; professional practice developed in such a way as to enable nurses to maintain an emotional distance from patients, with care tending to be reduced to a set of mechanical procedures. The emotional distance afforded by this form of practice protects nurses from an intolerable emotional intimacy with death and pain. These practices are supported by conscious cultural attitudes – for instance, the idea that a good nurse will carry out duties in a neutral way with all patients, regardless of their particular needs and personalities.

The notion that systemic stresses are managed by cultural practices can also be applied within the mental health field. We might therefore seek to investigate whether there was some such dynamic operating within the Vienna and Burghölzli groups. I shall consider the particular stresses operating in a psychiatric hospital like Burghölzli and compare these stresses with those implied in the Viennese group, whose members were treating ambulant neurotics in the context of their private practices. We can predict the stress each group may have suffered on the basis of the nature of their work. Differing anxieties in the workplace are likely to influence aspects of the group's culture in the service of defence.

One striking difference between the Vienna group and the Burghölzli is in the kinds of patients each served. At the Burghölzli, patients were psychotic and admitted in a custodial fashion with considerable restraints placed on their freedom. Not all were physically dangerous, but some were. Patients transgressed social norms as a *sine qua non* of being admitted there. Such a transgressive and unpredictable clientele must inevitably have led to strains on the staff and the institution, just as they do today. Defensiveness can then take the form of an objectifying, depersonalising attitude towards patients, thus serving to support a denial of anxiety (see Hinshelwood, 2004). Barbara Hannah tells a story that supports this. Jung was showing his childhood friend, Albert Oeri, around Burghölzli:

> In one of these wards, which housed the worst patients, the more restless were lying on their beds or standing around. Jung engaged some of them in conversation that could show where their trouble lay. Oeri found this so fascinating that he joined in the conversation himself, until a recumbent and apparently quiet patient suddenly leaped up in his bed and aimed a terrific blow at him from behind. Far from showing any concern at his friend's fright, Jung remarked with some pride that the man could indeed deliver real knockout blows.
>
> *(Hannah, 1976, p. 79)*

We will consider Jung's response to this alarming incident shortly.

Another form of anxiety concerns the question of professional rivalry. This was perhaps especially stressed in members of the Viennese group, for whom financial stability was at stake. Working in a hospital like Burghölzli provided security, albeit at the expense of a dependent relationship on the institution and the consequent need to comply with institutional expectations. By contrast, those in the Vienna group (at least those who were clinicians) were dependent on their patients. The privations that would later ensue in Vienna during the First World War demonstrated the extent to which members of Freud's circle depended on income from private practice (Jones, 1955). It is not known to what extent the Wednesday group served as a referral network, but if we are to assume that they did, this would have entailed a significant mutual dependence that would likely have been reflected in a need to maintain cordial relations between peers.

Collective defence in attitudes and practice

Different cultural attitudes arise partly from divergent working conditions and the nature of the patients each group served. As these divergences arouse different conflicts and anxieties, they provoke specific defensive cultures.

Burghölzli collective defence: To work closely with psychotic patients is to expose oneself to unpredictable and seemingly irrational behaviours, while often fearing a reactive disintegration of one's own mind (Hinshelwood, 2004). It is no coincidence that those institutions serving people experiencing psychosis tend to create a sense of concrete organisational solidity, as exemplified at the Burghölzli in terms of a hierarchical structure and strict daily regime. Additionally, efforts may be made by staff to emotionally distance themselves from patients (see Donati, 1989). This may be suggested in Jung's response, as described by Hannah (quoted above), when showing his friend around the wards. Jung seems to have exhibited a pride in the patient's violence rather than concern at his friend's fright. Emotional distancing of this kind is common in mental health institutions (Hinshelwood, 1999). It might therefore be appropriate to see Jung's attitude and response as indicative of the institutional culture in which he was working, thus reflecting a collectively promoted social defence.

Viennese collective defence: In contrast to the Burghölzli's culture of emotional distancing, in Vienna the group dynamic was shaped by anxieties concerning difference, jealousy and rivalry. Speaking of the Vienna group as it stood in 1908, Gay (1988) writes that they "held formal discussions aimed at 'reforming' procedures, and debated a proposal to abolish *geistigger Kommunismus*; henceforth, each idea should be identified as its originator's private property" (p. 177). The group's original openness prior to the encounter with the Zurich contingent was partly expressed in a communal "ownership" of the ideas discussed. However, it is plausible that this seeming egalitarianism represented a cultural reaction to something which the Vienna group collectively sought to deny – from an outside perspective, the extreme discrepancy of experience and talent between Freud and the other members of the group was quite clear.

Subsequent to their first encounters with Zurich, the private letters of both Eitingon and Abraham expressed what can be considered the Burghölzli view – that they were unimpressed by the followers that Freud had gathered around him and considered them dull (Mahony, 1997). It might be suggested that "open discussion" among the Viennese served as a means to avoid recognition of a more fundamental disparity in terms of native talent. In Vienna, it was essential for group members to pursue good personal relations with each other. Even the non-clinicians could be looked to as a source of referrals and therefore of possible income. The egalitarian culture of the Wednesday meetings could thus also be considered an expression of this mutual dependence. Financial pressures would likely provoke a defensive culture of acceptance and non-confrontation.

Between 1902 and 1907, the Viennese group could comfortably ignore underlying inequalities, rivalries and jealousy by agreeing unconsciously to deny them. From the breakdown in 1907–1910, we can infer an anxiety among the Viennese concerning the question of exposure to comparisons with others, especially Freud, and the financial implications of being professionally evaluated. After 1907, those cultural practices foregrounding acceptance and equality came under threat as the competitive attitudes from Zurich and its organisational competence invaded. Thus, the attitudes of the efficient Burghölzli culture disrupted the egalitarian atmosphere in Vienna. The result was that those anxieties which had been held in unconscious abeyance now emerged to threaten the Viennese. The painful reality of inequality started to become apparent in grumbling about the Swiss, and came to be reflected in the loss of members such as Alfred Adler.

In Zurich, meanwhile, the challenge posed by the Viennese to the defensive culture of emotional distancing left some members of the group exposed. Jung appears to have been particularly vulnerable to the temptations and anxieties associated with transgression. Many of the other members of the Burghölzli group simply moved away to avoid the dangers of psychiatric exposure; they became psychoanalysts working with an out-patient population and members of the international association now centred in Vienna. It might be argued that the emergence of the IPA seems to have provoked the fragmentation of the Burghölzli group. Bleuler came to abandon the psychoanalytic movement, thus rendering the spirit of the Burghölzli less creative and adventurous. The IPA, meanwhile, inherited the Burghölzli's organisational flair while perpetuating those unresolved conflicts that were originally reflected in the clash of the two groups.

Conclusion

Two group cultures have been described, exhibiting clear differences in organisational dynamics. It has been suggested that these differences might be understood to reflect collective defences against shared anxieties, and that the organisational dynamics of each group might inadvertently function so as to undermine the defences of the other. This being so, it might be supposed that this state of affairs constituted a significant factor in the break-up of the initial movement. It would seem that the events of the break-up align with what might be expected on the basis of social defences against each group's prevailing anxieties.

The psychological dimensions of a merger between two organisations are a challenging subject. There is virtually no literature on the unconscious phenomena of merger, nor on the potential for a clash between social defence systems. However, Jinette de Gooijer (2009) and Schalk, Heinen, and Freese (2001) both considered that the psychological effects of mergers stimulated persecutory anxiety. In particular, de Gooijer, in her thesis titled *The Murder in Merger*, describes the common fear based on unconscious phantasies of a murder of the organisation. When an organisation's survival comes to be threatened, so too is that of its members.

When the IPA formed in 1910, its job was to forge a working arrangement between the disparate cultures of Vienna and Zurich. While Jung supported psychoanalysis as a transgressive discourse, Bleuler continued to stand for strict institutional structure and boundaries. A case can therefore be made that the historical processes that gave rise to the developing psychoanalytic movement have less to do with the differences between Freud and Jung than is conventionally assumed, and more to do with group dynamics. I have postulated that the respective social defence systems operative within each group were mutually undermining, the consequences of which are still evident.

References

Bair, D. (2003). *Jung: A biography*. Boston: Little Brown.

Carotenuto, A. (1981). *A secret symmetry*. New York: Pantheon.

de Gooijer, J. (2009). *The murder in the merger: A systems psychodynamic exploration of a corporate merger*. London: Karnac.

Donati, F. (1989). A psychodynamic observer in a chronic psychiatric ward. *British Journal of Psychotherapy, 5*, 317–29.

Eisold, K. (2002). Jung, Jungians, and psychoanalysis. *Psychoanalytic Psychology , 19*, 501–24.

Ellenberger, H. F. (1970). *The discovery of the unconscious. The history and evolution of dynamic psychiatry*. New York: Basic Books.

Freud, S. (1914). On the history of the psycho-analytic movement. In J. Strachey (Ed.), *The standard edition of the complete psychological works of Sigmund Freud*, Vol. 14 (1–66). London: Hogarth.

Freud, S. (1928). Letter to Jung 1st January 1907. In W. McGuire (1974), *The Freud/Jung letters* (53–4). Princeton: Princeton University Press.

Gay, P. (1988). *Freud: A life for our time*. London: Dent.

Goertz, C., Bonduelle, M., & Gelfland, T. (1995). *Charcot: Constructing neurology*. Oxford: Oxford University Press.

Graf-Nold, A. (2001). The Zürich School of Psychiatry in theory and practice. *Journal of Analytical Psychology, 46*, 73–104.

Hannah, B. (1976). *Jung, his life and work*. New York: Putnam.

Haynal, A., & Falzeder, E. (2011). The Swiss. In P. Loewenberg & N. Thompson, (Eds) *100 years of the IPA* (182–95). London: Karnac.

Hinshelwood, R. D. (1999). The difficult patient: the role of "scientific" psychiatry in understanding patients with chronic schizophrenia or severe personality disorder. *British Journal of Psychiatry, 174*, 187–90.

Hinshelwood, R. D. (2004). *Suffering insanity*. London: Routledge.

Jaques, E. (1955). Social systems as a defence against persecutory and depressive anxiety. In M. Klein, R. Money-Kyrle & P. Heimann (Eds), *New directions in psycho-analysis* (478–98). London: Tavistock.

Jones, E. (1955). *The life and work of Sigmund Freud*, Vol. 2. London: Hogarth.

Jones, E. (1957). *The life and work of Sigmund Freud*, Vol. 3. London: Hogarth.

Kuhn, P. (2000). A scandal in Salzburg: Or Freud's surreptitious role in the 1908 Abraham–Jung dispute. *International Journal of Psychoanalysis, 81*, 705–31.

McGlynn, F. (1996). *Carl Gustav Jung*. London: Bantam.

Mahony, P. (1997). The budding International Association of Psychoanalysis and its discontents. In P. Mahony *et al.* (Eds), *Behind the scenes: Freud in correspondence* (47–80). Oslo: Scandinavian University Press.

Makari, G. (2008). *Revolution in mind: The creation of psychoanalysis*. London: Duckworth.

Menzies, L. I. (1959). The functioning of social systems as a defence against anxiety: A report on a study of the nursing service of a general hospital. *Human Relations, 13*, 95–121. Republished in I. Menzies Lyth (1988), *Containing anxiety in institutions*. London: Free Association Books; and in E. Trist and H. Murray (Eds) (1990), *The social engagement of social science*. London: Free Association Books.

Mühlleitner, E., & Reichmayr, J. (1997). Following Freud in Vienna. *International Forum of Psychoanalysis, 6*, 73–102.

Nunberg, H., & Federn, E. (Eds) (1962). *Minutes of the Vienna Psychoanalytic Society*, Vol. 1. New York: International Universities Press.

Schalk, R., Heinen, J., & Freese, C. (2001). Do organizational changes impact the psychological contract and workplace attitudes? A study of a merger of two home care organizations in the Netherlands. In J. de Jonge, V. A. Büssing, & W. B. Schaufeli (Eds), *Organizational psychology and health care at the start of a new millennium*. Mering: Rainer Hampp Verlag.

3

FATE, BROKENNESS, AND BEAUTY

Unconscious psychoanalytic themes

Mary Tennes

The format of this chapter—a pair of interlocking essays—was chosen as a way to approach the relationship between Freud and Jung more at an angle than head on. The fact that the two men drew together and split apart, that they talked for 13 hours without interruption in their first meeting yet in that same conversation confronted their most essential conflicts, expresses essential dilemmas not only between them personally but also within their explorations of psyche, self, and soul. My intent is to evoke rather than to explain, and to ask the reader to contend with multiple realities. Perhaps Freud and Jung, developing their ideas at a profound cultural juncture in which a constellation of conflicts emerged between the scientific and the spiritual, could only consolidate their theories and their selves through differentiation from one another. Yet within psychoanalysis itself the themes of their dialogue continued. What Jung makes explicit and lays out theoretically, Freud struggles with underground, inviting the reader to enter into the very tensions that he seemed to disavow. In focusing on that which lies in the shadows of Freud's work, this chapter attempts to reiterate and elaborate that invitation.

Fate

> Human life—indeed all life—*is* poetry. It's we who live it, unconsciously day by day, like scenes in a play, yet in its inviolable wholeness it lives *us,* it composes *us.* This is something far different from the old cliché "Turn your life into a work of art"; we are works of art—but we are not the artist.
>
> *(Andreas-Salome, 1991)*

Questions of human agency and human fatedness are as ancient as they are compellingly modern. What are we free to determine and what determines us? When Freud chose Oedipus as his mythological centerpiece, he (perhaps unwittingly) placed this question and the attempt to answer it at the heart of psychoanalysis. For at each juncture of Oedipus' story—his conception, his birth, his flight from Corinth, his blind pursuit of the murderer of King Laius—the attempt to defy the oracular prophecy of his fate becomes the guiding principle of the dramatic action. And that very defiance—the insistence upon the willful power to counteract or dismiss fatedness itself—appears to be the *hamartia*, the flaw, the error in orientation that allows the tragedy itself to unfold. The audience watching Sophocles' play is placed in an omniscient position, witness to the protagonist's attempts to mobilize himself against the forces that propel him towards a known outcome, so that the protest itself, the refusal to align with that which he cannot alter, becomes the focus and the subject.

Unlike the ancient Greeks, for whom "fate" was the totality of one's life path foretold and predestined, I use the word, in keeping with Nietzsche, to refer to the unalterable "is-ness" of our lives; that which we are born into by virtue of our genetics, our family, our culture, our circumstance, and that which evolves from these givens. We are "thrown," as Heidegger (1962) said, into a world that we do not choose, so that our essential being is characterized by "*Geworfenheit*" or "thrownness." We are cast into the constraints of existence, constraints that deeply challenge us, frustrate us, and present us with intense loss. At the same time, those very constraints become the container for the most acute experiences of beauty, the transient, contingent quality of our lives, defining our condition as one of "radical openness" (Ruti, 2014, p. 25). Interpreted through a modern lens, Oedipus demonstrates not only the willful and omnipotent desire to challenge the precariousness of this state of being but in addition the resistance to its inherent mystery. The presence of oracular knowledge in Sophocles' play speaks to that which exceeds the boundaries of our understanding, to "that which is unanalyzable—not in the sense of an unanalyzable patient, but in the sense of a remainder term—what is unanalyzable in each of us, that silence shared by Wittgenstein and the Sphinx" (Purcell, 1999, pp. 333–334).

Oedipus attempts, mightily, to evade and challenge not only his preordained path but also the uncanniness and mystery of its unfolding, and we watch as those attempts unravel as the truth overpowers his willful efforts to deny it. The play, then, can be seen to depict the tragedy of the refusal to surrender to that which challenges our known and familiar identifications. For our fate, in its irrefutable otherness, calls us up short as it defeats our egoic convictions and upends our identity as we have constructed it. Fate, in other words, is mysterious and paradoxical. Its hard unalterable edge is a source of helplessness and grief, yet at the same time, like the hard edge of a sculptor's chisel, with our cooperation it can help shape us into our most whole and unique selves.

Despite the fact that Freud sprinkles the word "fate" liberally throughout at least 227 letters, essays, and books, from as early as 1872 to his latest posthumously published works, the concept itself has no explicit place within his theory. He speaks of "accursed fate," "wicked fate," "the malevolence of fate," "jealous fate." Fate is a "taskmaster," has "purpose," is "inevitable," and cannot be "escape[d]." In both *The Interpretation of Dreams* (1900) and "The Theme of the Three Caskets" (1913), Freud directly references the *Moerae*, the three Fates of Greek mythology who "spin the destiny of man." And he coined the term *Schicksalzwang*, meaning "compulsion of destiny" (later translated as "fate neurosis"), to describe a syndrome in which the reiteration of destructive external circumstances suggests that a person is being pursued by a "malignant fate," a variation of a repetition compulsion in which the circumstances themselves become the lived expression of internal conflicts and impulses. Yet the concept of fate is not addressed by him theoretically. This is in keeping, perhaps, with the Fates themselves, who "refuse to speak except in ellipsis—a strange radical otherness […] This silence at the limit of theory lingers ambivalently in psychoanalysis" (Purcell, 1999, p. 345).

Jung, on the other hand, takes up the idea of fate explicitly and directly. In Whitmont's (1969) assessment of Jung, human freedom "rests essentially upon the choice to walk upright on our appointed path, namely when we consent to walk it, or to be dragged 'like cattle to the slaughterhouse' when we attempt to refuse" (p. 48). Jung describes the ego's relationship to what he calls the Self—our known identifications in relation to the larger totality of the psyche—and the need for the ego to recognize its relativized position, subordinate yet seeking alignment with that which is beyond its purview. The process of individuation, not an inevitable psychological development but one that, at some risk, may be chosen, entails a willingness to respond to the call of that which exists beyond the confines of who we know ourselves to be. The opening to the Other—to the "not I," the non-egoic, the shadowy, the denigrated, the feared, the longed for—entails a certain humble reckoning, a capacity to de-integrate (Fordham, 1958) in the service of a broader and yet simultaneously more unique identification. Essential to the Jungian paradigm are certain core assumptions: that our woundedness and our healing depend upon one another; that mystery is inherent; that wholeness underlies fragmentation. The Self with a capital S is an explicit deviation from the Freudian landscape, wherein the unconscious remains personal. Jung's objective psyche describes an unconscious which challenges the limits not only of our awareness but also of our individual and boundaried subjectivity. The assumption that an integrative purposefulness underpins the psyche means that for Jung the reckoning with fate, with the cards we have been dealt, is both the container and the vehicle for a transmuting process.

Freud circles in the darkness around the unnameable, or like Oedipus turns from the blinding beams of truth, or approaches them poetically, circuitously, at a slant (Tennes, 2016). Jung sheds light, uses language more definitively, overtly maps an approach to the very topics that Freud touches with caution. Freud immerses himself in the bodily and the transient, the inevitability of loss, and the necessity for mourning (Freud, 1916, 1917). Jung emphasizes that which underpins or transcends: the soulful, the symbolic, the transformative. It was over these differences that the relationship between the two men became severed and alienated. But perhaps that divisiveness can be thought of as an expression of a fundamental human difficulty that both Freud and Jung were, in very different ways, attempting to address: the challenge of encountering that which deconstructs and unravels who we know ourselves to be.

For the concept of fate itself, if understood in terms that are paradoxical rather than reductionist, points to a conceptualization of selfhood for which our language remains somewhat inadequate. How do we describe the profound interface of our capacity to be agential and our willingness to be, as Lou Andreas-Salome says, composed by life itself? Psychoanalytic theory is eloquent in its descriptions of our defenses against the unthinkable and the intolerable: our omnipotent attempts to control through a refusal of grief, our dissociative shattering of links in an attempt to evade the trauma of truth, our submissive and masochistic relinquishments of selfhood. We have complex conceptualizations of attempts to consolidate and regulate the self through the internalization and control of the very internal objects whose failures threatened catastrophe. We understand, in other words, why and how Oedipus railed against the realities he could not metabolize. And we, of course, have many nuanced theories about the ways in which psychoanalysis, through the immersion in and use of transference and countertransference, enables the unthinkable to be thought and the unbearable to be borne in the service of a more integrated self that is capable of tolerating rather than expelling the difficult.

Yet what lies between the spaces of psychoanalytic theory but remains partially obscured is a conceptualization of self which is more deeply paradoxical, which recognizes the inherent relationship between our capacity to encounter the grievous limits of our existence and our capacity to face the beautiful, the astonishing, and the limitless. The concept of fate itself holds within it the complex recognition that the constraints of our lives intensely and irrevocably define us and yet, at the same time, that who we are inherently transcends our self-definitions. For a surrender to our fate—I use the term "surrender," following Emmanuel Ghent (1990), as distinct from submission—goes hand in hand with the deconstruction of known ways of being, the "break[ing] down" of "false inner organizations which do not really belong to [us]" (Milner, 1969, pp. 384–385). The "ultimate direction" of surrender, says Ghent, "is the discovery of one's identity, one's sense of self, one's sense of wholeness, even one's sense of unity with other living beings" (1990, p. 111). Yet such unity is defended against intensely with, as Ghent points out, masochistic alternatives or, as Oedipus shows us, grandiose attempts to uphold a constrained and constricted identity. Ghent, in a footnote, states:

> It is worth noting here the relation between *healing*, making *whole*, and *holy*, all of which are etymological cognates. In this connection note Winnicott's description of false self as "missing the boat," or at times simply as "missing," "being absent." In the old testament the Hebrew word designating *sin* has as its literal meaning *to miss* as in "missing the boat," "missing an opportunity to be present, alive." The cure for *missing* is to become whole through surrender; the cure for sinning, in this sense, is to come alive, to be present in full awareness, authentic, centered in true self, holy. Rycroft has observed that "there would seem to be no necessary incompatibility between psychoanalysis and those religious formulations which locate God within the self. One could, indeed, argue that Freud's Id (and even more Groddeck's It), the

impersonal force within which is both the core of oneself and yet not oneself, and from which in illness one becomes alienated, is a secular formulation of the insight which makes religious people believe in an immanent God.

(p. 109)

What do we find in the footnotes, the cracks, the margins of psychoanalytic theory? Perhaps a recognition that the conflicts which split Freud and Jung apart were never entirely foreclosed or resolved.

Brokenness and beauty

Rabbi Bradley Shavit Artson tells a story about the Liberty Bell in Philadelphia:

> It was hung in the Philadelphia State House in 1753, and it sounded to summon the pre-Independence Colonial Legislature into session, and it was used after the Revolution for the Pennsylvania State Legislature as well. The intriguing idiosyncrasy of this bell is that when it arrived, it cracked right away. Not once, but twice, American craftspeople repaired the bell by filling in the crack with new metal. And yet it cracked again, and then it cracked again. Apparently the bell wanted to be broken; it had something to say. In the 1830s the abolitionist movement was gaining steam; Americans were awakening to the realization that slavery was economically harmful and morally repugnant. Some bold Americans started to organize against slavery as an ethical and political imperative. The abolitionists were the very first to label this bell the Liberty Bell [...] In 1846 [it] cracked for the final time, and at that point people stopped trying to fill the gap or to ring it [...] I realized that this bell—cracked and silent—resonates more loudly around the globe than any bell that is whole.
>
> *(2013, para. 1–4)*

We are now living again in broken times, when the harmful and the repugnant seem dominant, when the container of our society has been cracked and damaged. And perhaps we are challenged, at this moment in our history, to reconfigure, as our early compatriots did, our relationship to brokenness itself. What does it mean to recognize and tolerate brokenness rather than to cover it over, to "gather up" our brokenness, as Leonard Cohen[1] tells us, in order to heal? Psychoanalysis, of course, attempts to look beneath our symptomatic attempts to consolidate the self and to see, underlying such constructions, the sources of brokenness, the basic fault (Balint, 1968). But the paradoxical ways in which brokenness itself cracks us open to beauty and presence have been less explicitly explored and named.

The Japanese practice of *kintsugi*, literally meaning "golden joinery" is the art of mending broken pottery with lacquer resin dusted or mixed with powered gold. More than an attempt to simply repair, the process emphasizes the intensified beauty to be found in an approach to brokenness which highlights the cracks themselves. Expressive of the philosophy of *wabi-sabi*, a Japanese aesthetic which centers on the acceptance of transience, incompletion, and imperfection, *kintsugi* emphasizes the poignancy and resonance to be found in objects which, in their brokenness, speak to our own. The object becomes beautiful as its cracks are elaborated and integrated rather than covered over, as it moves us to claim rather than turn from our inevitably broken selves.

The openness to beauty, then, is perhaps inherently a form of surrender. The brokenness of both bell and bowl, when not resisted but aligned with, reconfigures the viewer, or invites the viewer to reconfigure themselves. Both necessitate the capacity to be available to the object, to let the object speak (Elkins, 1996). Such an orientation is a surrender to that which is other than one would choose or design, a surrender, in other words, to Otherness itself, to that which presents itself beyond our will or preconceptions. And a recognition, therefore, of the limitations of our subjective constructions, a willingness to be broken open ourselves.

Donald Meltzer and Meg Harris Williams (2008), focusing on "the apprehension of beauty," describe how the original, primary experience of beauty occurs in the baby's encounter with the mother's eyes and body—an intense experience of beauty and truth. But when the mother goes away, or her eyes become clouded and beauty recedes, the "aesthetic conflict" begins: how to not close down to what is stunning, how to find a way back, to wait through the disappearance for beauty to emerge again. The double meaning of the word "apprehend"—to be aware of and to fear—conveys the inevitable complexity that a true opening to the beautiful evokes. Beauty asks of us a certain faith,[2] a loosening of ego boundaries, a letting go of the rigid egoic holds that fend against loss.

Freud himself, writing in 1916, at another time of social upheaval and distress, focused himself on the challenges of sustaining a relationship to beauty. In his relatively obscure and unusual essay "On transience" (a text which itself exists on the margins of his work), he describes a summer walk through the mountain countryside with "a taciturn friend" and "a young but already famous poet"[3] in which the conversation turned towards the natural beauty around them. His companions became dispirited; beauty was intensely present, said the poet, but would vanish like all that is beautiful and so was "shorn of its worth by the transience which was its doom" (Freud, 1916, p. 305). Beauty, the friends felt, was "eclipsed by its negation" (Von Unwerth, 2005, p. 2), so becoming instead only a source of sorrow. Freud disagreed, not with the fact of transience but with the melancholy conclusion. The evanescence of existence, he protested, increases rather than diminishes beauty and value. His companions' despondency, he concluded, lay in their "revolt [...] against mourning" (Freud, 1916, p. 306); their difficulty with grieving mortality and limitation prevented them from sustaining joy as well. In a manner somewhat unusual for Freud, who tended towards a more pessimistic view of the human condition, in this text he emphasizes the deep value and pleasure to be found in that which, because of its transience, offers inspiration and a sense of worth:

> As regards the beauty of Nature, each time it is destroyed by winter it comes again next year, so that in relation to the length of our lives it can in fact be

regarded as eternal. The beauty of the human form and face vanish for ever in the course of our own lives, but their evanescence only lends them a fresh charm. A flower that blossoms only for a single night does not seem to us on that account less lovely [...] A time may indeed come when the pictures and statues which we admire today will crumble to dust, or a race of men may follow us who no longer understand the works of our poets and thinkers, or a geological epoch may even arrive when all animal life upon the earth ceases; but since the value of all this beauty and perfection is determined only by its significance for our own emotional lives, it has no need to survive us and is therefore independent of absolute duration.

(ibid., pp. 305–306)

This poetic prose piece, with its focus on the capacity to appreciate both natural and created beauty, was written at a time when:

the war broke out and robbed the world of its beauties [...] and let loose the evil spirits within us which we thought had been tamed forever [...] it robbed us of very much that we had loved, and showed us how ephemeral were many things that we had regarded as changeless.

(ibid., p. 307)

A broken time, in other words, not so unlike our own. Yet in the face of both personal and cultural mourning, Freud wrote a tribute not only to the intertwining of beauty and brokenness but to our capacity for openness and presence as we navigate the fleeting, fluid quality of our lives and of our selves.

Despite this testament, however, Freud struggled intensely with what it meant to encounter and surrender to the immediacy and power of beauty, as if the dialogue about transience that summer day in fact expressed a lifelong internal conflict. As Matthew Von Unwerth (2005) notes:

Even in his writings about those artists he most admired, such as Leonardo and Michelangelo, Freud's enjoyment of beauty depended on his ability to analyze it [...] Before experiences of beauty, such as that afforded by art, Freud had declared psychoanalysis powerless.

(pp. 126–127)

Moments of transporting beauty or ecstasy not mediated by interpretive thinking were almost entirely inaccessible to Freud, or so he claimed, and were linked by him to his well-known insistence that within himself he could find no trace of an oceanic feeling of unity, wonder, or awe (Freud, 1930, p. 65). "To me mysticism is just as closed a book as music," he wrote in 1929 (see Parsons, 1999, p. 175). The fear of losing a separate and fixed identity in opening to the beautiful and the ineffable in fact seems to drive Freud's thinking, and this barrier has been consolidated within psychoanalysis into a tendency to reduce or pathologize states of immersion and union (Rundel, 2015). For Freud, such states are seen to represent relics of the earliest boundary diffusion of the infant's ego and are to be transformed by more mature encounters with reality. Yet his seemingly conclusive interpretation of such experiences as expressions of infantile longing belies his lasting interest in them.

In fact, in his longstanding, quite astonishing exchange with his friend, Romain Rolland, Freud's preoccupation with questions about the unbounded, the beautiful, and the loving was ongoing and unresolved. Rolland was an esteemed novelist, musician, musicologist, historian, dramatist, art critic, political spokesman, poet, mystic, and Nobel laureate. He had read and admired Freud for 20 years before they first spoke, and Freud was well aware and deeply admiring of him in return. The dialogue between them (quoted in Parsons, 1999, pp. 170–179), initiated by Freud and lasting 13 years from 1923 to 1936 until both were elderly and ill, focuses almost entirely upon Freud's unsettled response to Rolland's mystical experiences and Rolland's attempts to correct what he saw as Freud's misunderstanding of them. Most noteworthy is Freud's clear and exuberant response to Rolland himself and his capacities. In his first letter, Freud began effusively, even as he then somewhat dismissively retracted his enthusiasm:

> That I have been allowed to exchange a greeting with you will remain a happy memory to the end of my days. Because for us your name has been associated with the most precious of beautiful illusions, that of love extended to all mankind. I, of course, belong to a race which in the Middle Ages was held responsible for all epidemics and which today is blamed for the disintegration of the Austrian Empire and the German defeat. Such experiences have a sobering effect and are not conducive to make one believe in illusions [...] My writings cannot be what yours are: comfort and refreshment for the reader.
>
> *(Freud, quoted in Parsons, 1999, p. 171)*

Rolland responded with a quick and incisive retort, sending Freud, within less than a week, a copy of his 1919 play *Liluli*, whose title character was the Goddess of Illusion. Written in response to Rolland's acute distress and sorrow about the state of the postwar world, the play was a fierce, farcical, and satiric critique of "illusions of all kinds" (Vermorel, 2009, p. 1240), including institutionalized religion. Clearly challenging Freud's view of him as the impenitent idealist, Rolland wrote a dedication: "To Freud, the Destroyer of Illusions" (p. 1240). Somewhat chagrined, Freud replied: "I find the subtle irony of your dedication well deserved, since I had completely forgotten *Liluli* when I wrote the silly passage in question in my letter" (p. 1240).

Thus began a conversation which continued in a similar vein for essentially the remainder of Freud's life, with Freud both awed and disconcerted by Rolland's mystical nature. In fact, of all the figures in Freud's world, Roland was the subject of some of his most glowing accolades. "I revered you as an artist and apostle of love for many years before I saw you" (Freud, quoted in Parsons, 1999, p. 172), Freud wrote in a letter of 1926, after their first and only meeting. "Your lines are among the most precious things which these days have brought me" (ibid.), he wrote in another. And, later on:

> I may confess to you that I have rarely experienced that mysterious attraction of one human being for another as vividly as I have with you; it is somehow bound up, perhaps, with the awareness of our being so different.
>
> *(ibid., p. 178)*

Yet when, in a letter of 1927, Rolland used the word "oceanic" to describe states of being that he felt were not addressed in Freud's conceptualization of religious experience,[4] Freud was deeply unsettled, waiting two years before responding and then telling Rolland that "your letter containing your remarks about a feeling you describe as 'oceanic' has left me no peace" (Parsons, 1999, p. 174). Indeed, *Civilization and Its Discontents*—a more precise translation of the title is *The Uneasiness in Civilization*—appears to have been written in those two years as a response to their conversation, and it begins with a description of this "exceptional" man whose "feeling of indissoluble connection, of belonging inseparably to the external world as a whole" (1930, p. 76) Freud felt compelled to explore.

In Rolland, Freud perhaps found a figure who returned him to unresolved dilemmas, to the crack in the container of his orientation which had first opened with Jung, who was similarly interested in experiences of the unbounded. In one letter to Rolland, in fact, Freud somewhat equates the two men, describing Jung as "a bit of a mystic himself" who, "hasn't belonged to us for years" (Parsons, 1999, p. 176). With Rolland, however, who was a peer but not a professional colleague, and whom Freud met at a later time when both men were sick and acutely aware of mortality, the conversation was less fraught than it had been with Jung and was characterized by a greater willingness to entertain uncertainty.

It might be suggested that a state of paradoxical uncertainty is in some degree fundamental to the experience of beauty. Beauty arises in the place where self and other, subject and object, meet, where there is both separateness and not, where one is undone and yet reconfigured by the other. To allow ourselves to be open to beauty, such as that encountered in the natural landscape by Freud and his friends on their walk in the countryside, is to allow ourselves to become aware of the fluid, transient nature of both self and other. We are changed by the beautiful and, in the words of the poet Richard Wilbur, the beautiful itself changes:

> as a forest is changed
> By a chameleon's tuning his skin to it
> As a mantis, arranged
> On a green leaf, grows
> Into it, makes the leaf leafier, and proves
> Any greenness is deeper than anyone knows
>
> *(Wilbur, 2004, p. 462)*

Forest and chameleon, mantis and leaf; each loses its separateness and becomes more itself through the other. Thus, the movement towards beauty invites an unravelling and deconstruction of the known parameters of the self, a "sundering," as Wilbur says, "of Things and things' selves for a second finding" (p. 462). What Freud was drawn to, yet balked at, was the paradoxical reality that, in order to more fully find the self, the self must first be lost. And yet, of course, this is the territory of psychoanalysis itself. As Anna Freud wrote, quoting Marion Milner, in her introduction to Milner's book *On Not Being Able to Paint*, the aesthetic and the psychoanalytic are both feared:

> There is the same unwillingness to transgress beyond the reassuring limits of the secondary process and "to accept chaos as a temporary stage." There is the same fear of the "plunge into no-differentiation" and the disbelief in the "spontaneous ordering forces" which emerge once the plunge is taken. There is, above all, the same terror of the unknown.
>
> *(A. Freud, in Milner, 1950, pp. xiii–xiv)*

Perhaps Freud struggled with the fact that his method opened him, beyond his own intentions, to realities which threatened to undo him. Indeed, perhaps most of us similarly struggle to remain open to brokenness and beauty, moving us, as they do, towards the undefinable and the ungraspable, towards new and unknown definitions of ourselves.

Coda

> And why are there resistances to this in the first place? Because lurking in the unconscious background there is always the primitive terror of losing oneself, of being engulfed into nothingness.
>
> *(Saketopoulou, 2015, p. 636)*

> I was afraid there'd be no doing if I did not say I, brood over I, fight for I. Now I'm letting I go, but eat my breakfast just the same, and it tastes better, for I'm not impelled to hurry to think of something which must be done to save I. So there's nothing to distract me from the taste of my marmalade and crisp toast [...] And as I glance out of the window I notice an apple tree, black branches against the white of frost-covered roofs—and it seems much better than brooding over my rights.
>
> *(Milner, aka Fields, 1936, pp. 196–197)*

The "primitive terror of losing oneself" arises in the face of surrender, a terror that becomes easily conflated—perhaps symbolically equated—with the letting go which accompanies the most significant movements towards presence and wholeness. To align with rather than to resist one's fate, to open ourselves to what is beautiful and transient, requires a willingness to let go of an insistent identification, a brooding over, and a fighting for the "I"—the known egoic self. Yet the letting go which surrender necessitates can seem not only to threaten dissolution at the most primitive levels of experience, but also to highlight the reality of our human frailty. Jung developed language to describe the inevitable and necessary pull, in an individuating process, towards the ego's reconfiguring of itself, its capacity to recognize its subordinate position, humbled by its partiality and limitations. Freud embodied and expressed the intense, inevitable, and often unconscious fears evoked by letting go. These preoccupations, however sidelined they were in his work, persisted nonetheless.

Indeed, to honor Romain Rolland's 70th birthday, when Freud himself was 80 and acutely aware of his own decline, he chose to write another piece: an intimate open letter to Rolland concerning "A disturbance of memory on the Acropolis." Freud spoke to Rolland of something that had happened years before when he visited Athens for the first time—an experience which he had first described in *The Future of an Illusion* as remarkable:

> I stood for the first time on the hill of the Acropolis in Athens, between the temple ruins, looking out over the blue sea. A feeling of astonishment mingled with my joy. It seemed to say: "So it really is true, just as we learnt at school!"
>
> *(Freud, 1927, p. 25)*

The direct encounter with the reality of what was before him was astounding to Freud, who struggled to believe what he was seeing. Soon afterwards, in conversation with Marie Bonaparte, he is reported to have said that the experience "had surpassed anything he had ever imagined" and that "the amber-colored columns of the Acropolis were the most beautiful things he had ever seen in his life" (Ernest Jones, quoted in Parsons, 1999, p. 81). The vividness of the reality, the starkly beautiful immediacy of what he had until that moment only held in his mind, was both stunning and overwhelming. Parsons (1999) suggests that Freud was bringing to Rolland an experience whose vibrancy was as close as Freud came to mystical awareness.

Nonetheless, Freud found the experience disturbing because, he says, his psyche was divided between the astonishment that the Acropolis was in fact real and the shock that he was astonished in this way. He goes on to say that:

> incredulity of this kind is obviously an attempt to repudiate a piece of reality; but there is something strange about it. We should not be in the least astonished if an attempt of this kind were aimed at a piece of reality that threatened to bring unpleasure: the mechanism of our mind is, so to speak, planned to work along just such lines. But why should such incredulity arise in something which, on the contrary, promises to bring a high degree of pleasure? Truly paradoxical behaviour! [...] But why?
>
> *(Freud, 1936, p. 242)*

Why, Freud wonders, would we balk at the intensely beautiful and desired? Why would we attempt to deny the very existence of that which we find most compelling? "Because," he answers, "one cannot expect Fate to grant one anything so good" (p. 242). Freud thus conceptualizes this "disturbance" as a retreat from possibilities one cannot fathom. He then enacts this very retreat by moving quickly away from a focus on the strange, the paradoxical, and the good, to formulate self-interpretations about Oedipal guilt and to diagnose his response as an instance of derealization. Yet derealization is generally characterized by a foggy, veiled, one-dimensional sense of unreality, a lack of emotional coloring and depth. Quite to the contrary, Freud's experience was one of intense and open-eyed contact with what was before him in all its richness: the co-existence of present and past, beauty and loss, limit and limitlessness, life and death. The language of the particular, the sensory, and the material seems to characterize such moments. Milner tastes the marmalade and crisp toast and sees the contrasting black branches against white frost-covered roofs. Freud stands by the temple ruins, with their amber-colored columns, looking out over the blue sea. The *thingness* of the world in its inviolable wholeness is thrown into sharp relief; things are essentially themselves, yet, at the same time, they are imbued with meaning, like vivid dream images, or like a lived poem.

I suggest, in a reinterpretation of Freud's analysis of himself, that such an opening is both frightening and astonishing because the known and isolated "I," as Milner says, has been suspended as the central organizing lens, exposing the exquisitely paradoxical nature of things. In the face of such experience, we, like Oedipus, like Freud, can balk at the threats to our identity, can resist and repudiate our own deconstruction, can fight for the "I" as we fear its evanescence. Yet reality itself in its beauty and transience challenges the ego's convictions about its own fixity while offering, at the same time, stunning images of the enduring: the still standing structures of a vanished world set against a backdrop of oceanic constancy. To "become whole through surrender [...] to come alive, to be present in full awareness" (Ghent, 1990), cracks open the container of our conscious orientation so that, cracked vessels ourselves, we can see the beauty and the continuity that our brokenness reveals.

In contending with the passage of time—his friend's birthday, his own past, his own mortality—Freud returned to an earlier experience, gathering and interweaving[5] it still, attempting to discover and to communicate something as of yet not fully grasped, something begun years earlier in dialogue with Jung. Listening to the unconscious voice of psychoanalysis, searching in the spaces between,[6] we find Freud searching too, with trepidation and courage, uncertainty and desire, for that which most unravels us yet leads us most fully to ourselves.

Notes

1   "There is a crack in everything/that's how the light gets in."
2   These words echo a line from Robert Frost's poem "Choose Something Like a Star."

3   Freud was referring to Lou Andreas-Salome and Rainer Maria Rilke, whose identities he was protecting. In fact, it has been argued that the walk itself may not even have occurred, nor may the place Freud describes actually have existed. Instead, the essay may function as an imaginative expression of central issues and conflicts that can be found throughout Freud's writings and life (Von Unwerth, 2005).

4   Rolland was responding to Freud having sent him a copy of *Future of an Illusion*. Rolland responded by agreeing with Freud's analysis of religion but added that "I would have liked to see you doing an analysis of *spontaneous religious sentiment* or, more exactly, of religious *feeling,* which is wholly different from *religions* in the strict sense of the word, and much more durable" (quoted in Parsons, 1999, p. 174).

5   "Memoria," says John O'Donohue (2010), "is always quietly at work, gathering and interweaving experience. Memoria is the place where our vanished lives secretly gather. For nothing that happens to us is ever finally lost or forgotten. In a strange way, everything that happens to us remains somehow still alive within us" (p. 138).

6   "Don't shoot for the stars; we already know what's there. Shoot for the space in between because that's where the real mystery lies"—this quote comes from Vera Rubin (2016), the female astrophysicist who, against great odds and with intense devotion to science, confirmed the existence of dark matter and in so doing revolutionized our understanding of the universe.

References

Andreas-Salome, L. (1991). *Looking back: Memoirs.* New York: Paragon House.

Artson, R. B. (2013, September 12). The crack is what lets in the light. Retrieved from www.huffingtonpost.com/rabbi-bradley-shavit-artson/the-crack-is-what-lets-in_b_3915053.html (accessed 30 January 2017).

Balint, M. (1968). *The basic fault: Therapeutic aspects of regression.* London: Tavistock.

Elkins, J. (1996). *The object stares back: On the nature of seeing.* New York: Simon & Schuster.

Field, J. (Milner, M.) (1936). *A life of one's own.* London: Virago.

Fordham, M. (1958). Individuation and ego development. *Journal of Analytical Psychology, 3,* 115–30.

Freud, S. (1900). The interpretation of dreams. In *Standard edition* (Vol. IV, pp. ix–627). London: The Hogarth Press.

Freud, S. (1913). The theme of the three caskets. In *Standard edition* (Vol. XII, pp. 289–302). London: The Hogarth Press.

Freud, S. (1916). On transience. In *Standard edition* (Vol. XIV, pp. 303–307). London: The Hogarth Press.

Freud, S. (1917). Mourning and melancholia. In *Standard edition* (Vol. XIV, pp. 237–58). London: The Hogarth Press.

Freud, S. (1927). The future of an illusion. In *Standard edition* (Vol. XXI, pp. 1–56). London: The Hogarth Press.

Freud, S. (1930). Civilization and its discontents. In *Standard edition* (Vol. XXI, pp. 57–146). London: The Hogarth Press.

Ghent, E. (1990). Masochism, submission, surrender: Masochism as a perversion of surrender. *Contemporary Psychoanalysis, 26,* 108–36.

Heidegger, M. (1962). *Being and time.* New York: Harper.

Meltzer, D., & Williams, M. H. (2008). *The apprehension of beauty: The role of aesthetic conflict in development, art, and violence.* London: Published for the Harris Meltzer Trust by Karnac.

Milner, M. (1950). *On not being able to paint.* London: Heinemann Educational Books.

Milner, M. (1969). *The hands of the living god: An account of a psycho-analytic treatment.* New York: International Universities Press.

O'Donohue, J. (2010). *Four elements: reflections on nature.* New York: Harmony Books.

Parsons, W. B. (1999). *The Enigma of the Oceanic Feeling: Revisioning the Psychoanalytic Theory of Mysticism.* New York: Oxford University Press. PEP Web. (2016). Retrieved from www.pep-web.org/ (accessed 30 January 2017).

Purcell, W. J. (1999). The agon with fate. *Psychoanalysis and Contemporary Thought, 22,* 343–63.

Rubin, V. (2016, February 4). [Web log comment].

Rundel, M. (2015). The fire of Eros: Sexuality and the movement toward union. *Psychoanalytic Dialogues, 25,* 614–30.

Ruti, M. (2014). *The call of character: Living a life worth living.* New York: Columbia University Press.

Saketopoulou, A. (2015). Sexual rapture, ego rupture and the role of transgression: A discussion of Megan Rundel's "The fire of Eros: Sexuality and the movement towards union". *Psychoanalytic Dialogues, 25,* 631–37.

Tennes, M. A. (2016). Tell all the truth but tell it slant: Psychoanalysis and the uncanny. Reading presented at Psychoanalytic Institute of Northern California, San Francisco.

Vermorel, H. (2009). The presence of Spinoza in the exchanges between Sigmund Freud and Romain Rolland. *International Journal of Psychoanalysis, 90,* 1235–54.

Von Unwerth, M. (2005). *Freud's Requiem: Mourning, Memory, and the Invisible History of a Summer Walk.* New York: Riverhead Books.

Whitmont, E. C. (1969). *The symbolic quest: Basic concepts of analytical psychology.* New York: Published by Putnam for the C.G. Jung Foundation for Analytical Psychology.

Wilbur, R. (2004). *Collected Poems 1943–2004.* Orlando: Harcourt Books.

PART II
New thinking on early debates

4

ON THE OTHERWISE ENERGIES OF THE HUMAN SPIRIT

A contemporary comparison of Freudian and Jungian approaches[1]

Barnaby B. Barratt

The concord, followed by discord and divergence, between Sigmund Freud and Carl Jung has affected a dozen decades of thinking about the character of knowing and being in our psychic life. One may well interpret their schism as a matter of personality and politics, but what remain are some important and fundamental questions about how one considers the human condition and how one hopes for its healing. In this chapter I will focus on Freud's and Jung's variant notions of *psychic energy,* using Jean Laplanche's (1992, 1992–1993, 2000–2006) reading of Freudian theory to sharpen this focus, and with some digression into other teachings about subtle energies. My general intent is an exploration of the ways in which the differences between Freud and Jung on this issue might be crucially relevant for our understanding of the psyche in these early decades of the twenty-first century.

Prefatory note

At the time of the dramatic turn-of-the-century germination of psychoanalysis and analytical psychology, in the span of the two decades from approximately 1895 to 1915, it was Jung who argued that the practitioner's personality, theoretical affiliations, and mode of clinical practice are inextricably entwined. As Freud (1912) acknowledged, we also owe to Jung the crucially important principle that one cannot be an analyst unless one has submitted to an extensive, and perhaps recurring, personal analysis. In this context, to commence this chapter with a certain amount of self-disclosure seems only appropriate, including an explanation of why I was enthusiastic to respond to the invitation to contribute to this anthology (although feeling not entirely competent to do so).

Like Jung, I have been—since adolescence and long before my psychoanalytic training—interested in the insights coming not only from the Abrahamic but also from the Dharmic and Taoic spiritual traditions. Unlike Jung, who seems to have felt that "Westerners" could not grasp yoga authentically, I have tried not only to study but also to practice within the lineages of tantric meditation (within both the Hindu tradition and the Buddhist *vajrayāna*). In addition to my formal education in England and the USA, I have lived, traveled, and studied in India, Thailand, China, and now southern Africa. All this has, I believe, enormously enhanced my understanding of psychoanalysis, of what healing is, and of what the human condition might be.

My psychoanalytic training was in the USA under the auspices of the American and International Psychoanalytic Associations, and included two lengthy periods of personal treatment. The didactic curriculum heavily emphasized not only the reading of Freud but also the structural-functional or ego-psychological school, from Anna Freud and Heinz Hartmann to Paul Gray and Fred Busch (via more of Jacob Arlow and Charles Brenner than one might imagine possible). As I recall, the syllabi included just four papers by Melanie Klein, two or three papers by Donald Winnicott, and some of the contributions of Heinz Kohut; no Wilfred Bion, and certainly no Jung! The rebellious consequence of this induction was that I became an ardent advocate of wide-ranging and far-reaching psychoanalytic curricula. As soon as I graduated, I started to study the Kleinian, neo-Kleinian, independent object-relational, interpersonal-relational, and Lacanian, as well as post-Lacanian, literatures. Having been recruited to the Institute's faculty, I developed a seminar for the candidates-in-training suitably titled "Comparative Psychoanalysis."

However, to this day, Jung and the post-Jungians remain far less familiar to me than other standpoints—although I have wrestled with this voluminous canon, and continue to do so. When I read texts by Jung and those who have followed in his footsteps, I often remain bewildered. Yet periodically I begin to feel that I might be some sort of a variant of what Andrew Samuels (1985) calls an "unknowing Jungian." In any event, I accepted with alacrity the invitation to participate in this project, although my expertise lies in a particular interpretation of Freudian ideas and so I am somewhat unsure whether what I want to present will be of credible interest to a Jungian reader. I ask for indulgence.

Interestingly, there is a sense in which both Freud and Jung start with "association," but in very different métiers. At the Burghölzli Hospital, Jung's studies in word association, first published in 1906, concerned the content of responses, reaction time, and emotional interference to single words presented by the researcher. By contrast, as he moved away from suggestion, catharsis, and hypnotic techniques between 1892 and 1898, Freud's interest was in the streaming of consciousness as censorship was relaxed and ideas or feelings are expressed pell-mell (Bankart, 1997; Ellenberger, 1970). To some degree, theoretical differences such as Jung's later views on the nature of the "personal unconscious," on the significance of dissociation rather than repression, and on the conditions of oedipality might be traced to this difference in their approach to associative phenomena.

As I indicated, the point of contact—both communicative and undoubtedly miscommunicative—between Freud and Jung on which I will focus is the notion of psychic energy or *Trieb* ("desire" or "drive" as libidinality). By way of amplification, I invoke a number of different approaches concerning the significance of psychic energy. Freud's oeuvre is not monolithic, nor is Jung's. I read Freud through Laplanche, emphasizing the writings prior to the development of objectivistic models such as that of the 1923 structural-functional theory, and I approach Jung's corpus in a way that examines the shifting of his ideas from 1912, when he was still very much under the influence of Freud, to those of the 1930s.

As is well known, introductory textbooks routinely summarize the divergence that occurred between 1906 and 1913 as pivoting on Freud's emphasis on the sexuality of libidinal vicissitudes contrasted with Jung's insistence on desexualizing the notion of psychic energy. Leaving aside the personal and political tensions between them, this summary assessment of their divergent paths is, in many respects, correct. It is clearly documented and has been much discussed (e.g., Brabant, Falzeder, & Giamperi-Deutsch, 2000; McGuire, 1974; Paskauskas, 1995). Also at issue are several derivative matters, such as Jung's tendency to recalibrate the oedipus complex, his later emphasis on dissociative processes, and his "soulful" explorations of the collective unconscious (McGuire & Hull, 1977). However, the disagreement concerning the nature of psychic energy can still be considered pivotal. This debate warrants revisiting, partly in light of recent scientific thinking concerning "subtle energies," and partly because, as I will suggest with some temerity, Freud and Jung both seem somewhat confused about their own ideas. I will begin with my interpretation of Freud, admitting forthrightly that there are, of course, other ways of reading his ideas.

A riff on Freud's notion of psychic energy

Freud's interest in "free-association" (*freie-Assoziation* or *freier Einfall*), which even to the end of his career he insisted is the *sine qua non* of his discipline (Freud, 1916–1917, 1924, 1925, 1937), is precisely with its *kinesis*. The movement from one association to the next, as a series of logical and rhetorical transformations, discloses underlying preconscious and deeply preconscious (that is, descriptively unconscious) themes that have eluded the speaker's self-conscious reflection. However, this streaming, chaining, or concatenation (*assoziative Verkettung* or *Verkettung von Einfällen*) of logical and rhetorical transformations that are not available to immediate reflection is further deranged by the disruption of an anarchic force that does not seem thematically organized. Thus, Freud's experience with free-associative discourse compelled him to write about the subtle energies of *Trieb* (drive, desire, or libidinality) as a "helpful notion" (*Hilfvorstellung*) that seemed necessary to explain the phenomena routinely evident via this method. There are deeply preconscious themes (in a Kleinian lexicon, "unconscious phantasies"), and then there is the disruptive eruption of libidinal energy or desire. By 1915, Freud will name these embodied traces, impulses, sparks, or waves of energy "thing-presentations," as contrasted with the representation of thoughts and wishes that can be verbally articulated and that furnish the conscious, preconscious, and deeply preconscious psyche.

Thus, a deeply preconscious representation (or "unconscious phantasy") may be *other* than those that are readily available to our self-consciousness, whereas a thing-presentation may be effective within us but is *otherwise* than that which can be represented (Barratt, 2016, in press a). It is as if these thing-presentations comprise a wild charge of subtle energy that latches on—as if randomly—to signifiers in the conscious concatenation of thoughts and wishes. Here, "as if randomly" implies that this "latching on" has meaning in terms of embodied desire but makes no sense in terms of the signifier's meaningfulness within the law and order of representational transformations. The otherwise effusion of thing-presentations, as they impinge upon the manifest text of consciousness, thus causes significant disturbances, perturbations, or commotions within the logical and rhetorical sense made by representational transformations between signifiers.

The subtle energy of thing-presentations, which Freud also called libidinality, *either* is generated by enigmatic (incomprehensible or "otherwise") messages imposed on individuals from their earliest infancy, as Laplanche describes so well, *or* is the trace of representations that have been decomposed as they were exiled across the "repression barrier." That is, when representations are repressed (as contrasted with suppression into some archive of preconscious ideation), they deteriorate into repositories (traces, impulses, sparks, or waves) of vibrational energy. After the repressively enforced decay of representations into charges of energy, these thing-presentations persist in our embodied experience and then insist themselves on our representational world. Repression is thus, in Freud's words, a "failure of translation." The energies that are beyond the "repression barrier" cannot be translated, sufficiently or adequately, back into representational form. Hence, I have dubbed them "otherwise" than representationality. But they continue to have a disruptively eruptive impact on the cogency, coherence, and continuity—the law and order—of the representational world. Free-associative processes open conscious discourse to this impact, which is why this method is essential to our capacity to appreciate the repressed unconscious and is rightly upheld as the *sine qua non* of Freud's discipline. Thus, the energies of thing-presentations exuberantly elude and exceed the purview of representationality, yet they are always with us as a dimension of our erotic embodied experience (as can be demonstrated by the chaotic moments in the streaming of free-associative discourse). For this reason, as Freud hinted, the repression barrier is to be understood as the psychic inscription of what he called the "incest barrier" (Barratt, 2012, 2013a, 2013b, 2016).

Without amplifying these issues further, it can be seen here how experience with free-associative discourse, and with our resistances to it, gave Freud insight into the importance of incest prohibitions (in relation to the development of our embodied experience and its apparent supersession by linguistically structured representationality) to a preliminary understanding of oedipal processes and complexities. That is, as the repression barrier is established with the child's induction into language, all pre-linguistic experience—to whatever extent it can be represented—must be gathered into the system of oedipalized representationality by processes of "afterwardsness" or *Nachträglichkeit*, and unrepresentable experience remains energetically embodied as "thing-presentations" (cf. Barratt, 2016; Green, 1972–1986, 1997, 2002; Laplanche, 1992, 1992–1993, 2000–2006). Yet, contrary to post-Freudian modifications of "psychoanalysis," Freud's discipline (at least in the first two decades of its articulation) remains inherently somatocentric and somatogenic.

From this introduction to Freud's implicit and explicit thinking between the years 1895 and 1915, we may note several major assumptions that he made about psychic energy, "drive," or desire. For the purposes of this chapter, I will mention five of these. Noting them will provide a basis from which to discuss other standpoints comparatively.

(1) *Ontological nonidenticality and the "threefold" psyche:* Whether Freud recognized this or not, he subverts the Cartesian dualism of mind/body by introducing what I have called an ontologically "threefold" character of the human condition (Barratt, 2016). He wrote of the subtle energies of *Trieb* as a "boundary notion"—a force flowing *between* biology and psychology, mediating their distinct operations. Thus, psychic energy is neither purely physical nor purely representational. It is not, for example, the same as the mechanisms that manifest in behavioral form but are genetically encoded—routines that ethology calls "fixed" or "modal action patterns," which have environmental triggers or "innate releaser mechanisms." Freud called the latter *Instinkte*, and, although this has been much confused by the Standard Edition of his works in English, he clearly separated these automatic biological operations or "instincts" from the notion of psychic energy or *Trieb*. So psychic energy is not in itself biological, but nor is it psychological, precisely because it is not equivalent to anything that can be adequately or sufficiently represented as a thought or wish in what we commonly call the "mind." As I have already indicated, psychic energy, as far as Freud is concerned, fuels representations (*cathects* or *decathects* them), moving them in and out of various conscious and preconscious states. But its meaningfulness is not itself representable and, in relation to the representational transformations that it fuels, it is elusive, excessive, and exuberant. Thus, psychic energy is neither identical with biological operations nor with the representations in which it invests in an apparently erratic or anarchic manner. However, although Freud called psychic energy a "helpful idea," there can be little doubt that he understood its force as a reality, rather than an abstraction.

(2) *Endogenous constitution and conservative principles:* In all his public statements, Freud clearly assumed that *Trieb* is endogenously constituted, that is, only found within the individual, rather than also flowing between individuals, or through and around the individual. This assumption that the genesis and vicissitudes of psychic energy are entirely endogenous is actually somewhat peculiar on Freud's part, although clearly it rendered his psychoanalytic theorizing more acceptable to conventional science. However, Freud secretly believed in telepathy, that is, communication operating beyond the physicality of the five senses. So there is some inconsistency here. We know that Freud himself must have recognized this, since he wrote to Ernest Jones that his belief was his "own affair" and that "the subject of telepathy is not related to psychoanalysis" (letter of March 7th, 1926, italics

omitted; Freud and Jones, 1908–1939). Yet the subject surely implies the transpersonal movement of subtle energies; that is, it contradicts the assumption of a totally endogenous constitution (cf. Barratt, in press b).

We owe to Laplanche a brilliant exegesis and extrapolation of Freud's thinking concerning the way in which libidinality emerges from biological operations yet involves enigmatic messages that bombard the organism from outside. That is, Laplanche opens us to the possibility of an exogenous—yet nonphysical—factor in the genesis of our libidinality. He interprets Freud's notion of *Anlehnung* to show how psychic energy "leans on," is "propped upon," or "follows from" innately programmed biological mechanisms, but is modified by the organism's bombardment with enigmatic messages. The latter are semiotic transmissions that are indecipherable, or otherwise than representationality. They come from outside the infant, notably from the caretakers and other aspects of the surrounds.

Freud also assumed that the subtle energy of libidinality operates according to the conservative principles of a closed "hydraulic" or thermodynamic system. Among other influences, the researches of Hermann Helmholtz (e.g., 1885) undoubtedly prompted Freud's assumption that psychic energy must follow the principles of classical Newtonian physics. It probably could not have been otherwise, since ideas such as those of energetic effects operating at a distance, of the spontaneous generation of energies, or of energy movements based on expansiveness, and so forth, would have seemed like mysticism to Freud. Again, there are some paradoxes and complexities here—if the initiation of the infant's drive or desire requires interaction with caretakers who bombard the uncomprehending child with enigmatic messages that mold the child's libidinality, then the sort of pure substantiality that Freud assumes of psychic energy is placed seriously in question.

(3) *The erotic embodiment of energized experiencing:* Although Freud—at least in most of his early writings—clearly understood psychic energy to be nonidentical with biological operations or *Instinkte*, he consistently asserted the embodied character of psychic energy, which is why he argued so strenuously for the term *libidinality.* He insisted that, both in its origins and in its primary vicissitudes, this energy is mobilized *erotically*, which means by *pleasure/unpleasure* in a manner that is *embodied*—a notion quite different from that of biological necessity. For example, the sucking reflex generates orality, but there is a hiatus between the biological mechanism and the libidinal energy that arises around it, and—as Laplanche extrapolates and explains—what occurs in this hiatus involves the reception of many enigmatic messages from caretakers and others from outside the event. Likewise, feeding satiates hunger, but the biological mechanisms involved are not equivalent to the erotic satiation of oral libidinality. Freud insists on the embodied and erotic character of psychic reality, even while holding on to an account of its constitution that seems to exclude exogenous factors such as the enigmatic semiotics (which emanate from the caretakers and are received by the uncomprehending infant). Yet, in his private views on telepathy, he leaves open the possibility of the

transmission of some sorts of energy or information, enigmatically, between the organism and the outside world. Such an occult transmission would not seem to be *sexual* in quite the way that Freud insisted on the erotic and embodied character of psychic energy.

(4) *Lifefulness and deathfulness principles of psychic energy:* A further feature of Freud's thinking about the subtle energies of psychic life depends on the way in which his 1920 essay is interpreted. *Beyond the Pleasure Principle* caused a certain amount of consternation within the psychoanalytic world and has generally been read as positing two new "drives" of life, *Lebenstrieb*, and death, *Todestrieb*. This approach subsequently provoked Paul Federn to postulate a suicidal drive, *Mortido*, and Eduardo Weiss to propose a destructive drive, *Destrudo*. The latter seems quite congruent with the Kleinian interpretation of *Todestrieb* that emerged in the 1930s and 1940s as indicative of innate aggressivity, destructiveness, and primal envy. Although the idea of *Thanatos* had been discussed in psychoanalytic circles prior to 1920 (e.g., Blumgart, 1916), it is Sabina Spielrein's 1912 paper that seems to have been most influential on Freud's 1920 speculations. Under the influence of Jung, who read the paper before it was presented to Freud, Spielrein wrote of the complicity of creation and destruction in every process of becoming. In line with this, Laplanche suggests that *Lebenstrieb* and *Todestrieb* should not be considered as two "new" drives in the Freudian cosmology, but rather as principles by which drives or desire operate. *Lebenstrieb* refers to the principle of "lifefulness" in which psychic energy is invested in our representational repertoire, whereas *Todestrieb* refers to the principle of "deathfulness" in which energy drains away from representationality (cf. Barratt, 2004, 2016).[2]

(5) *Healing as a perpetual "workplaying" with our contradictory constitution:* Finally to be noted here is an implication about the human capacity for healing. Because of the ontological nonidenticality of psychic energy and representationality—and also because the repression barrier, which is the intrapsychic inscription of the incest taboo, is ultimately implacable and impassable, which implies that there is always a "failure of translation" between modes of discourse that are within us—Freud never holds out the possibility of achieving a complete inner harmony or ideal state of alignment. Rather, the contradictoriness or "failure of translation" between desire—the libidinality of psychic energy or drive—and our inner world of representationality is unsurpassable and interminable (Barratt, 1984/2016, 1993/2016, 2013b, 2016). This contradictoriness, by which we are all constructed as humans, each with a distinct being-in-the-world, cannot be transcended. From this standpoint, healing can only be an ongoing "workplay" with the contradictoriness by which our "identity" is constituted. To aspire to some final state of noncontradictoriness is, from a Freudian standpoint, the pursuit of an illusion or delusion (Barratt, 1993/2016, 2016). There is, given Freud's premises about psychic energy, no resolution between desire and representationality, no state of total enlightenment to be attained, and no completion of the "journey of the soul."

Subtle energies and ancient wisdom

Freud's acquaintance with ancient wisdom traditions was perhaps rather minimal. We know that he was influenced by Arthur Schopenhauer (1811/1844), who was deeply impressed with Vedantic and Buddhist literatures. The influence of Friedrich Nietszche might also have inclined him toward Buddhist philosophy. Freud had at least a passing familiarity with the *Bhagavad Gita* and quoted from the *Upanishads*. He consulted with the Swiss novelist Bruno Goetz, who greatly admired Hinduism, had lively debates with Romain Rolland about spiritual experiences and oceanic feelings, conversed with Rabindranath Tagore and other visitors from India, and corresponded extensively with Girindrasekar Bose on matters that touched on South Asian cosmology (cf. Vaidyanathan & Kripal, 1999). Toward the end of his life, Freud's diaries also indicate that he talked about Buddhist philosophy with Yaekichi Yabe, a Japanese psychologist, and that he seemed impressed by the parallelism with psychoanalytic thinking (cf. Freud, 1929–1939, 1930; Freud & Ferenczi, 1908–1933; Freud and Jones, 1908–1939; Molino, 1998; Rubin, 1996; Safran, 2003).

However, Freud never considered in any detail the clear parallel (which is not to say equivalence) between his notion of psychic energy and similar ideas associated with spiritual doctrines. Yet almost every known indigenous culture has beliefs and experiential practices referring to the reality of subtle energies, which are neither identical with the material entities in which they may reside, nor entirely abstract or immaterial. In this respect, Freud may have been overcommitted to the rationality of the "modern era" that swept through Europe in the second half of the nineteenth century. However, he did remain somewhat connected to Kabbalist Judaism, which refers to the energies of *ohr* (light), *shefa* (flow), and similar notions (Bakan, 2004; Klein, 1987; Meghnagi, 1993). Moreover, directly or indirectly, he must have known something of the teachings concerning *prāna* within the Dharmic traditions (as well perhaps as the energies of *kundalini*), which are closely related to *chi* in Chinese Taoic teachings, *ki* in Japanese, *lom* in Thai, and indeed perhaps to other doctrines such as *mana* in certain Oceanic cultures, *orenda* or *spirit* for some Native American groups, and *od* in ancient Germanic cultures. This list could be extended. Without wishing to generalize or appear reductive in invoking these diverse and richly complex notions, I will now briefly suggest how these ideas might relate to the five characteristics of Freud's thinking previously outlined.

(1) *Ontological nonidenticality and the "threefold" psyche:* Nowhere, to my knowledge, is subtle energy, in the Dharmic teachings, understood to be identical with materiality, although inert material things (e.g., rocks, tables, bodily tissue) are often assumed to be coagulations of such energy. More saliently, it is clear that subtle energy cannot be identified with representationality, since the latter is usually characterized as *māyā*—the world of deception, illusions, and appearances. This is the world by which we maintain our "self," our egotism, or perhaps even our discrete ego organization (Schuhmacher & Woerner, 1986). Ideas—perceptions, conceptions, and emotions—may also be understood as accretions of energy. This is a

tenet very similar to Freud's notion that the emergence of representations and of the transformations between them depends on the investment of psychic energy. Thus, differentiated both from substantial things and from representational ideas (as formations of thought and wish), the nonidenticality of subtle energy in Dharmic cosmology is not at all unlike the neither/nor and both/and status of Freud's notion of libidinality.

(2) *Endogenous constitution and conservative principles:* However, subtle energy, in the Dharmic traditions, is emphatically not endogenously constituted or contained. Such energies are held to flow not only within the individual, but also through and around the individual, and indeed, throughout the cosmos. In this respect, Freud's tenet that psychic energy is more or less an individual acquisition or achievement aligns his thinking more with the Abrahamic notion of a "soul" as the quasi-incorporeal essence of a particular living being, which might be held to be mortal or immortal. If immortal, this somewhat corresponds to the Sanskrit notion of *jīvāt man*, as the spiritual essence of a living being that is bound to the cycle of life and death. However, given his adamant atheism, it seems very unlikely that psychic energy, as Freud imagined it, has any existence after life or that it is attached to an individual's "self" or identity in any particularized manner.

There is a similar discrepancy between Freud and the typical teachings of the Dharmic tradition in relation to the principles on which subtle energy is held to operate. There are meditation practices described in the yogic tradition and other aspects of the Dharmic teachings that advocate the conservation and accumulation of subtle energies and that warn against their wasteful expenditure. However, in general, Freud's Newtonian tendencies seem entirely foreign to most Dharmic doctrines. The latter tend to describe the cosmic circulation of subtle energies as almost inexhaustibly renewable, perhaps self-generating, and operating, if any-thing, as an "economy" of expenditure, expansiveness, liberation, release, or sac-rificial giving.

(3) *The erotic embodiment of energized experiencing:* In the Dharmic tradition, subtle energy can indeed be embodied, but it is unquestionably not only embodied but also cosmic. Whether, or in what sense, it is *erotic* might be a matter of dispute. If one reads the yoga sūtras of Patañjali, for example, it is evident that subtle energy can be described as "sexual" but might also be channeled into movements that would ordinarily be designated non-sexual. This perhaps depends on how one defines "sexual" and whether ascetic practices of abstinence can nonetheless be understood as erotic. By contrast, if one reads almost any of the great texts on *kundalini* and the deployment of subtle energy movements in tantric meditation, it is clear that subtle energies are ineluctably "sexual" even when engaged in an apparently desexualized manner (cf. Frost & Frost, 1989; Guenther & Trungpa, 1975; Saraswati, 1981, 1984; Woodroffe, 1928). It is well known that the tradition of *vajrayāna* and other tantric lineages—including the school from which the Dalai Lama hails—have often been discreet about the erotic character of the energies that are mobilized in the course of their meditation practices. In part, this is because most of the meditation methods—and, in the case of the Dalai Lama's Gelug-pa

school, *all* of them—are engaged under conditions that most of us would describe as total abstinence. In part, this is because historically the schools, such as the Kagyu or Sakya as well as numerous "Hindu" variants, whose methods are more explicitly sexual—in the ordinary sense of involving "sex acts"—have needed to be circumspect or wholly secretive about their practices, often to avoid persecution. The situation is perhaps similar to that of psychoanalysis in that many of Freud's contemporaries and those who followed him made a strenuous effort to protect psychoanalysis from the charge of immorality and pansexualism (e.g., Blumgart, 1918). The effort is, in my opinion, quite irrelevant, given Freud's notion of polymorphous perversity and the subsequent amendment of this to a theory of our polysexual potential (cf. Barratt, 2013b, 2016). I will return to this point when Jung's views are brought into focus.

(4) *Lifefulness and deathfulness principles of psychic energy:* Freud's 1920 formulation of the principles by which psychic energy is invested in biological operations and representational formations, or dissipated and withdrawn from them, seems wholly aligned with Dharmic insights. The complicity of movements of creation and movements of destruction seems almost to have been a perennial insight of cosmological thinking.

(5) *Healing as a perpetual "workplaying" with our contradictory constitution:* However—and this is perhaps an unacceptable generalization—there are few, if any, precepts in the Dharmic cosmology that are equivalent to Freud's dynamic notion of repression as a barrier to any possibility of a harmonious alignment between psychic energy and that in which it may be invested. Likewise, in the many schools of meditation with which I am familiar, there is no theorization as to why individuals do not pursue "enlightenment" that is substantially equivalent to Freud's notion of our "resistances" to free-associative discourse. In the Dharmic tradition, there is a notable promise of the possibility of *moksha*, liberation, enlightenment, or the achievement of a complete condition of inner and outer harmony; a goal that transcends *kāma* or the pursuit of pleasure. Freud's discoveries about the human condition hold out no such hope, and, in a sense, this is why his discipline has been characterized as a tragic vision of life. Human desire cannot be fulfilled, and, as Freud seems to have admitted early in his career, the best for which one can hope is a perpetual practice around the processes of suppression and repression. This sort of commitment to free-associative praxis is liberatory, in the sense that it frees psychic energy from its entrapment in repetition compulsivity, but not in the sense that a final and fulfilled state of liberation is attainable.

A reading of Jung on psychic energy

As is well known, Jung steeped himself in the ancient wisdom traditions (Bair, 2004; Clarke, 1994; Coward, 1985; Dunne, 2015). Even his seminal 1911–1912 publication, *Wandlungen und Symbole der Libido*, quotes from the Upanishads and the Rigveda. Moreover, in Volume 11 of his *Collected Works*, one sees clearly his considerably wide-ranging and sophisticated appreciation of both "Western" and

"Eastern" traditions. In terms of the "Western," this is exemplified by his 1928 essay "Psychoanalysis and the cure of souls," and from there all the way to his 1952 *Answer to Job*, which promulgates the divine "Quaternity" and expounds upon the fourth face of God as evil. This volume, however, is strikingly uninformative about his views on psychic energy. In the 1928 essay, for example, he indicts Freudian teachings as inadequate for the tasks that have to be addressed by Catholic and Protestant clergy. But in so doing he rather simplistically equates psychoanalytic practice with the expansion of conscious mastery over the (personal) unconscious. Jung thus overlooks Freud's distinction between representations (which may be deeply preconscious or descriptively unconscious) and the repressed dimension of thing-presentations—although it must be admitted that Freud himself participated in such confusion, for example with his 1933 idea that psychoanalysis is a "draining of the Zuider Zee" of unconscious contents.

To trace Jung's thinking about subtle energy systems, it seems necessary to organize his writings into two phases. First, one must grasp his ideas about psychic energy that led up to the 1914 break with Freud. Perhaps the three leading sources for this are his correspondence with Freud (Freud & Jung, 1906–1914), the 1912 Lectures on the "Theory of Psychoanalysis" presented in New York (Jung, 1912–1913), and his 1911–1912 publication *Wandlungen und Symbole der Libido*, which was later revised and published in 1916 as *The Psychology of the Unconscious* and then revised again as *Symbols of Transformation* in 1952 (the latter contains his 1920 paper "Concept of libido" and its successor, the 1922 paper "Transformation of libido"). These sources can perhaps be legitimately augmented by his 1928 paper "On psychic energy," which was published much later in "The structure and dynamics of the psyche." This grouping of texts can be compared with the writings of the 1930s, many of which address doctrines from the Dharmic tradition, although—as I shall show—they are often remarkably obscure in terms of Jung's notion of psychic energy.

Jung's 1912 lectures were clearly articulated under the shadow of his epistolary and conversational relationship with Freud. They are, in many respects, both a panegyric to Freud's discoveries and a reaction against Freud's theorization of his findings. In these lectures, Jung presents some arguments that are jarring to a Laplanchean reading of Freud's thinking and some that seem, in the context of his thesis, almost placatory toward Freud yet anticipatory of his subsequent theorizing.

The main line of dissent is well known and much publicized. Jung (1912–1913) equates libido with a general life-energy, "passionate desire," (p. 29)[3] or "vital force" (p. 30) that "far exceeds the bounds of any sexual definition" (p. 37). Against Freud, he argues that "we were deceiving ourselves when we believed that we could make the *libido sexualis* the vehicle of an energic conception of psychic life," and that we need "a new conception of libido" which is purely "energic" (p. 37); that is, libido "simply as a name of the energy which manifests itself in the life-process and is perceived subjectively as conation and desire" (p. 43). However, Jung's argument depends on a decidedly non-Freudian definition of sexuality as "the instinct for the preservation of the species" (p. 23). Unlike Freud, Jung seems to equate sexuality with "sex acts" in the usual sense of this term. Thus, adopting biological-behavioral assumptions about the nature of sexuality, he argues, for example, that whereas the original libidinal function of producing eggs and sperm might be considered "sexual," libido then becomes "desexualized" as the nutritive functions of infancy, as well as other functions. Jung asserts this because he claims that "the libido of a child is occupied far more with subsidiary functions of a mental and physical nature than with local sexual functions" (p. 36). However, aside from his brief and rather awkward flirtation with the idea of "component drives," it can be argued that Freud never actually conceived of libidinality in terms of "local sexual functions," let alone with the goals of reproduction (e.g., Freud, 1905). Yet, on the basis of such arguments, Jung claims to de-eroticize "the infant's sucking at its mother's breast" (pp. 22–46), and he posits a "pre-sexual phase of life" which is "characterized almost exclusively by the functions of nutrition and growth" (p. 35). Thus, Jung's main line of dissent seems to rest on a misunderstanding of the notion of sexuality as Freud promulgated it. This becomes evident when Jung asserts that "obtaining pleasure is by no means identical with sexuality" (p. 25, italics omitted). By way of such assertions, Jung dismisses, both overtly and covertly, Freud's tenet that psychic energy is mobilized *erotically*, both in its origins and in its primary vicissitudes, by *pleasure/unpleasure* in ways that are *embodied*.[4]

In short, at this early stage of his career, Jung seems to conflate psychic energy with biological functions, and, since not all biological operations are "sexual" in the narrow reproductive sense of this term, he argues that the notion of psychic energy must be de-eroticized. Thus, in a sense, Jung implicitly restores a dualistic depiction of our psychic life, contesting Freud's "threefold" assertion of the nonidenticality of energy with either biological or psychological realms. Consequently, Jung's 1912 lectures concede to Freud that psychic energy, being endogenous, probably operates on a hydraulic or thermodynamic principle. He states that "the law of conservation of energy" brings order into "the relationship" of energetic forces with each other (1912–1913, p. 27). Even in the 1952 revision of his book, he argues that "the concept of libido in psychology has functionally the same significance as the concept of energy in physics since the time of Robert Mayer" (p. 131, §189). Jung refers to Julius Robert von Mayer, the father of thermodynamics. However, here the assertion seems strange, since if one reads his writings of the 1930s, it appears that, by 1952, Jung had long since modified, if not entirely abandoned, his former attitude toward energetic notions.

Indeed, coming toward the end of his relationship with Freud, one can detect in Jung not only a break with any proclivity toward pansexualism, but also a break with Freud's primary emphasis on the significance of embodied experience. Accordingly, it must be noted that, even in the 1912 lectures, Jung begins to challenge the significance of the "incest complex" and thus of oedipality and, less directly, of the repression barrier. Correspondingly, he questions the etiological significance of childhood experiences and argues that "the cause of pathogenic conflict lies mainly in the present moment" (1912–1913, p. 84). The challenge to incest is hardly surprising, since Jung will later characterize the collective unconscious in terms of a return to the Mother for the purposes of rebirth. However, the diminution of the significance of the oedipal taboo against incest entails a dilution of the significance of repression, as well as opening the way for Jung to distinguish the personal unconscious from the collective. It opens the way for Jung to diminish the significance of the former and with it the significance of embodiment. In short, without launching too blatant an assault on psychoanalysis, Jung's lectures quite cunningly call into question all four of Freud's "fundamental coordinates" (Barratt, 2013a). He thus sets the course for his subsequent theorizing, in which the individual's trajectory now becomes a journey in relation to the archetypal unconscious. This is a journey that does not emphasize embodied experience—although, admittedly, some of Jung's followers have nevertheless written interestingly about bodily conditions (e.g., Ramos, 2004; Samuels, 1985; Schwartz-Salant, 1982; Woodman, 1985). These moves also enable Jung to mischaracterize psychoanalysis as merely a matter of "mastery over the unconscious" (which, as I already indicated, is an error Freud himself slipped into later in his life) and to create a psychology which is no longer somatocentric or somatogenic in the way that Freud's is.

Jung's migration away from somatics toward symbology is most clearly articulated in the writings of the 1930s. For example, his 1935 and 1939 commentaries on the great Tibetan texts focus more on the fate of the soul than on the vivacity of psychic energy. This is remarkable in that *vajrayāna* spiritual practice is emphatically focused on the energetic movements of "spirit," even though these movements are subsequently depicted in a very rich hermeneutic symbology of mandalas and so forth. Jung's focus is replicated in the 1936 essay on "Yoga and the West" as well as its successor, the 1943 paper on "The Psychology of Eastern Meditation." The latter again asserts that "Western man" attempts to conquer the (personal) unconscious and cannot, by means of yogic practices, attain spiritual enlightenment. For the Westerner, spiritual progress has to be achieved by exploration of the collective unconscious with all its archetypal symbols—and this seems to mean a contemplative practice rather than an energetic one. "Yoga and the West" mentions *prāna*, but only to suggest that Eastern yogic discipline might succeed in *uniting* the psychological and biological realms, but that this is unavailable to the dualistic thinking of the West—assertions that seem quite contrary to Freud's proclamations about his discoveries, since these imply the impossibility of any such unification and, indeed, dispute the sort of dualism to which Jung refers.

The more recently published notes taken from the 1932 seminar on *kundalini* yoga again focus on the issue of the journey of the soul. They also perhaps provide the clearest indication that Jung came to deny the reality of subtle energy (at least in anything like the manner that Freud presented it) and that he thus unequivocally demoted the energetic experiences of our erotic embodiment in favor of archetypal symbology. Interestingly, these lectures on kundalini or tantric yoga not only expose his views on psychic energy but also present significant modifications of the very teachings about subtle energies within our embodied experience that he purports to be interpreting. Here, I must outline the salient features of these doctrines.

In most Dharmic lineages, energy is held to move through the body, usually in an upward direction, through the *chakras* (although this sometimes may be reversed or complexified). The chakras are embodied nodes or plexuses of energetic organization, and the channels that run between and around them are called *nadis*. Chakras and nadis are typically held to be embodied, although the energy flowing through them may originate from outside our embodiment (and in some systems the individual is viewed as having additional chakras externally). As is now well known, the root chakra, the *mūlādhāra*, is approximately located in the perineal-genital area (associated with the generation of sexual energy); then the *svādhisthana* is in the sacrum (associated with the energy of movement and change), the *manipūra* in the abdomen (associated with the energy of power and strength), the *anāhata* in the heart (associated with the energy of connectivity and love), the *viśuddha* in the throat (associated with the energy of "giving voice" and truth-telling), the *ājnā* in the "third eye" (associated with the energy of intuition and intellect), and the *sahasrāra* in the crown (associated with enlightenment and liberation). Much spiritual practice in the Dharmic tradition is devoted to moving and balancing the energy movements between these nodes (Barratt, 2006; Johari, 1988). However, Jung's approach to appreciating this cosmological and experiential system is very remarkable in three ways.

First, he argues that libido or psychic energy "does not exist," but rather is "an abstraction, an idea" applied to the intensity of a natural force (1932, pp. 8–9). Yet he also concedes that it is "a good example of a *tattva*" (p. 8), which is a principle, truth, or reality. In a way that I find quite peculiar, he then seems to waver in his opinions by suggesting that such energy is "a concrete thing in the East" yet is "for us ... an abstraction, an idea" (p. 9). The problem here is that for Freud, libidinality has a "reality," a liminal existence "between" the physicality of the body and the representationality of the mind, and is thus, even if it is not measurable, far more tangibly embodied—and erotic—than any abstraction (Barratt, 2015, 2016). Furthermore, if psychic energy is "a concrete thing" for those acculturated in the East, it offers them spiritual and existential practices that are a dimension of their embodied experience, whereas it leaves Westerners only with contemplative practices that are imaginal, ideational, intuitive, or even intellectual.

The second striking aspect of Jung's exegesis relates to the first. It is remarkable in lectures on kundalini how little he actually speaks about energy *movements*, which are, from an Eastern point of view, essential to the very notion of kundalini, to our being-in-the-world, and to our spiritual-existential trajectory. Rather, in Jung's rendition, our journey again seems to become more contemplative than experiential—more disembodied than the praxis of free-associative discourse.

Thus, the third and probably most remarkable aspect of these lectures is that Jung proceeds to argue that since the two "root chakras"—the *mūlādhāra* and the *svādhisthana*—are asleep for Westerners, he is justified in rearranging the entire chakric cosmology. Rhetorically, he asks, "psychologically what is *mūlādhāra*? You think of it as that region down below the abdomen, having to do with sexuality and all sorts of unsavory [*sic*] things. But that is not *mūlādhāra*; *mūlādhāra* is something quite different" (p. 13), and then "we begin in our conscious world, so we can say that our *mūlādhāra* might be not down below in the belly but up in the head" (p. 17, italics in the original). Thus, Jung proceeds to associate the two chakras that are at the source and root of the cosmology—the earthiness of the *mūlādhāra* and the wateriness of *svādhisthana*—with the *ājnā chakra* that is the "eye" of intuition and intellectuality. In short, it could be said that Jung's rearrangement effectively de-eroticizes the human condition.

Coward (1985) rather mildly criticizes Jung for this feat, suggesting that nowadays "it is doubtful that Jung's 'rope trick' of standing *kundalini* yoga on its head and then lopping off the last two chakras as 'superfluous speculations with no practical value' would be accepted" (p. 123). Jung justified his procedure of rewriting the chakras as "adapting that system to ourselves" (1932, p. 18). The erotic dimension of being human is—at least for "us" Westerners—displaced into virtual insignificance. In Jung's terms, his "adaptation" serves to augment his theory of the process of individuation in relation to the collective unconscious, rendering the chakra system into a series of symbols, the contemplation of which enables us to understand more deeply the archetypal journey of the soul. In fairness, it must be added that Jung himself only claimed "important parallels" between analytical psychology and tantric or *kundalini* yoga—*vajrayāna* and Taoic visions—in as much as "their rich symbolism afford me invaluable comparative material for the interpretation of the collective unconscious" (quoted in 1932, p. xxix). However, the overall effect of Jung's "rope trick" is that kundalini-tantric spiritual practices are no longer about moving the "spirit" within our embodiment and thus re-aligning it with the spiritual momentum of the cosmos. Rather, tantric symbolism has been appropriated to suit Jung's contemplative "journey of the soul."

An aside on Reichian energetics

Reading Jung in this manner—which I hope is reasonably faithful to the trajectory of his thinking—it becomes questionable to what extent the notion of psychic energy was necessary to his work even in the years when he was still allied with Freud. Moreover, in his mature thinking, the notion seems to have been of little interest to him, as well as strangely disembodied and entirely subordinate to the transpersonality of the archetypal unconscious. It perhaps overstates the case—although perhaps it does not—to suggest that, in his early years, Jung resisted the erotics of a somatic psychology as articulated by Freud, whereas, in his mature years, he abandoned any sort of somatocentric or somatogenic vision of our humanity for one that is more or less "symbolocentric" and "symbologenic."

It seems irresistible to compare this theoretical migration to that undertaken by another brilliant mind who embarked under Freud's tutelage and then went beyond the Freudian ambit. Notoriously, Wilhelm Reich (1927, 1927–1953, 1933, 1936) extended the implications of Freud's formulations on libidinal energy. As is well known, early in his career he argued that healing depended on the full orgasmic discharge of such energy, the individual's "orgastic potency" that had been neurotically blocked by "character armoring." Orgastic potency was not merely a matter of "fucking," but of the capacity to experience emotionally the loss of one's ego organization or "self" and to immerse oneself in "spiritual" being—ideas that are essentially tantric (Barratt, 2013c; Reich, 1952). Release of character armor could be achieved by direct intervention upon the patient's body, thus making Reich unpopular with the psychoanalysts of the 1920s (although Freud himself regarded Reich's early work very favorably) and establishing him as one of the founders of "body psychotherapy" (Sharaf, 1983; Strick, 2015). After Reich fled from Nazism, this method of "vegetotherapy" was further developed into what is today called "bioenergetic analysis" (e.g., Lowen, 1994) and psychic energy was renamed "orgone" (Raknes, 2004). Convinced of the reality of this special form of subtle energy, Reich became very interested in establishing this reality in a manner that would satisfy both physicists and healers. He devoted himself to experimentation in "bioelectrics," eventually provoking vicious opposition from within the American Psychoanalytic Association and from the Food and Drug Administration.

In terms of my interpretation of Freud's early views on the subtle energies of psychic reality, it is clear that Reich understood orgone to be nonidentical with both "mind" as representationality and matter as the gross form of physical things. It is far from endogenously constituted, but rather, all pervasive. It is cosmic as much as psychic, and does not operate on conservative principles. Indeed, Reich's notion of the significance of orgone seems remarkably close to many of the teachings of the Dharmic tradition. Orgone is erotic, or perhaps more precisely, Reich started his investigations with research on the sexual energies of our embodied experience and came to define them in terms of the circulation of orgone, its release from blockages, and so forth. Moreover, in this frame of theorizing, the release of energy into kinesis is the essential feature of healing. It could be anticipated that Reich would have found Freud's principles of lifefulness and deathfulness very congenial.

Concluding notes

What is the importance of the mandate to re-encounter Jung in the context of contemporary theorizing? Indeed, what is the significance of this for all of us as we approach the third decade of the twenty-first century? Now more than ever, humanity seems to pirouette daily between hope and hopelessness. Even in the face of escalating crises, it does not seem to me an irrelevant or indulgently intellectual exercise to think about the composition of being human. Indeed, it seems more urgent than ever to grasp whether there is more to the human condition than the biological operations of our body, on the one side, and the ratiocinative functions of what might be called our logico-empiricist "mind," on the other. Is it farfetched to suggest that, in their different but unique ways, both Freud and Jung pointed toward a spiritual dimension within the composition of our humanity? Of course, Jung explicitly saw his contributions in this manner, but the psychoanalytic discovery of subtle energies also implies a break with Cartesian dualities—even if overtly Freud was, unlike Jung, quite preoccupied with the illusions, delusions, and political travesties committed in the name of theistic faith and organized religion.

Stopping very far short of announcing that his free-associative method might constitute a way of listening to the call of the Holy Spirit within us—an identification of subtle energy movements with the "Angel-as-Messenger," Gabriel or Jibra'il in the Abrahamic tradition—Freud's discovery nevertheless implies that, for any sort of liberation from our suffering, we must listen to the "voicing" of messages that are not simply either "of the body" or "of the ratiocinative mind" (Barratt, in press a, in press b). This otherwise voicing is a dimension that Reich, in his own eccentric manner, embraced, whereas Laplanche, I think, would have wished to retain a non-spiritual interpretation of its significance. Moreover, in a sense, Freud himself got lost after 1915—lost in his enthusiasms for constructing objectivistic models of mental functioning and for establishing his movement as a respectable science.

It seems very unlikely that questions about the otherwise energies of the human spirit will ever be resolved empirically, despite many recent efforts to do so (e.g., Gerber, 2001; Swanson, 2003, 2010; Tiller, 1997, 2001, 2007). But crucial questions remain, and I cannot detail further my own sense of the direction from which answers might come. Rather, I am going to end by insisting on the significance of the questions: Is the somatocentric way of reading Freud's early writings crucial to our understanding of the subtle energies that constitute desire and that animate the liveliness of life itself? Is our spirituality to be accessed through our embodied experience, including its erotic character, or is our sexuality inherently some sort of "unsavory" dimension of life, liable to be an impediment to the "journey of the soul"? What warranted the apparent migration of Jung's thinking (at least as I have read it) from psychic energy to symbology, and seemingly away from any sort of a somatogenic perspective? Moreover, is this to be understood as his personal resistance to both the erotic notion of libidinality and the repressive condition of the individual unconscious (and his notable preference for contemplation of the archetypes of the collective unconscious)? And what is the significance of Freud's greater interest in the dynamic kinesis of self-consciousness as contrasted with Jung's deep search for the coordinates of the eternal? In today's context, these are not obscure issues of intellectual history, but vitally pertinent to our understanding of ourselves and to the possibility of a human future.

Notes

1   The author would like to thank Julia June Parker-Barratt and Andrew Samuels for their comments on an earlier draft of this chapter.
2   As an aside, it may be noted that Laplanche's interpretation connects interestingly with Jones' (1927, 1929) ideas about *aphanisis* as the "fading of desire," which he suggests is most feared by all of us.
3   All quotes from the *Jung contra Freud* edition, published in 2011.
4   Another major line of argument against Freud pertains to Jung's work with psychoses. Against Freud, Jung states that "no one is likely to maintain that reality is a function of

sex" (p. 39). In distinction to the notion of a withdrawal of the libido from "reality," Jung argues that in psychotic conditions, especially in the prodromal phase, psychic energy is redirected toward what will later be called archetypal symbols. This argument is further elaborated in the 1952 revision of his 1911-1912 book.

References

Bair, D. (2004). *Jung: A biography*. Boston: Little Brown.

Bakan, D. (2004). *Sigmund Freud and the Jewish mystical tradition*. Mineola: Dover.

Bankart, C. P. (1997). *Talking cures: A history of western and eastern psychotherapies*. Pacific Grove: Brooks/Cole.

Barratt, B. B. (1984/2016). *Psychic reality and psychoanalytic knowing*. Hillsdale: Analytic Press. [Reissued in 2016 by Routledge.]

Barratt, B. B. (1993/2016). *Psychoanalysis and the postmodern impulse: Knowing and being since Freud's psychology*. Baltimore: Johns Hopkins University Press. [Reissued in 2016 by Routledge.]

Barratt, B. B. (2004). Desire and death in the constitution of I-ness. In: J. Reppen, J. Tucker, & M. A. Schulman (Eds.), *Way beyond Freud: Postmodern psychoanalysis observed* (264–279). London: Open Gate Press.

Barratt, B. B. (2006). *What is tantric practice?* Philadelphia: Xlibris/Random House.

Barratt, B. B. (2012). Boundaries and intimacies: Ethics and the (re)performance of "The Law" in psychoanalysis. *International Forum of Psychoanalysis, 24*, 204–15.

Barratt, B. B. (2013a). Free-associating with the bodymind. *International Forum of Psychoanalysis, 22*, 161–175. First published January 21 as DOI:10.1080/0803706X.2012.729860.

Barratt, B. B. (2013b). *What Is Psychoanalysis? 100 Years after Freud's "Secret Committee."* London: Routledge.

Barratt, B. B. (2013c). Sensuality, sexuality, and the eroticism of slowness. In: N. Osbaldiston (Ed.), *The culture of the slow: Social deceleration in an accelerated world* (136–53). Basingstoke: Palgrave Macmillan.

Barratt, B. B. (2015). On the mythematic reality of libidinality as a subtle energy system: Notes on vitalism, mechanism, and emergence in psychoanalytic thinking. *Psychoanalytic Psychology, 32*, 626–44.

Barratt, B. B. (2016). *Radical psychoanalysis: An essay on free-associative praxis*. London: Routledge.

Barratt, B. B. (in press a). Opening to the otherwise: The discipline of listening and the necessity of free-association for psychoanalytic praxis. *International Journal of Psychoanalysis*.

Barratt, B. B. (in press b). Sexuality, esoteric energies, and the subtleties of transmutation versus transformation. *International Journal of Transpersonal Studies*.

Blumgart, L. (1916). Abstracts from the "Jahrbuch für psychoanalytische und psychopathologische Forschungen." *Psychoanalytic Review, 3*, 90–114.

Blumgart, L. (1918). Summaries from the "Jahrbuch für psychoanalytische und psychopathologische Forschungen." *Psychoanalytic Review, 5*, 228–42.

Brabant, E., Falzeder, R., & Giamperi-Deutsch, P. (2000). *The correspondence of Sigmund Freud and Sándor Ferenczi: Volume I, 1908–1914*. Cambridge: Harvard University Press.

Clarke, J. J. (1994). *Jung and eastern thought: A dialogue with the orient*. London: Routledge.

Coward, H. (1985). *Jung and eastern thought*. Albany: State University of New York Press.

Dunne, C. (2015). *Jung: Wounded healer of the soul*. London: Watkins.

Ellenberger, H. F. (1970). *The discovery of the unconscious: The history and evolution of dynamic psychiatry*. New York: Basic Books.

Freud, S. (1905). Drei Abhandlungen zur Sexualtheorie. *Gesammelte Werke, 5,* 29–145. [Translated as: Three essays on the theory of sexuality. *Standard edition,* 7, 130–243.]

Freud, S. (1912). Ratschläge für den Arzt bei der Psychoanalytischen Behandlung. *Gesammelte Werke, 12,* 376–87. [Translated as: Recommendations to physicians practicing psychoanalysis. *Standard edition, 12,* 109–20.]

Freud, S. (1916–1917). Vorlesungen zur Einführung in die Psychoanalyse. *Gesammelte Werke, 11.* [Translated as: Introductory lectures on psychoanalysis. *Standard edition,* 15 & 16.]

Freud, S. (1920). Jenseits des Lustprinzips. *Gesammelte Werke, 13,* 3–69. [Translated as: Beyond the pleasure principle. *Standard edition, 18,* 1–64.]

Freud, S. (1924). Kurzer Abriss der Psychoanalyse. *Gesammelte Werke, 13,* 403–27. [Translated as: A short account of psychoanalysis. *Standard edition, 19,* 189–210.]

Freud, S. (1925). Selbstdarstellung. *Gesammelte Werke, 14,* 33–96. [Translated as: An autobiographical study. *Standard edition, 20,* 7–74.]

Freud, S. (1929–1939). *The diary of Sigmund Freud, 1929–1939* (translated by M. Molner). London: Macmillan, 1992.

Freud, S. (1930). Das Unbehagen in der Kultur. *Gesammelte Werke, 14,* 421–506. [Translated as: Civilization and its discontents. *Standard edition, 21,* 57–146.]

Freud, S. (1937). Konstruktionen in der Analyse. *Gesammelte Werke, 16,* 43–56. [Translated as: Constructions in analysis. *Standard edition, 23,* 257–69.]

Freud, S. & Ferenczi, S. (1908–1933). *The correspondence of Sigmund Freud and Sándor Ferenczi* (3 volumes, translated by Peter T. Hoffer). Cambridge: Belknap, 1993.

Freud, S. & Jones, E. (1908–1939). *The complete correspondence of Sigmund Freud and Ernest Jones* (edited by R. A. Paskauskas). Cambridge: Belknap, 1995.

Freud, S. & Jung, C. G. (1906–1914). *The Freud/Jung letters: The correspondence between Sigmund Freud and C. G. Jung.* Princeton: Princeton University Press, 1974.

Frost, G. and Frost, Y. (1989). *Tantric yoga: The royal path to raising kundalini power.* Boston: Weiser Books.

Gerber, R. (2001). *Vibrational medicine.* Rochester: Bear and Company.

Green, A. (1972–1986). *On private madness.* Madison: International Universities Press.

Green, A. (1997). *The chains of eros: The sexual in psychoanalysis* (translated by L. Thurston). London: Rebus Press, 2000.

Green, A. (2002). *Key ideas for a contemporary psychoanalysis: Misrecognition and recognition of the unconscious* (translated by A. Weller). London: Routledge, 2005.

Guenther, H. V., & Trungpa, C. (1975). *The dawn of tantra* (edited by M. Kohn). Berkeley: Shambhala.

Helmholtz, H. (1885). *Popular Lectures on Scientific Subjects* (translated by E. Atkinson). New York: Appleton.

Johari, H. (1988). *Chakras: Energy centers of transformation.* Rochester: Inner Traditions.

Jones, E. (1910–1935). *Papers on psychoanalysis.* Boston: Beacon Press, 1961.

Jones, E. (1927). The early development of female sexuality. *International Journal of Psychoanalysis, 8,* 459–72.

Jones, E. (1929). Fear, guilt and hate. *International Journal of Psychoanalysis, 10,* 383–97.

Jung, C. G. (1912–1913). The theory of psychoanalysis. *Collected Works, 4,* 83–226. [See also: *Jung contra Freud: The 1912 New York lectures on the theory of psychoanalysis* (translated by R. F. C. Hull). Princeton: Princeton University Press, 2011.]

Jung, C. G. (1912/1952). Symbols of transformation. *Collected Works,* 5. [Includes the 1920 paper, "The concept of libido" and the 1922 paper, "The transformation of libido."] Princeton: Princeton University Press, 2011.

Jung, C. G. (1928). The structure and dynamics of the psyche. *Collected works*, 8. [Includes the paper "On psychic energy."] Princeton: Princeton University Press, 2011.

Jung, C. G. (1932). *The psychology of kundalini yoga: Notes of the seminar given in 1932 by C. G. Jung* (edited by S. Shamdasani). Princeton: Princeton University Press, 1999.

Jung, C. G. (1936). Yoga and the west. *Collected works*, *11*, 529–37. Princeton: Princeton University Press, 2011.

Jung, C. G. (1943). The psychology of eastern meditation. *Collected works*, *11*, 558–75. Princeton: Princeton University Press, 2011.

Jung, C. G. (1952). Answer to Job. *Collected works*, *11*, 355–470. Princeton: Princeton University Press, 2011.

Klein, D. B. (1987). *Jewish origins of the psychoanalytic movement.* Chicago: University of Chicago Press.

Laplanche, J. (1992). *Seduction, translation, drives* (edited by J. Fletcher and M. Stanton). London: Institute of Contemporary Arts.

Laplanche, J. (1992–1993). *Essays on otherness* (edited by J. Fletcher). London: Routledge, 1999.

Laplanche, J. (2000–2006). *Freud and the "sexual"—essays 2000–2006* (translated by J. Fletcher, J. House, & N. Ray). New York: International Psychoanalytic Books, 2011.

Lowen, A. (1994). *Bioenergetics: The revolutionary therapy that uses the language of the body to heal the problems of the mind.* London: Penguin.

McGuire, W. (Ed.) (1974). *The Freud/Jung Letters* (translated by R. Mannheim & R. F. C. Hull). Princeton: Princeton University Press.

McGuire, W., & Hull, R. F. C. (Eds) (1977). *C. G. Jung speaking: Interviews and encounters.* Princeton: Princeton University Press.

Meghnagi, D. (Ed.) (1993). *Freud and Judaism.* London: Karnac.

Molino, A. (Ed.) (1998). *The couch and the tree: Dialogues in psychoanalysis and Buddhism.* New York: North Point Press.

Paskauskas, R. A. (1995). *The complete correspondence of Sigmund Freud and Ernest Jones, 1908–1939.* Cambridge: Belknap Press.

Patañjali (c. 400). *The yoga sūtras of Patañjali* (translated by S. S. Satchidananda). Yogaville: Integral Yoga Publications, 1990.

Raknes, O. (2004). *Wilhelm Reich and orgonomy: The brilliant psychiatrist and his revolutionary theory of life energy.* Princeton: American College of Orgonomy Press.

Ramos, D. G. (2004). *The psyche of the body: A Jungian approach to psychosomatics.* Hove: Brunner-Routledge.

Reich, W. (1927). *Genitality in the theory and therapy of the neuroses* (translated from *The function of the orgasm* by P. Schmitz, edited by M. Higgins & C. M. Raphael). New York: Farrar Straus and Giroux.

Reich, W. (1927–1953). *Selected writings: An introduction to orgonomy.* New York: Farrar, Straus and Cudahy, 1960.

Reich, W. (1933). *Character analysis* (translated by T. P. Wolfe). London: Vision, 1950.

Reich, W. (1936). *The sexual revolution: Toward a self-governing character structure* (translated by T. P. Wolfe). London: Vision Press, 1951.

Rubin, J. B. (1996). *Psychotherapy and Buddhism: Toward an integration.* New York: Plenum.

Safran, J. D. (Ed.) (2003). *Psychoanalysis and Buddhism: An unfolding dialogue.* Boston: Wisdom.

Samuels, A. (1985). *Jung and the post-Jungians.* London: Routledge.

Saraswati, S. S. (1981). *Yoga and kriya: A systematic course in the ancient tantric techniques of yoga and kriya.* Munger: Yoga Publications Trust.

Saraswati, S. S. (1984). *Kuntalinitantra.* Munger: Yoga Publications Trust.

Schopenhauer, A. (1811/1844). *The world as will and representation* (two volumes, translated by E. F. J. Payne). Mineola: Dover, 1966. [The second edition, issued in 1844, is almost certainly the one read by Freud and Jung.]

Schuhmacher, S., & Woerner, G. (1986). *The encyclopedia of eastern philosophy and religion: Buddhism, Hinduism, Taoism, Zen* (translated by M. H. Kohn, K. Ready, & W. Wünsche). Boston: Shambhala, 1989.

Schwartz-Salant, N. (1982). *Narcissism and character transformation: The psychology of narcissistic character disorders.* Toronto: Inner City.

Sharaf, M. (1983). *Fury on earth: A biography of Wilhelm Reich.* London: St Martin's Press.

Spielrein, S. (1912). Die Destruktionals Ursache des Werdens. *Jahrbuch für psychoanalytische und Psychopathologische Forschungen, 4,* 465–503. [Translated as: Destruction as the cause of coming into being. *Journal of Analytical Psychology, 39,* 155–86. Also translated as: Destruction as cause of becoming. *Psychoanalysis and Contemporary Thought, 18,* 85–118.]

Strick, J. E. (2015). *Wilhelm Reich, biologist.* Cambridge: Harvard University Press.

Swanson, C. (2003). *The synchronized universe: New science of the paranormal.* Tucson: Poseidia.

Swanson, C. (2010). *Lifeforce, the scientific basis: Breakthrough physics of energy medicine, healing, chi and quantum consciousness.* Tucson: Poseidia.

Tiller, W. A. (1997). *Science and human transformation: Subtle energies, intentionality and consciousness.* Walnut Creek: Pavior.

Tiller, W. A. (2001). *Conscious acts of creation: The emergence of a new physics.* Walnut Creek: Pavior.

Tiller, W. A. (2007). *Psychoenergetic science.* Walnut Creek: Pavior.

Vaidyanathan, T. G., & Kripal, J. J. (1999). *Vishnu on Freud's desk: A reader in psychoanalysis and Hinduism.* Delhi: Oxford University Press.

Woodman, M. (1985). *The owl was a baker's daughter: Obesity, anorexia nervosa, and the repressed feminine.* Toronto: Inner City Books.

Woodroffe, J. (aka Avalon, A.) (1928). *The serpent power.* Madras: Ganesh & Co.

5

SEA CHANGES

The iconic and aesthetic turns in depth psychology

Angela Connolly

> Nothing of him that doth fade
> But doth suffer a Sea-change
> Into something rich, and strange
>
> *W. Shakespeare, The Tempest*

It is undeniable that the postmodern era, with its refusal of meta-narratives, has marked a serious crisis in all schools of depth psychology. Nevertheless, it has also provided us with a unique opportunity to begin to rethink and revitalize the way in which we theorize and practice. Theories are not cast in stone, for as Jung famously declared, "One could as little catch the psyche in a theory as one could catch the world. Theories are not articles of faith, they are either instruments of knowledge and of therapy, or they are no good at all" (1954, para. 198). If we are to be able to go beyond Freud and Jung, we need to come to terms with the fact that our theories do not, and indeed cannot, represent absolute truths, but are merely heuristic devices that allow us to map our paths in the meanders of the unconscious. As Warren Colman writes, "They are like metaphorical maps to the ever-shifting territory of the psyche, subject to the idiosyncratic descriptions of the mapmakers and only roughly applicable to the particular psychic territory which the analyst is likely to meet" (2009, p. 200).

Over the years there have been many sea changes in the theoretical edifices and in the clinical practice of both psychoanalysis and analytical psychology, changes that are all too often rejected in favour of a dogmatic adherence to the gospel of our founding fathers. Nevertheless, as Giuseppe Civitarese notes in a 2011 article on the paradigmatic shifts in psychoanalysis, analysts are now beginning to speak

> a completely different language from Freud's original meta-theory. While in theory retained, they are actually shattered into a kaleidoscope of new

concepts that call for the continuous adoption of new points of view. Moreover, by virtue of the subtle interplay of cross-references, identifications and differentiations in which they are suspended, and of their deliberately unsaturated character, they demand from the analyst the constant exercise of doubt and critical attitude towards any form of school-related dogmatism.

(2011, p. 279)

Following the work of Fordham and the developmental school, however, as I noted in a previous paper,

> Many Jungians now have integrated models of practice and training that place a much greater emphasis on boundaries, frames and on working in and with the transference, just as the emphasis on object relations and on a relational model of clinical practice has further modified our theories and practice.
>
> *(Connolly, 2015, pp. 186–187)*

Today, however, we run the potential risk of losing the specificity of the Jungian method, with its insistence on the importance of the image and of the use of analogy and metaphor in the elucidation of clinical material. As Richard Carvahlo underlines, fantasy is an image-creating function "whose aim is one of revelation, to render whatever it is that we call 'mind' as if it were visible to itself in analogical form so that it is available to the subject for symbolic manipulation and scrutiny" (Carvahlo, 1991, pp. 331–332).

If the psychodynamic approach is to survive, it has become essential to open ourselves up to theoretical and clinical cross-fertilizations between the different psychoanalytical schools and between depth psychology and other related disciplines. Even more importantly, however, we need to be ready to accept the challenge posed by exchanges with other cultures that might have a very different approach to the psyche. In the words of the anthropologist Clifford Geertz,

> It is the asymmetries […] between what we believe or feel and what others do, that makes it possible to locate where we now are in the world, how it feels to be there, and where we might or might not want to go. To obscure those gaps and those asymmetries by relegating them to a realm of repressible or ignorable difference, mere unlikeness […] is to cut us off from such knowledge and such possibility: the possibility of quite literally, and quite thoroughly, changing our minds.
>
> *(1986, p. 114)*

In the present chapter I will be looking at two such shifts that have been brought about by the revaluation of the image and of aesthetics in philosophy, cognitive linguistics and cognitive aesthetics. The first is the iconic turn or the return of the image in psychoanalysis. The second is the return of interest in aesthetics in analytical psychology. At the outset, however, it is necessary to define what we actually mean when we talk about images. I will therefore begin with a brief excursus into the history and the phenomenology of the image.

Defining the image

As Paul Kugler notes, "In the history of Western thought, the psychic tendency to construct images has been portrayed primarily in two different forms: a) as a reproductive process portraying some more primary reality and b) as a productive process which creates original entities" (2005, p. 3). In general, however, until relatively recently, the image, art and aesthetics were regarded as inferior ways of accessing reality and of creating knowledge and new meanings. As Mark Johnson notes in *The Meaning of the Body*,

> From the very beginning of Western philosophy, art was never taken seriously as an essential mode of human engagement with and understanding of the world. The Platonic notion that art was *mimesis*, a form of imitation of the real, consigned it to a derivative and dependent status as a source of images and second-rate understanding, not a direct presentation of reality.
>
> *(2007, p. 210)*

From Plato onwards, Western civilization has been marked by continuous oscillations between iconoclastic moments of suspicion and distrust of the illusionary and imperfect character of images, and moments of profound iconophilia that stressed the power of images as a means to accessing the invisible or the transcendent. In the words of the art historian Barbara Maria Stafford, "From the iconophilic perspective, the earthly or natural image establishes a temporary resemblance with a hidden mystery that one cannot otherwise see. All of analogy's simile-generating figures are thus incarnational. They materialize, display and disseminate an enigma that escapes words" (2001, p. 24).

From the eighteenth century onwards, however, with the further declassification of aesthetic experience and perceptual apprehension as subjective and therefore inferior categories of knowledge, the power of the image to create new meanings was increasingly denied. Today, we are constantly bombarded by images, but they are merely empty simulacra, dead images that reflect nothing but themselves and are incapable of any productive capacity (Baudrillard, 1994, pp. 6–7). All images, however, whether considered mere copies of existing reality, reproductions of a more primary reality or productive creations of something hitherto unknown, share a common denominator: they are linked to acts of representation. As Elio Franzoni, an Italian professor of aesthetics, states,

> The multiple meanings of the term "image" are in fact evidenced by the past and present history of the philosophy of the artistic experience and theories which nevertheless reveal a common denominator: the image is always

linked to "representational" acts and when it is not in itself "representation of", it is the mediation that makes it possible.

(2001, p. 1)

While for Freud the image is merely a sign (a representation of something known, even if repressed), for Jung the image is above all a symbol, a means or mediatory process through which it becomes possible to represent and gain access to something invisible and unknown.

Freud, Jung and the image

Freud, reflecting his lifelong commitment to science and to rationality, was profoundly ambivalent about the value of the image. Nowhere is this clearer than in his theorizing on dreams. The elements of the dream are produced by the transformation of thoughts and words into visual images, and, in this way, they represent a movement from more evolved ways of thinking to the more regressive and archaic pictorial language of infancy and of primitive man. As he writes in the "Introductory lectures on psychoanalysis", dreams "hark back to states of intellectual development which have long been superseded – to picture language, to symbolic connections, to conditions, perhaps, which existed before our thought-language had developed" (1916, p. 199). Furthermore, Freud demonstrates a marked distrust of the authenticity of dream images, which he sees as inauthentic and inherently suspicious:

> The conception of dream elements tells us that they are ungenuine things, substitutes for something else that is unknown to the dreamer (like the purpose of a parapraxis) substituting for something the knowledge of which is present in the dreamer but which is inaccessible to him.
>
> *(Freud, 1916, p. 113)*

As Christopher Bollas states, "this leads him to regard the dream text as a pernicious and deceitful representation" (1987, p. 68). For Freud, dream images are purely reproductive and therefore incapable of producing new meanings. The task of the analyst is therefore merely one of translating the image back into words so as to render intelligible the meaning of the dream. As Donald Meltzer puts it, "Freud views the problem of understanding symbols as one of re-translation, since symbol-formation itself is seen as a process of translation, movement in form without alteration or increment in meaning" (1983, p. 20). Freud concentrated all his attention on the dream text. He did this, as Bollas notes, "specifically to identify the dream thoughts that sponsored the dream – in order to translate the image back into words" (Bollas, 1987, p. 69). He ignored the importance of the dream as an experience with its own particular qualities; an experience which, according to Bollas, "brings us into contact with our own internal and highly idiomatic aesthetic: that aesthetic reflected by the ego style typical of each of us" (ibid., p. 81).

In contrast with Freud's suspicion of images, for Jung the visual image always has primacy over the word. As George Hogenson states, "Even the casual reader of Jung will be struck by his fascination with figural representations, the work of art, the pictorial [...] for Jung the visual image is as important as language is to Freud" (2009, p. 333). Jung distinguished clearly between signs and symbols, and he believed that dream images are symbolic in as much as they "represent an attempt to elucidate, by means of analogy, something that still belongs entirely to the domain of the unknown or something that is yet to be" (Jung, 1953, para. 494). Images are therefore productive of new meaning; they cannot be translated, but only amplified through analogy in an attempt to elucidate some of their possible meanings. Despite this position, Jung's need to find a scientific justification for his theories concerning the collective unconscious and archetypes led him to neglect the role of aesthetics in the creation and in the psychological function of images. As Paul Bishop says with reference to alchemical symbols, "Placing emphasis on the importance of intuition (*Anschauung*) Jung recognized the aesthetic appeal of such symbols, although he was reluctant to go one step further and regard this appeal in itself as central to their psychological function" (2009, p. 87). Symbolical images work, therefore, through analogical processes, and, according to Stafford, analogy is "a vision of ordered relationships, articulated as similarity in difference. This order is neither facilely affirmative nor purchased at the expense of variety" (2001, p. 9). The difficulty in analogy, therefore, is finding enough similarity to warrant giving a common name to disparate items while acknowledging their significant variations. Analogy should not be confused with establishing identity or isomorphism. This, however, is exactly what Jung did when he conflated images taken from very different cultural and historical contexts, as I have shown in a previous paper on Jung's approach to alchemical imagery (Connolly, 2013). Conflating images in this way led Jung to believe that while the content of images varies, the underlying form can be reduced to a limited number of uniform and eternal patterns. As the Italian philosopher and Jungian analyst Mario Trevi writes, "Jung's mistake was to hypothesize a repetitive, and in any case improvable, fixity in that rich world of forms where eventual similarities are based not on improbable a priori structures but on the all too human relative constancy of man's needs" (1993, p. 62). If the underlying form of the image is therefore in some way innate and unchanging, aesthetics would have nothing to say about the creation and function of images. Jung always tends to oppose aesthetic formulation to understanding, insisting that "aesthetic formulation, when it predominates, leaves it at that and gives up any idea of discovering a meaning" (Jung, 1916/1953, para. 180).

Another unfortunate result of this is that the image is seen as in some way secondary to the archetype. Warren Colman in his recent book, *Art and Image*, insists instead on the primacy of the image:

> I want to argue that any kind of form or structure is secondary to the process whereby archetypal images are created through the activity of

symbolic imagination. That is, symbolic imagination is not shaped by pre-existing psychic forms so much as being the means by which it is possible to conceive of such forms in the first place. Ontologically, the image is primary and the abstract forms represent further levels of symbolic thought being constituted by rather than being constitutive of symbolic imagination.

(2016, p. 16)

A further problem is evident in that Jung conceived of the image as something purely internal, springing entirely from the unconscious. Jung writes: "Consciousness has no direct relation to any material objects. We perceive nothing but images, transmitted to us indirectly by a complicated nervous apparatus" (1933, para. 745). The result of this outlook was that Jung failed to adequately take into consideration the role of the body and the wider material environment in the creation of meaningful images. A neglectful attitude of this kind has been challenged by philosophers such as Merleau-Ponty:

The body is our general medium for having a world. Sometimes it is restricted to the actions necessary for the conservation of life, and accordingly it posits around us a biological world; at other times, elaborating on these primary actions and moving from a literal to a figurative meaning, it manifests through them a core of new significance: this is true of motor habits such as dancing. Sometimes, finally, the meaning aimed at cannot be achieved by the body's natural means; it must then build itself an instrument and it projects thereby around itself a cultural world.

(1962, p. 146)

Likewise, Stafford (2007) stresses that the image comes into play in the interface between mind and body, between body and world:

Rather than seeing images as the mere illustration of some modular function, the range and variety of the cognitive *work* they perform needs to be better understood. Avoiding both Plato's claim that they are necessarily the sensible copies of paradigmatic ideas and more recent phenomenological claims that they are entirely generated from the brain's intrinsic activity, I treat them as boundary events [...] the medium or interface where world and subject get co-constructed, that is echoically presented to one another's view.

(p. 212)

Today, thanks to cross-fertilization between different analytical schools and different cultures, we are now in the position to begin to critique the theories of our illustrious predecessors and to make use of the image and of aesthetics to extend our theories in new and exciting ways.

The iconic turn or the return of the image in psychoanalysis

The recent encounter between psychoanalysis and Asian culture has led to a revaluation of the importance of the image in the experience of the dream and in the way analysts approach and interpret images. Christopher Bollas in his recent publication, *China on the Mind*, sketches out some of the implications that contact with Asian culture might have for the Freudian model of mind and for therapy. Bollas distinguishes between two different states of consciousness: one dominated by the paternal order, which is causal, metonymic, diachronic, representational (privileging content over form) and dependent on words; and one under the sway of the maternal order, which is metaphoric, synchronic, presentational (privileging form over content) and dependent on image. Bollas states that the maternal order

> has been subjected to an ongoing repression within the psychoanalytical movement, but since this presents an Eastern way of being and relating, is it possible that growing commerce between West and East will de-repress the maternal order and challenge the hermeneutically bound causal-inclined paternal focus that has dominated psychoanalytical discourse?
>
> *(2013, p. 29)*

Similarly, the English analyst Kenneth Wright suggests that Freud's approach to the unconscious is based on a paternal mode in which the unconscious self is perceived "as a subject to be conquered rather than a creature to be drawn into life" (2015, p. 950). For Freud, dream interpretation is a question of translating visual images – the "thing presentation" – into words. The philosopher Susanne Langer (1947) distinguishes between discursive symbols and non-discursive or presentational symbols. Whereas the discursive symbols of common language and of systems such as mathematics and physics are arbitrary and conventional signs whose meaning is unequivocal and which are bound by the rules of the system in which they take form, presentational symbols such as those found in dreams, myths, music, poetry and art enclose within themselves multiple levels of indeterminate meanings. According to Langer, works of art (and we might suppose this applies equally to dreams) are expressive forms whose function is to give voice to feelings, bearing in mind that

> the word feeling must be taken here in its broadest sense, meaning *everything that can be felt*, from physical sensation, pain and comfort, excitement and repose, to the most complex emotions, intellectual tensions, or the steady feeling-tones of a conscious human life.
>
> *(Langer, 1947, p. 15)*

Helping patients to understand and integrate these kinds of symbols requires a careful use of analogy and metaphor to begin to explore possible meanings. As Colman says, "No single interpretation can ever encompass their meanings and no matter how interpretations are made, their meaning can never be exhausted" (2016, p.

93). Premature or insensitive interpretations can detract from the patient's experience of the dream, and the potential for real harm is apparent where the patient is unable to represent to herself her own subjective affective experiences because of a failure of early maternal mirroring or attunement. As Wright notes,

> If words are thrust upon the unrepresented, as might happen with a patient who was not yet able to imagine his experiences with the help of image-based maternal forms – in other words where experience is unrepresented – the situation is dire. In effect, the other has commandeered and named his experience before it was born, thus robbing him of the possibility of becoming himself.
>
> *(2015, p. 947)*

It is here that we can learn something from the Eastern approach. Kawai (1976) suggests that in Japan the boundary between consciousness and unconsciousness is much vaguer than that found in Western individuals, and that while the ego complex is the centre of consciousness in the West, in the East this place is occupied by the Self. This means that the approach to the unconscious requires not so much a direct line of attack through words and linear thinking, but rather, the establishment of connections with the self through images which are arrived at via more circular routes. In the Eastern approach to the unconscious, as the Japanese Jungian analyst Megumi Yama writes, it is necessary "to allow the images to begin to emerge, express and unfold themselves and to refrain from pushing for verbal articulation before what has been invisible is ready to be made manifest" (2013, p. 69).

Italian psychoanalysis has been characterized in recent years by a new openness towards the possibility of integrating certain key Jungian concepts. This has permitted non-Jungian analysts to begin to rethink the traditional Freudian approach to dream images. Domenico Chianese and Andreina Fontana, in their 2010 book *Immaginando*, advocate for the need in psychoanalysis of an "iconic turn" capable of integrating the image into Freudian theory and practice. They suggest that such a turn might go beyond semantic approaches to the generation of meaning:

> From our part, it is not a question of any incautious ambition to reject a tradition to which we feel we belong, but more a question of rethinking it. For us as analysts, words and thoughts are central but we believe that language and thinking have their original foundation in perceptual experience, as that implicit horizon of the world of the sensible, of aesthetics, worlds that feed language and thought, and that language and thought represent the inexhaustible experience of these worlds.
>
> *(2010, p. 164)*

While the aim of Chianese and Fontana is not to assert the primacy of the image over the word, they acknowledge the longstanding psychoanalytic error of reducing images to words or of perceiving images to be inferior to words. As they state,

> Images are simply not words; they are not structured semantically or syntacti-
> cally as language is, they bring to light worlds that are different than those that
> emerge from words. The logic of the image cannot be reduced to predicative
> and conceptual logic.
>
> *(ibid., p. 147)*

The authors trace out the history of the gradual re-emergence of the image in analysis, starting from certain passages of Freud himself, who, in the 29th lesson in the
"New introductory lectures" of 1933, states that "the primary foundation of dreaming is not so much the fulfilment of a wish, even if this remains the dream's objective
and defines its content, but hallucinatory activity itself, the need to represent" (cited
in Botella and Botella, 2005, p. 42). The approach Chianese and Fontana offer is
most directly influenced by the elaboration of Bionian ideas provided by the Milan
school of psychoanalysis and in particular by the work of Antonino Ferro. Chianese
and Fontana are also explicit in the need to begin a dialogue with Jung (he is cited
three times in their work). Nonetheless, the authors acknowledge that their principal
debt is to the Italian analytical psychologist and sandplay therapist, Paolo Aite. As
they write, "Reading the book, *Paessaggi della psyche*, in which Aite describes his long
experiences as an analyst, the desire comes to re-open that dialogue between Jung
and Freud that was so dramatically interrupted in that far off 1913" (2010, p. 190).

The result of this approach is a new emphasis on the dream as a visual, aesthetic
experience which cannot be simply translated into words without betraying the
dream experience and its meaning. As they put it,

> The meaning we attribute to the dream (which remains a "visual experi-
> ence," an "aesthetic experience" which can only partially be reduced to dis-
> course), the significance we attribute to the unconscious (which is reductive
> to think of in terms of a language in as much as it has an essential and foun-
> dational relationship with the visual), the significance we give to the field in
> therapy which we need to think of not only, and not so much, as a field of
> words but rather as the field of the image.
>
> *(Chianese and Fontana, 2010, p. 147)*

Chianese and Fontana advocate, therefore, not only for a return to the image but,
perhaps more importantly, for the need of an aesthetic attitude in our approach to
the dream. Paradoxically, it is exactly this that has been ignored by analytical psychology for so long, since, despite the work of Hillman and the archetypal school,
very few of us look at the aesthetic quality of dream metaphors or of our own
interpretations.

The aesthetic turn in analytical psychology

We have seen that Jung's tendency to oppose sensuous perception and rational directed
thinking, on the one hand, with purely subjective imaginative fantasy thinking, on

the other, led him to deny that aesthetics was involved in meaning-making and in cognitive processes. One result of this is that, as John Beebe notes, "aesthetics has remained, theoretically, a bit off limits for our psychology, and it has rarely been seen as applying to what we might do with patients" (2010, p. 170). In recent years, however, it has become increasingly clear that metaphoric imaginative thinking is grounded in the body and in the world and that it has important cognitive functions. As the work of authors such as Lakoff and Johnson has shown, even the most abstract forms of thought are inherently metaphorical: "most of the conceptual structures of a natural language is metaphorical in nature. The conceptual structure is grounded in physical and cultural experience" (Lakoff & Johnson, 1980/2003, p. 107). On this basis, Mark Johnson argues that we need to see aesthetics as fundamental to the understanding of how human beings experience and create meaning. In his words, "Aesthetics concerns all the things that go into meaning – form, expression, communication, qualities, emotion, feeling, value, purpose, and more" (2007, p. 212).

John Beebe, perhaps reflecting his lifelong engagement with film, feels that an aesthetic attitude is an important therapeutic tool and that the aesthetic attitude "confronts both analyst and patient with the problem of taste, affects how the therapy is shaped and 'framed' and can grant a dimension of grace to the analyst's mirroring of the struggles that attend the patient's effort to be a more smoothly functioning human being" (2010, p. 165). Beebe delineates three specific aesthetic dimensions which he feels have been all too often neglected in psychotherapy: taste, shape, and grace. Likewise, Mark Winborn suggests that "many of the experiences associated with analytical process – such as the experience of depth, the emergence of meaning, transcendence, coherence, narrative flow or moments of meeting – can be viewed through the lens of aesthetic experience" (2015, p. 94). In particular, Winborn focuses on three distinct aesthetic experiences: the aesthetics of the setting; the aesthetics of interpretation; and the aesthetics of narrative. Both Beebe and Winborn argue for the need that the analyst should develop an aesthetic attitude, and that this is essential if we are to be able to take into account and further develop the aesthetics of the analytical process. What I wish to explore is, on the one hand, what we analysts need to do to develop this aesthetic attitude and, on the other, the role of this aesthetic attitude in developing our metaphoric capacity – an ability that will help us to make better use of our own imaginative processes and reverie, and to better amplify or interpret our patients' dreams and symbolic material.

Developing an aesthetic attitude

Paul Bishop has argued that Goethe's approach to aesthetics can give us new insights into the significance of archetypal experiences: "What Jung termed an 'archetypal experience' might be better understood, relieved of misleading mystical connotations, and understood along Goethean lines, under the category of the aesthetic" (2009, p. 75). In a 1789 essay on the qualities which characterize good art, Goethe delineates three different approaches to artistic creation that distinguish the average artist from the successful artist: simple imitation, manner and style (1789/1986, p. 72). If simple imitation requires only a pedantic attention to detail in order to produce a facsimile of the original, manner instead strives to find a pictorial language that is capable of expressing the spirit of the artist directly and characteristically. It is only style, however, that "rests on the most fundamental principle of cognition, on the essence of things – to the extent that it is granted to us to perceive this essence in visible and tangible form" (ibid., pp. 71–72). Good art therefore requires that the artist's work "will have such content and such form that it appears natural and at the same time seems above nature" (ibid., p. 81).

I would like to suggest that these Goethean considerations on aesthetics can provide us with important insights into how analysts can begin to develop an aesthetic attitude. I think it is fair to suggest that most analysts begin, consciously or unconsciously, by imitating their own analyst – his/her setting, style of relationship and modes of interpretation – just as they tend to adhere as faithfully as possible to the theoretical corpus and the rules of practice learned during training. As Bion once remarked, "It is impossible to undergo analysis without learning about psychoanalysis as practiced by one particular psychoanalyst; this is a misfortune rather than an advantage" (1984, p. 27). Gradually, however, through the experience of clinical practice, the analyst begins to develop her own private theories, which are more in correspondence with the clinical facts as she encounters them – theories that are more consonant with her own "personal equation." This will often contrast (or perhaps even conflict) with the theory she adheres to officially, for, as Fonagy noted in a 2002 panel on the issue of difference in method, "Theory is largely not about clinical practice and there is a gulf between public theories and the more private implicit or unconscious theories that actually guide individual practice" (2002, p. 453). Warren Colman seems to be describing something very similar when he writes that

> There is a transformation of the generalities in which all theories are concerned ("universals") into becoming familiar with the particulars out of which such theories are made. The more one becomes able to recognize theory in practice, the less relevant the theory seems to become since the universal generalities are replaced by a long series of unique particulars, albeit that these are organized in terms of a range of increasingly pre-conscious schemas.
>
> *(2013, p. 202)*

It is only when the analyst is capable of perceiving the essence of things and of rendering them in "visible and tangible form" that she could be said to be a truly successful analyst. Colman compares this to that intangible quality that makes an artistic performance emotionally moving or spiritually inspiring, and, as he notes, this is not merely a question of clinical experience or practice, for it requires a "spark that comes from the inner depths of an artist or an analyst's individual being from the self" (ibid., p. 203). As Bion puts it, "It is only after you have qualified [as an analyst] that you have a chance of becoming an analyst. The analyst you become is you and you alone" (1987, p. 15).

The aesthetics of metaphor

If most metaphors are conventional in the sense that they form part of the same linguistic and conceptual context into which an individual is born and raised, what is at stake in analysis is the ability to respond to the patient's material though the use of original and appropriate metaphors. A fundamental character of any original or poetic metaphor is its capacity to bring together and unite imagination and feeling, cognition and sensation, in order to create a new meaning. According to Hester in *The Meaning of Poetic Metaphor*, the capacity to create good metaphor depends essentially on "seeing as", where this process is defined as "an intuitive experience-act by which one selects from the quasi-sensory mass of imagery [...] the relevant aspects of such imagery" (1967, p. 213).

Jung always made a clear distinction between the symbol (indicating something unknown that cannot be articulated conceptually) and the sign (indicating something known). He is much less clear, however, in his conception of the status of the metaphor. Smythe and Baydala (2012) note that symbols can possess a denotative function, describing or defining something literal and relatively self-contained, but that what is relevant is their expressive function, which is both metaphorical and open-ended. In their account, the expressive metaphorical function of a symbol cannot be understood conceptually and as such cannot be evaluated for its truth function. It can, however, be evaluated in aesthetic or moral terms for what Goodman calls "its rightness of rendering" – its capacity to resonate with and illuminate the personal or cultural context from which it arose (2012, pp. 66–70). Warren Colman likewise stresses the importance of the aesthetic evaluation of the dream metaphors when he states: "we do not judge a metaphor in terms of whether it is 'correct' [...] metaphors are to be judged by whether they are apposite and illuminating" (2005, p. 658).

This creative act of "seeing as", essential for the creation of original dream metaphors, can, however, fail for three different reasons: the metaphor created is part of the conceptual system of conventional metaphors and adds nothing new; there is not sufficient similarity between the two terms of the metaphor to justify bringing them into relationship; or there is a refusal to accept difference and there is too much similarity between the terms. If there is insufficient similarity between the two terms of the metaphor to justify bringing them into relationship, then what we have is a kind of pseudo-metaphor. This is essentially defensive in that it is created purely to ward off affects, either because they are too charged to be contained or because the inner space for containment is inadequate. On the other hand, if there is an incapacity to accept difference and there is too much similarity between the terms, then we are left with concrete metaphors which are purely iconic and which exhibit no differentiation between the thing in itself and its mental presentation – this is what we typically find in dreams associated with trauma and psychosis. It is exactly here that the analyst's metaphoric capacity can help her to recognize that the patient's ability to make use of metaphor to represent the inner world is missing or deficient. To attribute symbolical significance to pseudo-metaphors or concrete metaphors (and it is irrelevant in this context whether the content is interpreted in terms of archetypes or in terms of transference and counter-transference) is at best useless and at worst positively harmful. In such cases, what is needed is the reconstruction or construction *ex novo* of the various functions and apparatuses that are essential for the creation of the visual metaphors necessary to dream and the linguistic metaphors that we utilize to narrate our dreams.

All this suggests that when we look at a dream, it is not sufficient to take into consideration the conceptual articulation of the meaning of the dream contents; we must also be able to assess the aesthetic value of the dream metaphors: their originality; the power of their expressive capacity to give form to unprocessed experiences; and their ability to link together different experiences so as to hold the creative tension between thought and sensation, feeling and intuition. This enables something new to be added to both the personal and the collective context. Likewise, when we interpret or amplify such images, it is not the correctness of our responses that counts but their metaphorical power, their expressive capacity to facilitate emergent processes in the development of the images. It is when a metaphor becomes capable of holding this creative tension that it becomes truly symbolic in as much as it assumes to itself that quality of being operative – of constituting itself as a "generator of activity" which, as Trevi (1986) says, "is located in the mid-point between two activities (or if one prefers, two functions): the com-positive activity that produces it and the com-positive activity that it produces" (p. 68).

Conclusion

When the dialogue between Freud and Jung broke down so dramatically in 1913, for many years this created a barrier to any possibility of cross-fertilization between the two schools of depth psychology. On the one hand, there was Freud, with his model of a mind-psyche confined within the boundaries of the individual body and with his paternally based method emphasizing the causal, the diachronic, the representational and the linguistic. On the other was Jung, with his model of a radically interconnected mind and his more maternal method of therapy, which focused above all on the metaphoric, on the presentational, on the synchronic and on the image. Both men, however, sought at all costs to ground their psychology in the science of their time, and, given the status of aesthetics as an inferior kind of knowledge, neither took this outlook into consideration. The result was that both tended to privilege content over form. Today, the revaluation of aesthetics as a means to exploring the process of meaning-making offers both psychoanalysis and analytical psychology an important opportunity to reopen this dialogue between our two different schools.

References

Aite, P. (2002). *Paessaggi della psiche: Il gioco della sabbia nell'analisi*. Torino: Bollati Borighieri Editore.

Baudrillard, J. (1994). *Simulacra and simulation* (Trans. S.F Glaser). Ann Arbor: University of Michigan Press.

Beebe, J. (2010). Psychotherapy in the aesthetic attitude. *The Journal of Analytical Psychology*, *55*(2), 165–87.

Bion, W.R. (1984). *Attention and interpretation*. London: Marsfield Reprints.

Bion, W.R. (1987). Clinical seminars. In *Clinical seminars and other works*. London: Karnac.

Bishop, P. (2009). *Analytical psychology and german classical aesthetics: Goethe, Schiller and Jung*. (Vol. 2. *The constellation of the self*). London and New York: Routledge.

Bollas, C. (1987). *The shadow of the object: Psychoanalysis of the unthought known*. London: Free Association Books.

Bollas, C. (2013). *China on the mind*. New York: London.

Botella, C., & Botella, S. (2005). *The work of psychic figurability: Mental states without representation*. Hove and New York: Routledge.

Carvahlo, R. (1991). Mechanism, metaphor. *Journal of Analytical Psychology*, *36*, 331–41.

Chianese, D., & Fontana, A. (2010). *Immaginando*. Milano: Franco Angeli.

Civitarese, G. (2011). The unconscious. *International Journal of Psychoanalysis*, *92*(2), 277–80.

Colman, W. (2005). Sexual metaphor and the language of unconscious phantasy. *Journal of Analytical Psychology*, *50*(5), 641–60.

Colman, W. (2009). Theory as metaphor: Clinical knowledge and its communication. *Journal of Analytical Psychology*, *54*(2), 199–217.

Colman, W. (2013). Reflections on knowledge and experience. *Journal of Analytical Psychology*, *58*(2), 200–19.

Colman, W. (2016). *Act and image: The emergence of symbolic imagination*. New Orleans: Spring Journal Inc.

Connolly, A.M. (2013). Cognitive aesthetics of alchemical imagery. *Journal of Analytical Psychology*, *58*(1), 4–34.

Connolly, A.M. (2015). The delivery of training: Personal experiences as a trainer in other cultures. In C. Crowther & J. Wiener (Eds), *From tradition to innovation: Jungian analysts working in different cultures*. New Orleans: Spring Journal Books.

Fonagy, P. (2002). Panel on controversial discussions. *International Journal of Psychoanalysis*, *83*, 453–58.

Franzoni, E. (2001). *Fenomenologia dell'invisibile: al di là dell'immagine*. Milano: Raffaello Cortina Editore.

Freud, S. (1916). Introductory lectures on psycho-analysis. In J. Strachey (Ed.), *The standard edition of the complete psychological works of Sigmund Freud* (Vol. *15*, pp. 1–240). London: Hogarth.

Freud, S. (1933). New introductory lectures on psycho-analysis. In J. Strachey (Ed.), *The standard edition of the complete psychological works of Sigmund Freud* (Vol. *22*, pp. 1–182). London: Hogarth.

Geertz, C. (1986). The uses of diversity. *Michigan Quarterly Review*, Winter, 105–23.

Goethe, J.W. (1789/1986). Essays on art and literature, in J. Grearey (Ed.), E. von Nardroff and E.H. von Nardroff (Trans.), *The collected works* (Vol. *3*). Princeton: Princeton University Press.

Hester, M.B. (1967). *The meaning of poetic metaphor*. The Hague: Mouton.

Hogenson, G. (2009). Archetypes as action patterns. *Journal of Analytical Psychology*, *54*(3), 325–39.

Johnson, M. (2007). *The meaning of the body: Aesthetics of human understanding*. Chicago: University of Chicago Press.

Jung, C.G. (1916/1953). The transcendent function. In G. Adler & R.F.C. Hull (Eds. & Trans.) *The collected works of C.G. Jung* (Vol. *8*, pp. 67–91). Princeton: Princeton University Press.

Jung, C.G. (1933). The real and the surreal. In G. Adler & R.F.C. Hull (Eds. & Trans.), *The collected works of C.G. Jung* (Vol. *8*, pp. 382–4). Princeton: Princeton University Press.

Jung, C.G. (1953). The structure of the unconscious. In G. Adler & R.F.C. Hull (Eds. & Trans.), *The collected works of C.G. Jung* (Vol. 7, pp. 269–304). Princeton: Princeton University Press.

Jung C.G. (1954). Medicine and psychotherapy. In G. Adler & R.F.C. Hull (Eds. & Trans.), *The collected works of C.G. Jung* (Vol. *16*, pp. 384–93). Princeton: Princeton University Press.

Kawai, H. (1976). *Pathology of Japan as a society of maternity*. Trans. M. Yama. Tokyo: Chuokoron-sha.

Kugler, P. (2005). *Raids on the unthinkable: Freudian and Jungian psychoanalysis*. New Orleans: Spring Journal Books.

Lakoff, G., & Johnson, M. (1980/2003). *Metaphors we live by*. Chicago: University of Chicago Press.

Langer, S. (1947). *Problems of art*. New York: Charles Scribner's Sons.

Meltzer, D. (1983). *Dream life*. Perthshire: Cluny.

Merleau-Ponty, M. (1962). *Phenomenology of perception*. London and New York: Routledge & Kegan Paul.

Shakespeare, W. *The tempest*. First Folio. Accessible online: www.gutenberg.org/cache/epub/2235/pg2235.html (accessed 30 January 2017).

Smythe, W.E., & Baydala, A. (2012). The hermeneutic background of C.G. Jung. *Journal of Analytical Psychology*, *57*(1), 57–75.

Stafford, B.M. (2001). *Visual analogy: Consciousness as the art of connecting*. Cambridge: MIT Press.

Stafford, B.M. (2007). *Echo objects: The cognitive work of images*. Chicago: Chicago University Press.

Trevi, M. (1986). *Metafore del simbolo: Ricerche sulla funzione simbolica nella psicologia complessa*. Milano: Raffaello Cortina Editore.

Trevi, M. (1993). *Saggi di critica neojunghiana*. Milano: Feltrinelli.

Winborn, M.D. (2015). Aesthetic experience and analytical process. *International Journal of Jungian Studies*, 7(2), 94–108.

Wright, K. (2015). The circus animals' desertion. *Rivista di Psicoanalisi*, *61*(4), 933–53.

Yama, M. (2013). Ego consciousness in the Japanese psyche: Culture, myth and disaster. *Journal of Analytical Psychology*, *58*(1), 52–73.

PART III
Post-Kleinian reflections

6

BION AND JUNG

Intersecting vertices

Mark Winborn

The intersection between the work of Wilfred Bion and Carl Jung offers an engaging conversation within the larger discourse between analytical psychology and contemporrary psychoanalysis. Their lives share similarities, both in terms of early childhood and traumatic events, as well as difficult periods of resistance to their ideas from factions within the psychoanalytic community. In addition to their life experiences, both Bion and Jung focus their work along similar lines—e.g., an emphasis on psychic reality, transcendent aspects of the psyche and experience, and the mutuality of influence in the analytic situation. In the present chapter, areas of convergence between the theoretical systems of Bion and Jung will be explored, as well as points of complementation and divergence. Finally, areas of exchange between post-Bionian and post-Jungian authors will be reviewed. While the manner in which Jung and Bion present their respective ideas is vastly different, it will be seen that the vertices outlined by these two men have laid an important framework for the dialogue between analytical psychology and contemporary psychoanalysis. I am writing from the perspective of someone who was trained as a Jungian psychoanalyst but who has developed an appreciation for Bionian and post-Bionian perspectives. My vertex of interpretation will inevitably be influenced by my Jungian background, and this chapter would likely have emerged differently if written by someone trained from a Bionian perspective.

Background

While Bion and the post-Bionian authors create a conceptual bridge between Jungian thought and contemporary psychoanalysis, there has always been a strong segment of resistance within the Jungian world towards incorporating psychoanalytic ideas. Only in recent decades has this resistance shown signs of diminishing, just as the resistance in the psychoanalytic world to acknowledging Jung's contribution has likewise softened. Anne Alvarez, a Kleinian analyst, acknowledges this shift:

> We need the psychoanalytic perspective to help us see the acorn in the oak tree, the baby in the child or the lost breast in the child's cuddly soft teddy. But we may need the developmentalists and Jung's perspective to help us to see the oak tree in the acorn, the man the child will become and is in the process of becoming.
>
> *(1992, p. 177)*

Samuels (1996) summarizes the evolution in contemporary psychoanalysis which has permitted greater receptivity to Jung: "Post-Freudian psychoanalysis has gone on to revise, repudiate, and extend many of Freud's seminal ideas [...] Many of the central issues and features of contemporary psychoanalysis are reminiscent of positions taken by Jung in earlier years" (p. 472). This change in attitude is reflected in an observation by Freudian scholar Paul Roazen: "Few responsible figures in psychoanalysis would be disturbed today if an analyst were to present views identical to Jung's in 1913" (1976, p. 272). A similar statement is also made by Robert Wallerstein:[1]

> If the Jungian viewpoint had arisen today, it would be accommodated within the body of psychoanalysis the way Kohut has been, rather than Jungians feeling they had to leave. The kind of unity that Freud tried to impose was an impossible one because it demanded a real orthodoxy.
>
> *(in Hunter, 1994, p. 333)*

Paralleling these developments in the psychoanalytic community, a group of psychoanalytically informed Jungians emerged in London around the influence of Michael Fordham. This group[2] has come to be referred to by Jungians as the "Developmental School" (Samuels, 1985), and their orientation has developed to become an influential voice in analytical psychology.

Openings and reconciliation

Two primary themes have emerged in psychoanalysis which set the stage for a closer dialogue between Bion and Jung: (1) a greater openness to psycho-spiritual themes in the analytic encounter (Gordon, 2004; Tennes, 2007; Rosegrant, 2012; Brown, 2016, 2017) and (2) an increased interest in the creative and generative aspects of the unconscious (Newirth, 2003; Safran, 2006; Aron & Atlas, 2015). These emerging themes in the psychoanalytic literature have created impetus for a reconsideration of Jungian theory.

Gordon (2004) draws on the work of Wilfred Bion, Donald Winnicott, Christopher Bollas, James Grotstein, and Michael Eigen, as well as some influences from relational psychoanalysis, to support his call for the restoration of wonderment and the experience of numinosity (Otto, 1958) to the psychoanalytic dialogue. As Gordon puts it,

There is a basic human tendency to seek experience of the numinous ... We are presupposed in this way. Relatively recently ... these efforts have been largely disconnected from their original wonderment and replaced with *primarily* rational or practical intentions. And the results have been devastating. With the removal of numinous experience from everyday life, a central dimension of self-experience has been flattened, its potential richness desiccated ... In the extreme, this gives rise to the feelings of emptiness and purposelessness that are the background canvas of so many of our patients' lives, no matter the particulars that first bring them to treatment.

(2004, p. 6)

Gordon goes on to state, more succinctly, "There also seems to be a concomitant universal *psychic* imperative: to seek experience that connects us, temporarily but repeatedly, with the transcendent" (2004, p. 7).

Similarly, Tennes (2007) points out that psychoanalytic theory has avoided embracing the mysterious and unknowable, particularly in the analytic encounter. Like Gordon, she also references Bion, Eigen, Grotstein, and Bollas as the primary psychoanalytic authors who have incorporated the ineffable unknown as a centerpiece in their analytic frameworks. Tennes proposes that psychoanalysis as a field is on the verge of a paradigm shift: a move towards greater openness to spiritual dimensions of experience. Her discussion centers around the "transpersonal" aspects of experience which point beyond the intersubjective to an encounter with "ontological otherness" (2007, p. 515). Bion's notion of "O"[3] is the psychoanalytic concept Tennes highlights as best expressing the ontological otherness of the objective ground of being. In the context of this discussion, she states:

The theory and practice of Jungian analysis is without doubt the approach that most extensively explores the integration of spiritual realities into depth psychotherapy [...] Because Jungian theory has tended to be overlooked within psychoanalytic circles, however, the spiritual dimension articulated there remains split off from psychoanalytic thought, however well developed it may be.

(p. 512, fn 4)

Rosegrant (2012), like Gordon and Tennes, also examines the emerging role of the transpersonal in psychoanalysis, but does so through the analytic theories of Jung and Bion. He points out that both figures attend to a layer of experience beyond the personal, thus reflecting "a commitment for connecting with a higher truth outside of personal experience" (p. 721).

Newirth (2003) and Safran (2006) focus attention on the generative, creative aspects of the unconscious rather than on the transpersonal. Safran indicates:

There has been a recent resurgence of interest in the unconscious by relational analysts, as exemplified in the work of such theorists as James Grotstein and Michael Eigen as well as some of Stephen Mitchell's later writing.

But the picture of the unconscious that emerges from these authors is a different one from Freud's unconscious and from the writing of many European analysts. The unconscious that emerges in these writings is one that is creative and generative, rather than one that is dangerous or destructive. And the emphasis of these authors is on harnessing unconscious forces or being guided by them, rather than taming or modulating them.

(2006, p. 394)

Since the transpersonal, generative, and creative aspects of the unconscious are all central to Jung's model of psychic functioning, these notions might serve a conceptual bridging function for those in the psychoanalytic community moving towards rapprochement with Jung.

The encounter between Jung and Bion

The direct dialogue between Jung and Bion largely began and ended in 1935 at Jung's Tavistock lectures. Bion, then a young psychiatrist hoping to become a psychoanalyst, attended three of the five lectures Jung gave at the Tavistock Clinic from September 30th to October 4th. The transcripts of those lectures (Jung, 1968) reveal Bion asking questions following Lectures One and Two. Bion was accompanied to one of the lectures by his analysand Samuel Beckett. During that lecture, Jung spoke on the difficulty some patients experience in "being born." This apparently had a significant impact on both Bion and Beckett in terms of better understanding Beckett's experience of his early childhood and the influence of those experiences on his writer's block (Bléandonu, 1999). It does not appear that Jung had any further contact with Bion, nor does he appear to have been familiar with Bion's writings.

Bion, for his part, did not publicly acknowledge any similarities between his theories and those of Jung until late in life. As Grotstein points out, this omission should not be considered specific to Jung, as Bion didn't tend to reference other psychoanalytic authors either: "Bion [...] was not a scholar who would cite other people's works" (Grotstein in Culbert-Koehn, 1997a, p. 16). Grotstein summarizes his perception of Bion's relationship to Jung as follows:

So I think that with Bion's own notions of myths, of transcendence and transformations, and of prenatal, unborn selves, we are clearly hearing someone who was very much influenced by Jung and/or working parallel to him without knowing it [...] Bion is also one of the very few people in the psychoanalytic field who really respects religion, spirituality, the numinous, the ineffable. And that certainly is Jung.

(Grotstein in Culbert-Koehn, 1997a, p. 16)

Despite Bion's failure to cite Jung directly in his work, when asked during a 1976 interview whether his notion of a "primordial mind" was related to Jung's concept of archetypes, Bion replied, "I think he [Jung] was probably talking about the same thing. There exists some fundamental mind, something that seems to remain unaltered in us all" (Bion, 1994, p. 247). It may be that Bion had more interest in Jung than he admitted publicly. The existence of an annotated copy of Jung's autobiography, *Memories, Dreams, Reflections* (Jung, 1965), in Bion's library would seem suggestive (Aguayo, 2016).

Jung and Bion: Similarities and contrasts

Bion and Jung both had tremendous respect for the concept of psychic reality and molded their approaches to reflect this. They both emphasized the centrality of unconscious-to-unconscious communication between analyst and analysand. Both created psychoanalytic models based on their experiences in working extensively with psychotic individuals. They each emphasized the importance of containing experiences; Jung emphasizing the alchemical metaphors of the *vas hermeticum* and the alchemical bath, while Bion relied on the image of containment provided by the mother's mind for the infant's emerging psychic experience. Both place great importance on transcendent dimensions of experience as well as the mysterious, unknown, complex, and infinite aspects of psyche. They share a focus on innate predisposing factors, which Jung refers to as archetypes and which Bion calls preconceptions. Bion, like Jung, had tremendous respect for spiritual/religious experience. They both articulate a prospective aspect of psyche; for Jung, this was conceptualized as the individuation process and for Bion, it took the form of the mind "coming into being." Intuition is seen as an important clinical tool for both figures. Finally, both men have a rather arcane style of writing that can be daunting and difficult to penetrate for newcomers.

I will now review several areas of overlapping focus shared by Bion and Jung, as well as highlighting some contrasts.

Jung and Bion: Gnostic mystics

Jung and Bion share an important commonality in emphasizing gnostic and mystical experience in their conceptualizations of the psyche. They share common influences from the gnostic-mystical tradition, such as Meister Eckhart and St John of the Cross. By "mysticism," I am referring not to particular mystical beliefs or practices, but to the immediate experience of a numinous or transcendent reality. And by "gnosticism," I am referring to knowledge gained through direct experience of the transcendent rather than the specific beliefs of Gnostic religion. Grotstein refers to Bion, Lacan, and Jung as the "three great mystics of psychoanalysis" (in Culbert-Koehn, 1997a, p. 21). Grotstein summarizes these trends in Bion and Jung as follows:

> I think the common ancestry of that is the Gnostics and later Meister Eckhart [...] And I think the early mystics understood, and the Gnostics understood,

something which the early church divided off and decided to ban, the concept of the God within, because, low and behold, I think we're beginning to understand, thanks to Jung and to Bion, and maybe indirectly to Lacan, that the concept of the unconscious is as close to God as we get.

(ibid., p. 27)

Jung's emphasis on the gnostic and mystical aspects of experience can be discerned in this excerpt from a letter written in 1945:

The main interest of my work is not concerned with the treatment of neuroses but rather with the approach to the numinous. But the fact is that the approach to the numinous is the real therapy and inasmuch as you attain to the numinous experiences you are released from the source of pathology. Even the very disease takes on a numinous character.

(Jung, 1973, p. 377)

Interestingly, these themes became more pronounced in the writings of both Bion and Jung as they matured in years. The mystical and gnostic themes in Jung and Bion are explored in greater depth by Grotstein (1981), Dehing (1990), Merkur (2010), and Segal (1992).

Views of the unconscious

In terms of the unconscious, what we see with Jung and later with Bion is a move away from the topographical model of the mind proposed by Freud. In Freudian theory the concept of the unconscious is largely treated as a noun, a location where certain psychic contents are deposited or reside. De Azevedo (2000) refers to this notion as the "substantive unconscious" in contrast to what she terms the "adjective unconscious"—a conception of the unconscious as process, "as a quality, or a state, ever temporary, dynamic, and subject to the constant changes going on in the individual's internal psychic world as well as to external conditions" (p. 75). It is largely in the adjective understanding of the unconscious that Bion and Jung find common ground. While Jung does often refer to the unconscious as noun (see Sullivan, 2011, pp. 18–19), he also conveys a strong sense of the adjective unconscious: "The self is not just a static quantity or constant form, but is also a dynamic process" (Jung, 1959b, para. 411). Here it is important to note that Jung refers to the self as both the center and the circumference of the psyche; hence, at times Jung uses self, and qualities of the self, almost synonymously with unconscious experience.

In Bion, this adjective aspect of unconscious experience is most clearly developed in his theory of thinking (Bion, 1993). Relying on his concepts of beta elements, alpha function, alpha elements, and transformation, Bion outlines an unconscious dynamic that forms an evolving capacity for thinking and relationship to self and other. According to Levine and Civitarese (2016), Bion "conceptualized the unconscious not simply as a structure and place of hidden contents, but as an ever expanding, inexhaustible domain and a psychoanalytic function of the personality" (p. xxii).

Complexity of the psyche

The vast complexity of the psyche is a feature of the unconscious that captivates both Jung and Bion. Jung (1965) writes:

> It is important to have a secret, a premonition of things unknown. It fills life with something impersonal, a numinosum. A man who has never experienced that has missed something important. He must sense that he lives in a world which in some respects is mysterious; that things happen and can be experienced which remain inexplicable; that not everything which happens can be anticipated. The unexpected and the incredible belong in this world. Only then is a life whole. For me the world has from the beginning been infinite and ungraspable.
>
> *(p. 356)*

Bion expresses a similar respect and awe for the complexity of the psyche in this passage from *Attention and Interpretation* (1970):

> The domain of personality is so extensive that it cannot be investigated with thoroughness. The power of psycho-analysis demonstrates to any practicing psycho-analyst that adjectives like "complete" or "full" have no place in qualifying "analysis." The more nearly thorough the investigation, the clearer it becomes that however prolonged a psycho-analysis may be it represents only the start of an investigation. It stimulates growth of the domain it investigates.
>
> *(p. 69)*

Transcendence

Grotstein identifies transcendence as a parallel area of exploration for Jung and Bion: "Another place of correspondence is his concept of [...] I call it transcendence, he [Bion] calls it transformations. There I think Jung and Bion are going along parallel tracks" (Grotstein in Culbert-Koehn, 1997a, p. 16). Transcendence refers to levels of experience which move beyond the personal and solely subjective. Jung uses a variety of terms to address this level of experience: "archetypal," "collective unconscious," "objective psyche," and "self." An example of this transcendence can be found in Jung's description of the self:

> I usually describe the supraordinate personality as the "self," thus making a sharp distinction between the ego, which, as is well known, extends only as far as the conscious mind, and the whole of the personality, which includes

the unconscious as well as the conscious component. The ego is thus related to the self as part to whole. To that extent the self is supraordinate. Moreover, the self is felt empirically not as subject but as object.

(1959a, para. 315)

Elsewhere, Jung indicates:

But as one can never distinguish empirically between a symbol of the self and a God-image, the two ideas, however much we try to differentiate them, always appear blended together, so that the self appears synonymous with the inner Christ [...] Anything that man postulates as being a greater totality than himself can become a symbol of the self.

(1958, paras 231–232)

Bion chooses the term "O" to represent all that is infinite in contrast to finite, all that is unknowable in contrast to known, and all that supersedes personal experience (Bion, 1965). He refers to states of union with "O" as "at-one-ment" (1965, p. 163). Bion is intentionally vague about what "O" is, other than "the thing-in-itself," preferring to leave the definition and experience of "O" unencumbered by previous associations. This is in contrast to Jung's discussions of self, archetype, and collective unconscious, where he elaborates at length the many associations he identifies between transcendent aspects of experience and the patterns found in myths, fairytales, alchemy, and religion.

Embrace of unknowing

A central aspect of Bion's model is his emphasis on what he terms "negative capability" in the analyst (Bion, 1970). Negative capability is a term Bion borrowed from the British poet John Keats, who defined negative capability as the capacity to embrace uncertainty, live with mystery, and make peace with ambiguity "without any irritable reaching after fact and reason." This emphasis on negative capability is reflected in Bion's reliance on non-sensuous intuition, the use of reverie, and his recommendation to "approach every session without memory or desire" (Bion, 1967, p. 272). It is also reflected in his selection of terms to describe his model of the psyche—Bion intentionally selected terms he felt were abstract, undefined, unsaturated by preconceived meanings, and open to interpretation in new ways. Bion felt that only by approaching the analytic session with this attitude and frame of mind would the analyst be able to discern what is emerging in the field in relationship to "O," rather than defaulting to a categorization of experience based on concepts, terms, and patterns previously experienced.

An embrace of the unknown is present in Jung, but is often more subtly stated, e.g., "Doctor and patient thus find themselves in a relationship founded on mutual unconsciousness" (1954/1966, para. 364). Elsewhere, Jung addresses the unknown more specifically:

The unconscious is not simply the unknown, it is rather the unknown psychic; and this we define on the one hand as all those things in us which, if they came to consciousness, would presumably differ in no respect from the known psychic contents, with the addition [...] of the psychoid system, of which nothing is known directly.

(1960, para. 382)

From a synthetic Jungian-Bionian perspective, Michael Fordham develops the theme of the unknown more fully in his paper 'On not knowing beforehand' (1993b).

Both Jung and Bion emphasize the analyst's reliance on intuition as an important aspect of the relationship to the unknown.[4] Grotstein highlights this point: "Both Jung and Bion particularly emphasized the importance of intuition. Intuition is really looking inward" (Grotstein in Culbert-Koehn, 1997a, p. 18). Jung's description of intuition is informative:

The peculiarity of intuition is that it is neither sense perception, nor feeling, nor intellectual inference [...] In intuition a content presents itself whole and complete, without our being able to explain or discover how this content came into existence. Intuition is a kind of instinctive apprehension ... it is an irrational function of perception. As with sensation, its contents have the character of being "given," in contrast to the "derived" or "produced" character of thinking and feeling contents.

(1921, para. 770)

Jung (1960) also identifies a close relationship between intuition and the manifestation of symbolic material: "Symbols were never devised consciously, but were always produced out of the unconscious by way of revelation or intuition" (para. 92). The same reliance on intuition that exists in Jung also figures prominently in Bion:

I am supposing that there is a psychoanalytic domain with its own reality—unquestionable, constant, subject to change only in accordance with its own rules even if those rules are not known. These realities are "intuitable" if the proper apparatus is available in the condition proper to its functioning [...] The conditions in which the intuition operates (intuits) are pellucid and opaque.

(1992, p. 315)

In Bion's thinking, intuition is closely connected with his concept of reverie. Reverie is the primary way that the analyst accesses, perceives, experiences, and works with the states and psychic elements of the analytic field. Being in reverie involves an opening up to one's own internal stream of consciousness and unconscious promptings—opening to ideas, thoughts, feelings, sensations, memories, images, urges, and fantasies. Reverie also involves being receptive on many levels to the experience and communication, both explicit and implicit, of the other person's presence in the room. The potential range of reverie experiences stretches from the strange or horrific to the ordinary, and at times opens to glimpses of the transcendent. While reverie has some similarities to Jung's method of active imagination (Jung, 1916),[5] reverie is actually closer to Jung's concept of *participation mystique*— a term adopted by Jung to refer to a blurring of boundaries in the experience between subject and object.[6]

Teleological thrust

Teleology is the explanation of phenomena by the purpose they serve rather than through the identification of the causes of the phenomena. As Alvarez (1992) says, "The prospective, forward-looking and aspiring element in human nature has always been important in Jungian analytic theory" (p. 175). Janus, the two-faced god of the Romans, is always facing both forward and back. The teleological perspective in psychoanalysis adds a forward-looking vision, i.e., where psyche is moving, to the backward-looking vision associated with the more traditional causal perspective in psychoanalysis. A teleological orientation is central in the Jungian and Bionian perspectives. In Bion, this is articulated through his concept of the "Man of Achievement" (Bion, 1970, p. 125). A Man of Achievement is an individual who possesses "negative capability" and the "language of achievement"; the "language of achievement" refers to a form of language which is sufficiently grounded in experience and connected with "O" that it makes "possible a degree of 'publication' in that formulations exist which have achieved durability and extensibility" (1970, p. 1). Bion goes on to state:

> In his sphere the psycho-analyst's attention is arrested by a particular experience to which he would draw the attention of the analysand. To do this he must employ the Language of Achievement. That is to say, he must employ methods which have the counterpart of durability or extension in a domain where there is no time or space as those terms are used in the world of sense.
>
> *(1970, p. 2)*

The language of achievement is rooted in the capacity to utilize intuition and emotional experience for learning. It contrasts with destructive attacks on thinking and the development of the apparatus for thinking. A teleological thrust is explicitly addressed in Jung's (1960) definition of a symbol:

> By a symbol I do not mean an allegory or a sign, but an image that describes in the best possible way the dimly discerned nature of the spirit. A symbol does not define or explain; it points beyond itself to a meaning that is darkly divined yet still beyond our grasp, and cannot be adequately expressed in the familiar words of our language.
>
> *(para. 644)*

The teleological thrust in Jung is also strongly represented in his concept of the transcendent function (1916), which Jung proposes as the mechanism by which opposites of psychological experience are transformed via a higher synthesis into a new third thing. Grotstein notes that the emphasis on intuition in Jung and Bion is closely tied with sensing the teleological thrust of the psyche:

> I think they both [Jung and Bion] were going in the same direction, in a kind of poetic language which indicated what we see and know is limited by our senses. There is a coherence beyond. I think that's one of the principal things that unites Jung with Bion, that there is something beyond, before, and in the future—what Bion called *A Memoir of the Future*.
> *(Grotstein in Culbert-Koehn, 1997a, p. 18)*

Dreamwork

The function of dreamwork for both Bion and Jung shifts away from the classical approach wherein the analyst's task is to translate from the manifest to latent content, thus revealing the underlying wish, feeling, or fantasy that is threatening to the ego of the analysand. For Jung, the dream speaks for itself and reveals its meaning in the language of symbols; not to obscure, but because symbols are the language of the unconscious. In Jung's model (1954/1966), dreams also function to facilitate the creation of the personality: "every dream is an organ of information and control, and why dreams are our most effective aid in building up the personality" (para. 332). Jung views dreams as having a function beyond the maintenance of repression; i.e., that dreams confront the dreamer with new situations: "Increased knowledge of the unconscious brings a deeper experience of life and greater consciousness, and therefore confronts us with apparently new situations" (1964, para. 677).

Like Jung, Bion began with Freud's notion of "dream-work" and again broadened its meaning to encompass disparate phenomena. Freud's idea of dreams serving the pleasure principle remained intact, but Bion supplemented this with an understanding of how dreams could also serve the reality principle by giving representation to raw emotional experience. The dream portrays the emotional state of the dreamer, and it is incumbent on the dreamer and the analyst to comprehend the emotional state being presented. In the Bionian model, dreaming is considered to occur both when sleeping and when awake. In waking states, the conscious mind is not aware of dreaming, but the individual continues their unconscious efforts to dream themselves into existence. Jung also hypothesizes the possibility of waking dreams: "It is on the whole probable that we continually dream but that consciousness makes such a noise that we do not hear it [...] one does not dream, one is dreamt. We 'suffer' the dream, we are its objects" (quoted in Jacobi, 1977, p. 73).

Dreaming, in Bion's model, refers to unconscious psychological work that a person does with their emotional experiences. It is through this work that we attempt to dream ourselves into being. We have no direct experience of the waking dream—we can only recognize its existence through the behavioral and narrative derivatives that filter into our conscious thoughts and actions. Listening from Bion's perspective is not just listening through a different set of theoretical constructs; it is listening in an altogether different way. In Bion's model of dreaming, the emphasis shifts away from the meaning and symbolic content of dreams and refocuses our attention on the process of dreaming as an experience (or non-experience) of being. Note the teleological parallel between Jung's model of individuation and Bion's idea of "dreaming ourselves into existence."

Pre-structuring of experience

Ideas regarding the pre-structuring of experience are common to both Jung and Bion. Jung addresses the pre-structuring of experience through his theory of archetypes. Archetypes are thought of as unconscious universal structures or inherited templates which organize psychic energy along certain repeatable patterns. These innate patterns or predispositions influence the formation of experience and become manifest through images or symbols. Jung is careful to point out that it is "not a question [...] of inherited ideas but of inherited possibilities of ideas" (1959a, para. 136).

The pre-structuring of the unconscious appears in Bion's work in the concept of "preconception" (Bion, 1993). In Bion's model, infants are born with preconceptions. The baby searches for and eventually finds realizations of these preconceptions in the outer world; a search that is essential for survival. An example of this would be the infant's innate search for the mother's breast. When a preconception finds a realization in the environment, a conception is created. As Bion (1994) frames the issue, "Why should there not be what we would call mental vestiges, or archaic elements, which are operative in a way that is alarming and disturbing because it breaks through the beautiful calm surface we ordinarily think of as rational, sane behavior?" (p. 236). When asked whether there was a similarity between Bion's notion of preconceptions and Jung's notion of archetypes, Grotstein responds: "I think quite a bit. In fact, I think it's the same thing. Preconceptions, like archetypes, intuit, anticipate their future" (Grotstein in Culbert-Koehn, 1997a, p. 29).

Transformation of experience

Both Jung and Bion articulate models of transformation in their theories. For Bion, this is most evident in terms of his theory of thinking (1993, pp. 110–119). Bion refers frequently to "thinking" in his writing, but his idea of thinking is not synonymous with cognition or intellectual acts. He is using the word "thinking" as a shorthand term for the capacity "to be" through the reflective embodied experience of emotion. Hence, emotional experience is the foundation from which the capacity for increasingly complex forms of reflection emerges. The work of analysis still involves the work of understanding symbolic content so as to reveal unconscious meanings, but analysis also becomes a process of metabolizing un-symbolized aspects of experience which have never been conscious or "thought." Bion refers to these bits of un-symbolized experience as beta elements. Because beta elements operate outside awareness and have not yet been represented, they are not available for thought, reflection, or learning, and are not subject to repression.

Bion speaks of "alpha elements" to refer to bits of experience which have coalesced sufficiently to be reflected upon by the individual or in the presence of another person. Alpha elements are produced from the impressions of experience which have been made storable and available for dream thought. Alpha elements are the building blocks of experience, and they have the potential to become connected together to form dream thoughts. "Alpha function" is the process by which beta elements become transformed into alpha elements. Analytically, this refers to the capacity of the analyst to contain elements of the patient's psyche through engaging in reverie with the patient's beta elements in order to facilitate their transformation into alpha elements. For the patient to learn from experience, the alpha function of the analyst must metabolize the emotional experience of the patient until the patient develops sufficient alpha function to participate in the process through a mutually constellated alpha function.

Alpha function is similar to Jung's concept of the transcendent function (1916), except that in Jung's model the transcendent function operates to generate symbolic material and functions intrapsychically, while alpha function operates intersubjectively and on the level of the pre-representational. We can think of alpha function as operating on a more fundamental level of transformation than the transcendent function—the level of very discrete, almost imperceptible shifts which transform undigested elements of experience into usable bits of experience. These transformed bits become the building blocks of the symbolization process expressed by the transcendent function. As Cwik (2011) indicates, these small transformative experiences reflect "micro-activations of the transcendent function resulting in new images, thoughts, and feelings that appear to the analyst" (p. 31).

Mutual influence

Intersubjectivity theory holds that there are two subjectivities present in the analytic relationship, and that they mutually create an interactive psychological field in which elements of the individual psyches cannot be clearly distinguished. This is in contrast to the traditional Freudian view of the analytic dyad as being composed of two distinct and isolated psyches; what Stolorow and Atwood (1994) refer to as "the myth of the isolated mind." Jung's theories on analytic interaction foreshadow the fundamental tenets of an intersubjective approach:

> For two personalities to meet is like mixing two different chemical substances: If there is any combination at all both are transformed. In any effective psychological treatment the doctor is bound to influence the patient: But this influence can only take place if the patient has a reciprocal influence on the doctor. You can exert no influence if you are not susceptible to influence.
>
> *(1954/1966, para. 163)*

Jung states elsewhere: "In any thoroughgoing analysis the whole personality of both patient and doctor is called into play" (1965, p. 132). A similar attitude can also be discerned in Bion's work:

> In psycho-analysis: when approaching the unconscious—that is, what we do *not* know, not what we *do* know—we, patient and analyst alike, are certain to be disturbed. Anyone who is going to see a patient tomorrow should, at some point, experience fear. In every consulting room there ought to be two rather frightened people: the patient and the psycho-analyst. If they are not, one wonders why they are bothering to find out what everyone knows.
>
> *(1990, pp. 4–5)*

Ogden (1994) identifies Bion as a precursor to intersubjective theory, especially in Bion's development of the notion of projective identification as a means of communication.

Summary of Bion's model contrasted with Jung's

Bion's model is without a specifically delineated goal other than the transformation of un-metabolized experience into elements of experience that can be reflected upon. He is intentionally vague in describing these elements and functions. Bion's approach provides a complement to the Jungian model of transformation, which has more specific and higher-ordered outcomes associated with the concepts of the transcendent function and individuation. Bion's focus is on recognizing and gathering up small bits of unintegrated experience, rather than on uncovering, finding meaning, or narrating. Higher-order processes such as the discovery of meaning, individuation, or improved relational capacity become attainable as these unintegrated bits of experience cohere as larger units of usable experience. In this regard, Bion's model is operating on a level of experience which precedes the process of symbolic activity that is typically the focus of Jungian analysis.

The dialogues

Jungian dialogue with Bion

Significant Jungian interest has been expressed towards Bion, with references to Bion's work appearing in Jungian literature dating back to 1957.

Michael Fordham

The dialogue between Jung and Bion might have ended with Bion's attendance at Jung's 1935 Tavistock lectures had it not been for the pioneering efforts of Michael Fordham. He was the first significant figure in the Jungian community to incorporate the developments that had occurred in psychoanalytic theory and practice following Jung's resignation as President of the International Psychoanalytical Association in 1914. Fordham was a child psychiatrist at the London Child Guidance Clinic from 1934 through much of World War II. During this period, he came to feel that the tools provided by his Jungian training were insufficient to the needs of working with severely disturbed children. Fordham found new resources to draw from when he was exposed to the work of Melanie Klein, particularly *The Psycho-Analysis of Children* (1932), which he reports reading "with amazement and emotional shock" (Fordham, 1993a, p. 65).

Fordham's effort to integrate Klein's psychoanalytic method with Jung's theories was met with resistance by many in the Jungian community. It created doubts about his loyalty to Jung's ideas and eventually led to a split among the Jungians practicing in London. To supplement his Jungian training, Fordham sought supervision with a Kleinian analyst, attended a two-year infant observation seminar at the Tavistock Clinic in London, and at age 79, entered analysis with Kleinian-Bionian analyst Donald Meltzer. Fordham was also later exposed to Bion's work, which he incorporates extensively in *Explorations into the Self* (1985). Summarizing that exposure, Fordham says: "It has seemed to me that Bion has presented much matter which needs to be assimilated by analytical psychologists" (1985, p. 2). Elsewhere, Fordham (1995) states: "Bion's extraordinarily rich but difficult thought has a curious familiarity, which I believe derives from a similarity with many of Jung's formations" (p. 223).

Fordham was significantly influenced by Bion's concepts of beta elements, alpha elements, and alpha function as he extended Jung's theory of individuation into infancy: a process he termed "deintegration-integration of the primary self" (Fordham, 1985). Fordham's deintegrate-integrate model of individuation is much closer to Bion's model of transformation via alpha function than Jung's model of the transcendent function. He also acknowledges the influence of Bion's (1993) "attacks on linking" in the development of his "defenses of the self" (Fordham, 1974). Fordham's dedication to a pluralistic, integrated vision of analytic theory and practice can be discerned in the title of one of his last books, *Freud, Jung, Klein: The Fenceless Field* (1995). In this same volume, Fordham outlines eight areas in Bion's theoretical system which find correspondence in Jung (1995, pp. 223–224).

Barbara Stevens Sullivan

By far the most extensive examination and integration of Bionian and Jungian thought is offered by Barbara Stevens Sullivan (2010) in her book *The Mystery of Analytical Work: Weavings of Jung and Bion*. Sullivan identifies points of commonality and complementation in their work. Major themes addressed by Sullivan include the creativity of the unconscious, the processes by which experience is registered, the nature of psychopathology, the pursuit of truth and individuation, how listening occurs in analysis, and observations on the process of change and transformation.

A unique aspect of Sullivan's approach is her emphasis on relatedness and her effort to cast Bion and Jung in relational terms, which she acknowledges is a reflection of her own personality. Perhaps this would please Bion, who intentionally left his concepts loosely defined or "unsaturated" so that there was room for his readers to develop their own interpretations of his work.[7] However, Sandler (2005) indicates that efforts to cast Bion as a relationalist, or to suggest that Bion had a greater interest in the analytic relationship than the individual's mind, are unwarranted (p. 410). I agree with Sandler's assessment of Bion in this regard. My own reading of Bion suggests that Bion's work can readily be conceptualized as fitting within the intersubjective/relational perspective in psychoanalysis which emerged shortly after Bion's death, but that a number of the overarching characteristics of relational psychoanalysis are not congruent with Bion's model of psychoanalysis. Nevertheless, Sullivan does the Jungian world a significant service by highlighting how an incorporation of Bionian concepts and practices into a Jungian framework can expand the way Jungians experience their patients and the analytic process. She also does the Bionian psychoanalytic community a service by explicating Jung's conceptual framework from a Bionian perspective, allowing Jung's ideas to be more easily assimilated by those unfamiliar with Jung. Sullivan nicely summarizes the relationship between Bion's opus and that of Jung as follows:

> I believe that it is the late Bion whose ideas regarding O, doubt, Faith, the impossibility of Knowing and the consequent need to focus instead on moving-toward-knowing, on endlessly becoming rather than existing in a fixed shape is the Bion whose ideas can be thought of as "Jungian" in nature [...] Analysts like Ferro, Grotstein and the Symingtons see Bion's later work as bringing us to a new kind of analysis ... For this Jungian, the late Bion is a brilliant expander of Jung's perspective.
>
> *(2012, pp. 689–690)*

JoAnn Culbert-Koehn

JoAnn Culbert-Koehn has lectured widely on the intersection of Jung, Klein, and Bion and published a number of articles on Bionian/Jungian themes (1997a, 1997b, 1997c, 1998, 2000, 2011). Culbert-Koehn goes so far as to describe a "Jung/Bion tradition" (1998, p. 71). Her work is particularly informative when describing the impact that the Kleinian and Bionian conceptual frameworks have had on her work as a Jungian analyst:

> Klein's work and Bion's work add to what I can observe and describe. Klein's work has been particularly helpful in elucidating what Jung described as the personal shadow within the context of the transference–countertransference interaction in the here and now of the analytic relationship. Bion's ideas help me understand the pain and turbulence of psychic change and how to help a patient increase his or her capacity to bear the psychic pain necessary for transformation ... Bion's writing was very helpful to me in understanding the importance of containment, catastrophic anxiety and its relationship to birth,

the pain of bearing the unknown, and the hatred of psychic change … I have found that these theories augment what I can see, describe, and help patients integrate. I have not found that they conflict with the broad view of the psyche that I was introduced to in my Jungian training.

(Culbert-Koehn, 2000, p. 448)

Culbert-Koehn also finds value in Bion's ideas about the process of change as related to the capacity to tolerate psychic pain:

One of the underlying factors in the lack of change, it seems to me, is an inability to tolerate psychic pain. I have found Bion's writing most helpful in addressing this issue. His idea is that the analyst is a container for undigested psychic contents. The analyst in each session takes in what is intolerable psychic pain and digests or metabolizes it in a way that it can be returned to the patient in a form of psychic contents that are digestible and available for mentalization […] It was Bion's idea that an analysis would enable a patient to tolerate the catastrophic anxiety involved in psychic change.

(2000, p. 451)

Other Jungian authors[8]

Winborn (2014) and Mathew (2005) provide detailed explorations of Bion's (1962) concept of reverie from a Jungian perspective. They both demonstrate how reverie fits well with the imaginal-metaphoric emphasis in Jungian theory and offer suggestions for assimilating reverie into Jungian practice. As Mathew (2005) beautifully states, "Reverie is, I believe, both a process and a state of mind […] It is reverie that extends psyche's vision beyond the doors and windows of our minds into the cathedrals of our souls" (p. 391).

Cwik (2011) provides a well-developed synthesis of Jungian and Bionian conceptualizations, particularly focusing on Bion's concepts of reverie and waking dreaming as well as Jung's concept of active imagination. He outlines a continuum of affective, somatic, and imaginal experience in the transference-countertransference matrix of the analytic encounter. Cwik proposes the term "associative dreaming" to capture the continuum of potential experiences in the analytic encounter and offers examples of how various elements gathered from this continuum can be utilized in session. This notion of associative dreaming provides a rich example of the synergistic complementation that is possible between Jungian and Bionian theory.

Dehing (1994) offers a creative conceptual integration in his utilization of Bion's conceptual framework of "thinking" to provide a detailed "hypothesis about the mechanisms by which archetypal structures achieve psychic reality" (p. 459), which Dehing argues is not sufficiently articulated by Jung. In addition, Dehing also proposes that "the whole 'containing' operation itself is archetypally determined" (p. 460). Thus, Dehing utilizes the theoretical systems developed by Jung and Bion as reciprocal lenses or vertices to develop new insights about each system.

Godsil (2014) provides an exploration of trauma and disruptions in capacity for mental representation through the theories of Bion, Jung, and Fordham. She gives special focus to the trauma which Bion experienced firsthand during World War I, as well as offering a close discussion of triggers for reversal of alpha functioning and the development of beta screens or bizarre objects.

Carvalho, in a series of articles (2002, 2008, 2014a, 2014b), investigates the intersections between Jung, Bion, and Matte Blanco. While his analysis is mutually supportive of all three theorists, Carvalho's primary emphasis is to provide external theoretical support for certain aspects of Jung's conceptualization of the unconscious and unconscious processes. To do so, Carvalho utilizes Bion's concepts of "O" and beta elements, along with Matte Blanco's (1998a, 1998b) conceptualization of an unconscious that is a multi-dimensional, stratified, operating bi-logically,[9] and possessing an infinite number of possible unconscious sets.

Addison (2016) provides an in-depth comparison of Jung's psychoid concept and Bion's proto-mental concept. Bion's proto-mental concept refers to undifferentiated feeling states and was an aspect of his theory of groups which evolved into his concept of beta elements. Jung's psychoid concept refers to an inferred connection between psyche and matter. Addison indicates that both of these concepts point to the centrality of the soma in analytic work and articulate a combined mind-body monism in which mind and body are seen as two aspects of the same thing.

There are a number of case studies which combine Jungian and Bionian perspectives. In a case of an adult client who experienced infantile trauma through separation, Cavalli (2014) supplements her Jungian background with Bion's conceptualization of the capacity to think. Her patient's experiences of "O" mediated through the analyst's alpha function allowed representations of her early separation experience to form where no representation had previously existed. Sullivan (2007) documents a Jungian-Bionian analysis of an aging female patient who had previously been in a classical Jungian analysis. Sullivan explains the trajectory of the case through the lens of Bion's concepts of alpha function, attacks on linking, increased capacity to develop alpha elements, and an emergent capacity to become psychologically "alive." Bovensiepen (2002) illustrates how the transcendent function and the symbolic attitude[10] can be disrupted and how these capacities can be restored in analysis through the experience of shared reverie. Several Jungian analysts (Proner, 2005; Cavalli, 2011; Schmidt, 2012; McAlister, 2014; and Mizen, 2014) also present case studies of severely disturbed patients organized around the concept of psychic skin as developed by Esther Bick and Frances Tustin. These authors blend the concept of psychic skin with Bion's theories on psychosis, undigested beta elements, reverse alpha function, and transformations in "O," as well as Jung's theories of archetypes, psychosis, and teleology.

In closing this section, I would be remiss if I failed to mention several Jungian authors who often incorporate Bion's ideas in their books. Some of these authors include Kenneth Lambert (1981), Nathan Schwartz-Salant (1989), Fred Plaut (1993), Mara Sidoli (2000), Donald Kalsched (1996, 2013), and Marcus West (2007, 2016).

Bionian dialogue with Jung

The number of psychoanalysts practicing from a Bionian perspective who also incorporate ideas from Jungian theory is relatively small. The main figures to have acknowledged Jung's contributions to psychoanalysis and incorporated his ideas into their work are James Grotstein, Michael Eigen, and Neville Symington. Giuseppe Civitarese has also begun to acknowledge an appreciation for Jung's work. One of the few pieces of collaborative scholarship involving both Jungian and psychoanalytic authors is by Horne, Sowa, and Isenman (2000). They examine the issue of causality, tracing the philosophical roots of causality and then comparing how causality is addressed in the theoretical systems of Freud, Bion, and Jung.

James Grotstein

References to Jung appear in many of Grotstein's books and articles. He has published in Jungian journals, made presentations at Jungian conferences, and served as mentor to several Jungian analysts. Grotstein (2006) describes his initial reaction to reading Jung: "What immediately struck me were the differences between how Jung and Freud—and for that matter, Klein—conceive of the unconscious, and, in retrospect, how two-dimensional their views now seem without the numinous dimension" (p. xi). Grotstein (2006) notes the sympathy between Bion's model of the psyche and that of Jung: "after reading [Bion's] later works, one cannot help regarding him as a closet Jungian [...] It remains a mystery why Bion, who obviously appreciated Jung's thinking, never really acknowledged Jung" (p. xiii). The thrust of Grotstein's response to Jung is also reflected by Culbert-Koehn (2015), who recalls, "I had heard Jim say at a conference in L.A. that Bion was closer to Jung than Freud" (p. 753).

Grotstein credits Jung as an influence throughout his work—particularly Jung's writing on the transcendent, the intersubjective third, archetypes, the collective unconscious, mystical experience, and the psychopomp. It is somewhat surprising that Grotstein does not mention Jung's (1948) theory of complexes in his writing, even though Grotstein speaks extensively of complexes and internal objects. In some instances, Grotstein appears to implicitly subsume Jung's complex theory into Jung's theory of archetypes—a tendency that can be rather misleading. Grotstein's treatment of the numinous, transcendent, and ultimately unknowable foundations of experience, sometimes referred to in his work as God or the Godhead, possesses clear parallels to Jung's concept of self, and figures prominently throughout Grotstein's writings (1997a, 1997b, 1998, 2000, 2001, 2006).

In my reading of Grotstein, I do sometimes wish for a closer analysis of Jung's theories; as Culbert-Koehn puts it, "I would like to see Jung not just referenced and credited but explicated" (1998, p. 73). Grotstein arguably reaches his most creative synthesis of Kleinian, Bionian, and Jungian thought in *Who Is the Dreamer Who Dreams the Dream?* (2000). The subtitle, *A Study of Psychic Presences*, would work equally well as an introduction to Jung's (1948) theory of complexes. I believe

Grotstein's most original contribution to synthetic Kleinian-Bionian-Jungian thought is his proposal of a "transcendent position" (Grotstein, 1997b, 2000), which moves beyond Klein's (1946) "paranoid-schizoid" and "depressive" positions. In Grotstein's conceptualization, the transcendent position is necessary to account for the experience of "O" and to speak of psychological experiences that go beyond part-object and whole object functioning:

> Thus I believe that another position, which I call the transcendent position, is required to accommodate the conception of transformations and evolutions in "O." Whereas the paranoid-schizoid position prepares for the ability to know K, and the depressive position allows for the actual knowing of K, K is always the object to be known. In the transcendent position, the object dissolves into the ultimate, ineffable Subject. There is no object in the transcendent position. "O" not only involves a transformation and evolution from the paranoid-schizoid and depressive positions, it also involves a resonance with a total subjectivity. One intuits—internally "senses"—the objectlessness of the object without ever contemplating it, yet experiences its presence. *In the transcendent position, the individual must forsake the presence of the object in order to look inward into his or her own subjectivity. Thus, in the transcendent position one experiences the quintessence of subjectivity that transcends (for the moment) object relations.*
>
> *(Grotstein, 1997b, p. 10, italics in original)*

Also significant among Grotstein's contributions is his elaboration of Bion's model of dreaming, which he interpolates with a guiding psychic presence similar to Jung's (1959b) idea of self. Grotstein (2000) elaborates a model of dreaming that reflects a dialogue between parts of the psyche which interact to do the work of dreaming the individual into existence. In Grotstein's (1979) own words,

> The Dreamer Who Understands the Dream is as mysterious as the Dreamer Who Dreams the Dream. It is the self in relationship to "I." A self in association with a Divine Self seems to be able to experience the Truth of a dream—as the Truth within a dream.
>
> *(p. 118)*

Grotstein's description exhibits elements quite similar to Jung's description of the activity of the self and of the relationship between the self and the ego:

> The term "self" seemed to me a suitable one for this unconscious substrate, whose actual exponent in consciousness is the ego. The ego stands to the self as the moved to the mover, or as object to subject, because the determining factors which radiate out from the self surround the ego on all sides and are therefore supraordinate to it. The self, like the unconscious, is an a priori existent out of which the ego evolves. It is, so to speak, an unconscious prefiguration of the ego. It is not I who create myself, rather I happen to myself.
>
> *(Jung, 1958, para. 391)*

Michael Eigen

A prolific author with numerous books and articles, Michael Eigen frequently and appreciatively references Jung. In Eigen's (2011) words, "I love Jung. I certainly have been influenced by Jung in a deep way. So was Bion. So was Winnicott. So was Marion Milner, all influenced by Jung" (p. 18). Eigen is one of the few psychoanalysts who have consistently received invitations from Jungian conferences and publications (Eigen, 1991, 1993, 2014). He initially became exposed to and excited by Jung's works as an undergraduate, and before reading Freud. His first analytic experience was with a Jungian analyst. Most of his books incorporate Jungian ideas to some extent, particularly Jung's ideas about spirituality, transcendence, the Godhead, psychosis, typology, mythology, archetypes, and synchronicity.

Eigen's most in-depth incorporation of Jung's work occurs in *The Psychotic Core* (1986), where he builds on the ideas of Jung and Bion to develop his perspective on the nature and treatment of psychosis. Eigen states: "It is hard to imagine work with psychosis today without Jung's contribution" (p. 16). Rather than crafting carefully structured arguments as to the correspondence between various authors, Eigen induces the reader with his stream of consciousness reflections, revealing associative linkages between analytic concepts, spiritual intuitions, and feeling states. Ideas from Bion, Lao Tzu, Winnicott, Buddhism, Jung, the Kabbalists, and Lacan drift in and out of his narrative like the spontaneous riffs and phrases of an accomplished jazz musician. What Eigen reveals through his improvisational process is an underlying spirit which unites these disparate sources. This sense of unity is reflected in the following passage:

> David Bohm, a physicist, talked about two modes of being, the explicate and implicate orders. Loosely speaking, the explicate order refers to all the things that are on the surface that you can see, the distinctions between things [...] The implicate order involves the deep unknown that you can't see. Everything is interconnected below the surface. Everything grows with everything else in ways we see and don't see [...] You don't see the unseen connection [...] All these schools fought each other and still fight each other. Yet they're deeply interconnected and meet each other, whether or not this is seen and digested [...] Bion, Klein, Lacan, Jung are all stripes on a tiger.
>
> *(Eigen, 2011, p. 104)*

Neville Symington

Symington also makes frequent use of Jung's conceptual framework in his writing (1997, 1998, 2007), often drawing on or highlighting Jung's concepts of shadow, participation mystique, and complex theory. He also makes frequent reference to Jung's ideas about religion and religious experience while also subjecting these ideas to critical evaluation (1998).

Giuseppe Civitarese

While he does not specifically explore or incorporate Jungian metapsychology in his work, Giuseppe Civitarese, a prominent post-Bionian from a younger generation of analysts than Grotstein, Eigen, and Symington, refers to Jung affirmatively in a recent book *The Necessary Dream* (2015). In the introduction, Civitarese states: "I should have dedicated at least as much space to Jung, Ferenczi, Winnicott, and Kohut" (2015, p. xiv). Civitarese's attention to important nuances in various analytic approaches to dreams assists the Jungian reader in seeing how compatible Bion's theory of dreaming is with Jung's, and in a way that complements Jung rather than merely duplicating his perspective.

Conclusion: Personal reflections on the intersection of Jung and Bion

For a Jungian, the initial exposure to Bion's ideas can be somewhat overwhelming. The terms adopted by Bion seem abstract and minimalist—almost mathematical—in nature. However, I've come to appreciate that Bion's theories have many parallels to Jung and that Bion's work extends many of Jung's ideas in ways that are useful to the analytic setting. Bion offers ways of engaging and reflecting upon what is happening in the analytic hour at a very close, moment by moment, level of interaction. As Godsil (2014) puts it, "Bion has more to contribute to Jungian theory at a micro-level of process" (p. 60). While some of these nuances are implied in Jung, they are rarely brought to full development.

It strikes me that many analysts who become interested in Bion's model are drawn to him after acquiring their fundamental training in some other psychoanalytic orientation. Perhaps this is because the Bionian model itself doesn't offer a highly differentiated metapsychology. As Levine and Civitarese (2016) put it, "Rather than emphasizing a particular psychic content [...] he [Bion] tried to help open and prepare the mind of the analyst [...] for the encounter with the patient" (p. xxi). Bion's model focuses much more on the analyst's stance as it relates to psychological experience. Bion is also much more focused on articulating processes rather than structures. Because of these tendencies, Bion's model suggests a rather open system which can be readily adapted to other theoretical orientations, thus opening up new experiences or perspectives.

In Bion's model of dreaming, the emphasis shifts away from the meaning and symbolic content of dreams and refocuses our attention to dreaming as an experience (or non-experience) of being. Thought of in this way, dreaming is not a process intended to protect the dreamer from unacceptable ideas. Rather, it is a means of soaking consciousness in the stream of unconsciousness. This becomes a means of connecting symbolic meaning to our lived experience; of dreaming ourselves into existence.

I also find in Bion a significant counterweight against reification of psychological constructs and against saturation of interpretation. For those trained in the

Jungian framework, it is sometimes difficult not to become caught up in pursuing the broad narrative brushstrokes so vividly depicted in the imagery of myth, fairytales, alchemy, and religion. As Colman (2007) puts it,

> Bion is always aware of the danger that a model may become concretized and thus mistaken for a realization of that model. Simply put, this means taking the metaphor literally so that instead of it being an analogy, it is seen as identical to what is being described.

> *(p. 568)*

Or, as Grotstein (1981) states,

> When [Bion] suggests the abnegation of memory and desire, I believe him to mean one should desaturate ideas of dogma so that the analytic container can be opened for new possibilities rather than having to be saturated with Klein or Freud or Jung or the like.

> *(p. 534)*

The concepts and techniques of analytical psychology form a robust and useful model for analytic interaction and process. However, at times these tools are not sufficient by themselves. A specific strength of the Jungian model is its deep emphasis on the metaphoric nature of psychological experience. Facility, comfort, and familiarity with metaphoric material are gained through an immersion in the archetypal. However, in working with more traumatized, primitive, or personality disordered patients, there is often a need for a different approach. The theories and methods of analytical psychology are oriented towards the engagement of psychological structures, particularly complexes, and are not always readily adapted for work with less developed psychic states and processes—particularly with patients who have little capacity to participate in the process of dreaming themselves into existence.

The contemporary dialogue between Bionian and Jungian perspectives is already substantial, yet there are many additional exchanges to be made. Exploring the intersection between Jung and Bion, I find a greater fluidity in the way I listen, think, feel, and respond in the analytic hour.

Notes

1 Past-president of the American Psychoanalytic Association and the International Psychoanalytical Association.
2 No longer geographically confined to London or the UK.
3 I.e., absolute truth, ultimate reality, the experience of the numinous, the fundamentally unknowable (Bion, 1965, 1970).
4 The importance of intuition for both Jung and Bion is more fully delineated by Williams (2006).
5 A process of engaging in a dialogue with internal images and figures.

6 See Winborn (2014) for a more complete discussion of this comparison.
7 Bion's attitude is well reflected in the following statement: "The way that I do analysis is of no importance to anybody excepting myself, but it may give you some idea of how you do analysis, and that is important" (1994, p. 224).
8 This listing is not exhaustive, and there are certainly many authors worthy of inclusion who are left out because of the limitations of space.
9 Referring to the two processing modes of symmetry and asymmetry.
10 Both are concepts developed by Jung to articulate how symbols are formed and related to/utilized psychically.

References

Addison, A. (2016). Jung's psychoid concept and Bion's proto-mental concept. *Journal of Analytical Psychology, 61*, 567–587.

Aguayo, J. (2016). Personal communication.

Alvarez, A. (1992). *Live company: Psychoanalytic psychotherapy with autistic, borderline, deprived and abused children*. London: Routledge.

Aron, L., & Atlas, G. (2015). Generative enactment: Memories from the future. *Psychoanalytic Dialogues, 25*(3), 309–324.

Bion, W. R. (1962). *Learning from experience*. London: Karnac.

Bion, W. R. (1965). *Transformations*. London: Karnac.

Bion, W. R. (1967). Notes on memory and desire. *Psychoanalytic Forum, 3*, 272–280.

Bion, W. R. (1970). *Attention and interpretation*. London: Karnac.

Bion, W. R. (1990). *Brazilian seminars*. London: Karnac.

Bion, W. R. (1992). *Cogitations*. London: Karnac.

Bion, W. R. (1993). *Second thoughts*. London: Karnac.

Bion, W. R. (1994). *Clinical seminars and other works*. London: Karnac.

Bléandonu, G. (1999). *Wilfred Bion: His life and works*. New York: Other.

Bovensiepen, G. (2002). Symbolic attitude and reverie. *Journal of Analytical Psychology, 47*, 241–257.

Brown, R.S. (2016). Spirituality and the challenge of clinical pluralism: Participatory thinking in psychotherapeutic context. *Spirituality in Clinical Practice, 3*(3), 187–195.

Brown, R.S. (2017). *Psychoanalysis beyond the end of metaphysics: Thinking towards the post-relational*. London & New York: Routledge.

Carvalho, R. (2002). Psychic retreats revisited. *British Journal of Psychotherapy, 19*, 153–171.

Carvalho, R. (2008). The final challenge: Ageing, dying, individuation. *Journal of Analytical Psychology, 53*, 1–18.

Carvalho, R. (2014a). A vindication of Jung's unconscious and its archetypal expression: Jung, Bion, and Matte Blanco. In A. Cavalli, L. Hawkins, & M. Stevens (Eds.), *Transformation: Jung's legacy and clinical work today* (pp. 41–58). London: Karnac.

Carvalho, R. (2014b). Synchronicity, the infinite unrepressed, dissociation and the interpersonal. *Journal of Analytical Psychology, 59*, 366–384.

Cavalli, A. (2011). On receiving what has gone astray, on finding what has got lost. *Journal of Analytical Psychology, 56*, 1–13.

Cavalli, A. (2014). From not knowing to knowing. In A. Cavalli, L. Hawkins, & M. Stevens (Eds.), *Transformation: Jung's legacy and clinical work today* (pp. 193–210). London: Karnac.

Civitarese, G. (2015). *The necessary dream*. London: Karnac.

Colman, W. (2007). Symbolic conceptions. *Journal of Analytical Psychology, 52*, 565–583.

Culbert-Koehn, J. (1997a). Between Bion and Jung: A talk with James Grotstein. *The San Francisco Jung Institute Library Journal, 15*(4), 15–32.

Culbert-Koehn, J. (1997b). Prenatal and perinatal influences in contemporary Jungian analysis. In Mary Ann Mattoon (Ed.), *Zurich 95: Open questions in analytical psychology* (pp. 574–586). Einsiedeln, Switzerland: Daimon Verlag.

Culbert-Koehn, J. (1997c). The intersection between Bionian and Jungian vertices. Retrieved from www.sicap.it/merciai/bion/papers/culbe.htm (accessed 30 January 2017).

Culbert-Koehn, J. (1998). Where is James Grotstein? *Journal of Analytical Psychology, 43,* 69–75.

Culbert-Koehn, J. (2000). Classical Jung meets Klein and Bion. *Psychoanalytic Dialogues, 10,* 443–455.

Culbert-Koehn, J. (2011). An analysis with Bion: An interview with James Gooch. *Journal of Analytical Psychology, 56,* 76–91.

Culbert-Koehn, J. (2015). James Grotstein: Obituary. *Journal of Analytical Psychology, 60,* 752–755.

Cwik, A. J. (2011). Associative dreaming: Reverie and active imagination. *Journal of Analytical Psychology, 56,* 14–36.

de Azevedo, A. A. (2000). Substantive unconscious and adjective unconscious. *Journal of Analytical Psychology, 45,* 75–91.

Dehing, J. (1990). Jung and knowledge: From gnosis to praxis. *Journal of Analytical Psychology, 35,* 193–211.

Dehing, J. (1994). Containment – an archetype?: Meaning and madness in Jung and Bion. *Journal of Analytical Psychology, 39,* 419–461.

Eigen, M. (1986). *The psychotic core.* Northvale: Aronson.

Eigen, M. (1991). Winnicott's area of freedom. In N. Schwartz-Salant & M. Stein (Eds.), *Liminality and transitional phenomena* (pp. 67–88). Wilmette: Chiron.

Eigen, M. (1993). Notes on the counterpart. In M. Stein (Ed.), *Mad parts of sane people in analysis* (pp. 37–51). Wilmette: Chiron.

Eigen, M. (2011). *Faith and transformation.* London: Karnac.

Eigen, M. (2014). Variants of mystical participation. In M. Winborn (Ed.), *Shared realities: Participation mystique and beyond* (pp. 130–143). Skiatook: Fisher King.

Fordham, M. (1974). Defences of the self. *Journal of Analytical Psychology, 19,* 192–199.

Fordham, M. (1985). *Explorations into the self.* London: Karnac.

Fordham, M. (1993a). *The making of an analyst.* London: Free Association Books.

Fordham, M. (1993b). On not knowing beforehand. *Journal of Analytical Psychology, 38,* 127–136.

Fordham, M. (1995). *Freud, Jung, Klein – the fenceless field.* London: Routledge.

Godsil, G. (2014). Reversal and recovery in trauma. In A. Cavalli, L. Hawkins & M. Stevens (Eds.), *Transformation: Jung's Legacy and clinical work today* (pp. 59–78). London: Karnac.

Gordon, K. (2004). The tiger's stripe: Some thoughts on psychoanalysis, gnosis, and the experience of wonderment. *Contemporary Psychoanalysis, 40,* 5–45.

Grotstein, J. S. (1979). Who is the dreamer who dreams the dream and who is the dreamer who understands it? *Contemporary Psychoanalysis, 15,* 110–169.

Grotstein, J. S. (1981). Wilfred R. Bion: The man, the psychoanalyst, the mystic. *Contemporary Psychoanalysis, 17,* 501–536.

Grotstein, J. S. (1997a). Bion, the pariah of "O". *British Journal of Psychotherapy, 14,* 77–90.

Grotstein, J. S. (1997b). Bion's transformation in "O" and the concept of the transcendent position. Retrieved from www.sicap.it/merciai/bion/papers/grots.htm.

Grotstein, J. S. (1998). The numinous and immanent nature of the psychoanalytic subject. *Journal of Analytical Psychology, 43,* 41–68.

Grotstein, J. S. (2000). *Who is the dreamer who dreams the dream? A study of psychic presences.* Hillsdale: Analytic.

Grotstein, J. S. (2001). The unconscious, the infinite, and god. *Fort Da, 7*, 56–69.

Grotstein, J. S. (2006). Forward. In A. Casement & D. Tacey (Eds.), *The idea of the numinous* (pp. xi–xv). London: Routledge.

Horne, M., Sowa, A., & Isenman, D. (2000). Philosophical assumptions in Freud, Jung and Bion. *Journal of Analytical Psychology, 45*, 109–121.

Hunter, V. (1994). *Psychoanalysts talk.* New York: Guilford.

Jacobi, J. (1977). *The psychology of C. G. Jung.* New Haven: Yale University Press.

Jung, C. G. (1916). The transcendent function. In *CW8* (pp. 67–91). Princeton: Princeton University Press.

Jung, C. G. (1921). *Psychological types: CW6.* Princeton: Princeton University Press.

Jung, C. G. (1948). A review of complex theory. In *CW8* (pp. 92–104). Princeton: Princeton University Press.

Jung, C. G. (1954/1966). *The practice of psychotherapy: CW16.* Princeton: Princeton University Press.

Jung, C. G. (1958). *Psychology and religion: CW11.* Princeton: Princeton University Press.

Jung, C. G. (1959a). *The archetypes of the collective unconscious: CW9i.* Princeton: Princeton University Press.

Jung, C. G. (1959b). *Aion: CW9ii.* Princeton: Princeton University Press.

Jung, C. G. (1960). *The structure and dynamics of the psyche: CW8.* Princeton: Princeton University Press.

Jung, C. G. (1964). *Civilization in transition: CW10.* Princeton: Princeton University Press.

Jung, C. G. (1965). *Memories, dreams, reflections.* New York: Vintage.

Jung, C. G. (1968). *Analytical psychology: Its theory and practice.* New York: Random House.

Jung, C. G. (1973). *Letters,* Vol. 1. Princeton: Princeton University Press.

Jung, C. G. (2012). *The red book.* New York: Norton.

Kalsched, D. (1996). *The inner world of trauma.* London: Routledge.

Kalsched, D. (2013). *Trauma and the soul.* London: Routledge.

Klein, M. (1932). *The psycho-analysis of children.* London: Hogarth.

Klein, M. (1946). Notes on some schizoid mechanisms. *International Journal of Psychoanalysis, 27*, 99–110.

Lambert, K. (1981). *Analysis, repair, and individuation.* London: Karnac.

Levine, H., & Civitarese, G. (2016). *The W.R. Bion tradition: Lines of development – evolution of theory and practice over decades.* London: Karnac.

McAlister, M. (2014). Beneath the skin. In A. Cavalli, L. Hawkins, & M. Stevens (Eds.), *Transformation: Jung's legacy and clinical work today* (pp. 155–173). London: Karnac.

Mathew, M. (2005). Reverie: Between thought and prayer. *Journal of Analytical Psychology, 50*, 383–393.

Matte Blanco, I. (1998a). *The unconscious as infinite sets.* London: Duckworth.

Matte Blanco, I. (1998b). *Thinking, feeling and being.* London: Routledge.

Merkur, D. (2010). *Explorations of the psychoanalytic mystics.* Amsterdam: Rodopi.

Mizen, R. (2014). On the capacity to suffer one's self. *Journal of Analytical Psychology, 59*, 314–332.

Newirth, J. (2003). *Between emotion and cognition: The generative unconscious.* New York: Other.

Ogden, T. (1994). *Subjects of analysis.* Northvale: Aronson.

Otto, R. (1958). *The idea of the holy,* trans. J. Harvey. New York: Oxford University Press.

Plaut, F. (1993). *Analysis analysed.* London: Routledge.

Proner, B. D. (2005). Bodily states of anxiety. *Journal of Analytical Psychology, 50*, 311–331.

Roazen, P. (1976). *Freud and his followers*. London: Penguin.

Rosegrant, J. (2012). Why Bion? Why Jung? For that matter, why Freud? *Journal of the American Psychoanalytic Association, 60,* 721–745.

Safran, J. D. (2006). The relational unconscious, the enchanted interior, and the return of the repressed. *Contemporary Psychoanalysis, 42,* 393–412.

Samuels, A. (1985). *Jung and the post-Jungians*. London: Routledge.

Samuels, A. (1996). Jung's return from banishment. *Psychoanalytic Review, 83,* 469–489.

Sandler, P. C. (2005). *The language of Bion*. London: Karnac.

Schmidt, M. (2012). Psychic skin: Psychotic defences, borderline process and delusions. *Journal of Analytical Psychology, 57,* 21–39.

Schwartz-Salant, N. (1989). *The borderline personality*. Wilmette: Chiron.

Segal, R. (1992). *The gnostic Jung*. Princeton: Princeton University Press.

Sidoli, M. (2000). *When the body speaks*. London: Routledge.

Stolorow, R. D. & Atwood, G.E. (1994). Chapter 17: The myth of the isolated mind. *Progress in Self Psychology, 10,* 233–250.

Sullivan, B. S. (2007). Alphabetizing in old age. *Journal of Analytical Psychology, 52,* 1–196.

Sullivan, B. S. (2010). *Mystery of analytical work: Weavings from Jung and Bion*. London: Routledge.

Sullivan, B. S. (2011). Truth and lies. *Fort Da, 17,* 8–24.

Sullivan, B. S. (2012). Review of Mawson, Chris (Ed.). *Bion today*. London & New York: Routledge, 2011. *Journal of Analytical Psychology, 57,* 688–690.

Symington, N. (1997). *The making of a psychotherapist*. London: Karnac.

Symington, N. (1998). *Emotion and spirit*. London: Karnac.

Symington, N. (2007). *Becoming a person through psychoanalysis*. London: Karnac.

Tennes, M. (2007). Beyond intersubjectivity: The transpersonal dimension of the psycho-analytic encounter. *Contemporary Psychoanalysis, 43,* 505–525.

West, M. (2007). *Feeling, being and the sense of self*. London: Karnac.

West, M. (2016). *Into the darkest places: Early relational trauma and borderline states of mind*. London: Karnac.

Williams, S. (2006). Analytic intuition: A meeting place for Jung and Bion. *British Journal of Psychotherapy, 23,* 83–98.

Winborn, M. (2014). Watching clouds together: Analytic reverie and participation mystique. In M. Winborn (Ed.), *Shared realities: Participation mystique and beyond* (pp. 70–96). Skiatook: Fisher King.

PART IV

Self psychology

7

WEAVING THE DREAM FIELDS OF JUNG AND KOHUT

An integrative approach

Marcia D.-S. Dobson

Kohut and Jung take quite different approaches to dreams. This is despite the fact that both of their theories consider the discovery of the self to be the final goal of analysis. Kohut, unlike Jung, did not place much store in the idea of an archetypal or collective unconscious that could, through primordial images and universal patterns, assist the individuation process. Kohut, rather, looked to dreams as representing "self-states" that could help in the understanding of the development of the narcissistic transferences in the therapeutic process. How compatible are these approaches?

Weaving together the dream fields of Jung and Kohut is an intriguing and nostalgic venture for me. There is something here that needs to be uncovered, searched out, and brought to resolution. Let me attempt to emphasize the personal importance of this undertaking by relating the journey that brought me here. As a small child, I met Dr. Jung at Burghölzli in Zurich. Later, and for many years, I used Jung's work as a way to help my students explore the meaning of ancient myths and religion by examining their own dreams. After studying Jung semi-formally, having benefitted from two years in Jungian therapy, and now anticipating becoming a Jungian analyst, I made an impulsive choice one August to attend Stephen Aizenstat's dream seminars at Pacifica Graduate Institute in Carpenteria, California. This led, five years later, to my graduating with a PhD in clinical psychology with an emphasis in depth psychology. During this time, I discovered and began to teach self psychology. Family tragedies involving childhood death tumbled my mind into earlier losses, and sent me in 2003 to seek analysis. I decided to enter treatment with a self psychologically trained psychoanalyst.

I will never forget how I felt when I brought my first dream to treatment. It was a dream I was proud of, and that entranced me with its storybook quality:

> I am going down a long winding hill to a large mill pond with a quaint house next to it occupied by a couple. At the bottom of the hill, right smack in the middle of the road there stands a rather large dog. It is alive, but instead of

having fur, its coat is composed of a thick quilt of bright patchwork designs that is zipped up its back. As I look beyond the dog to the mill pond, the water wheel moves the water in such a way that it keeps flooding over the banks and I have no idea how I will ever cross to the other side.

When I related the part about the quilted dog to my analyst, he startled me with a soft chuckle. I don't remember his offering any sort of interpretation. Somewhat disappointed, I questioned him about this. He replied simply and with a gentle smile, "I interpret when I can." His comment had a settling and gathering effect that relaxed me and made me feel that I was in good and caring hands. This dream and others at the beginning of the analysis sifted down into the silt of a deep pool of unconscious meanings. Not long after that, I started to grieve.

What was I to make of my analyst's apparent reticence to interpret? His comment could be taken as a reflection of his belief that this was a founding dream for the forthcoming analysis that ought not to be hastily translated. Or, one could imagine that this was a different kind of analysis in which dreams were going to have a different function. Or, maybe he simply felt unable to interpret the dream. In any case, I was startled into a kind of nostalgia for my Jungian dream homes, which now appeared to be left in the background, while at the same time feeling the glow of a powerful warmth and possibility in the apparent nurturance of the analytic relationship. I turned to Heinz Kohut's work on dreams to seek answers.

Self-state dreams

In 1971, Kohut made an abrupt break from Freudian dream theory in identifying what he called "self-state" dreams. Against Freud, he suggested that there are dreams that do not benefit from trying to uncover latent content. No matter how much one tries to excavate such dreams, nothing further is revealed. Indeed, such an undertaking may actually lead to a further sense of fragmentation on the part of the dreamer. Kohut came to feel that dreams of this kind represented the present state of the dreamer's psyche/soma, often specifically in relation to the analyst and the analytic relationship. Kohut (1974) gives the following example:

> When a patient who is feeling chaotic and emotionally overburdened comes in and complains of a bad smell in the office I do not ask him: "What occurs to you about the fact you smell something today?" as if it were something portentous or might reveal a primal scene. It may have to do with a primal scene, but that comes later and arises in a different way.
>
> *(p. 150)*

Kohut adds that self-state dreams are very frequently expressions of an imbalanced mental state:

> During [...] states of traumatic overburdenedness of the psyche, these dream images are a visual commentary about how the patient preconsciously feels;

and to ask for association to these dreams is not only useless—they don't lead anywhere—but putting this demand on the patient just adds to his burdens.

(ibid.)

The only fitting interpretation at such moments should be based on an attitude of protectiveness that indicates one is in touch with the patient's off-kilter feeling. Kohut's (1977) most often-quoted definition of the self-state dream is as follows:

It is a dream that attempts, with the aid of verbalizable dream-imagery, to bind the non-verbal tensions of the traumatic states. Dreams of this [...] type portray the dreamer's dread vis-a-vis some uncontrollable tension-increase or his dread of the dissolution of the self. The very act of portraying these vicissitudes in the dream constitutes an attempt to deal with the psychological danger by covering frightening nameless processes with namable visual imagery.

(pp. 109–110)

From a Kohutian perspective, my early dream in the analysis can be seen as an expression of my self-state at that time. I was the dog, protected with a thickly quilted coat, and held together like patchwork. The dog had a childlike sense—like a stuffed animal—perhaps representing my need to be protected and cared for. I was well zipped up, not yet ready to open up, or perhaps even to have my dream examined. The couple in the house may have represented the analytic couple. In front of the dog was the flooded mill pond, perhaps metaphorically showing the magnitude of grieving that had yet to be accomplished. My analyst's not interpreting the dream, but holding me in the session warmly and with a fatherly chuckle of appreciation, gave me a bodily sense of being protected and cared for despite my desire to involve us both in conversation with the intent of figuring out the dream. In fear of fragmentation, I was perhaps covering frightening, nameless processes with nameable visual imagery. Later, I was to discover that my analyst felt I was too engaged with what Winnicott (1971) might call "fantasying" rather than "dreaming"—that I would rather remain cocooned in dream material than face the genuine pain of my real world. As a child, I had a repetitive dream of going into a toy store and being able to have anything I wanted. I would choose a toy and hug it tightly, expecting it to be in my arms when I awoke, always to be disappointed.

Self psychologists since Kohut have expanded and developed his notion of the self-state dream. Paul Ornstein (1986) notes that dreams help with tension regulation and can be understood as an expression of the ways in which patients deal with chronic injuries to self-esteem: "we shall soon learn that the dream is always about the self" (p. 101). Robert Stolorow (1992) suggests: "By vividly reifying the experience of self-fragmentation, the dream symbols bring the state of the self into focal awareness with a feeling of conviction and reality that can only accompany sensory perceptions" (pp. 282–283). James Fosshage, a self psychologist with a Jungian background, builds on Kohut's notion of self-state dreams to show that many dreams stem from unconscious processes that work to keep the psyche in balance. Images in the dream are amplifications that help the psyche to firm and right itself when fragile. According to Fosshage, "the supraordinate function of dreams is the development, maintenance (regulation), and when necessary, restoration of psychic processes, structure, and organization" (1983, p. 650). Elsewhere, he states: "Dream mentation, like waking mentation can reinforce or *transform* [our patterns of organizational experience]" (2000, p. 104).[1]

All of the authors mentioned above are concerned with dreams as performing functions that help to restore balance to a psyche that is experiencing states of fragmentation not easily responsive to the more linear and interpretive processes of waking mentation. Dreams communicate in a symbolic language, authentic in itself, to achieve psychic organization and, as Fosshage suggests, transformation. Stolorow emphasizes that the self can only be brought into focus by *embodying* our fragmentary experiences in dream images. None of these authors, however, emphasize the notion of a Jungian archetypal world that speaks through myths and dreams to evoke a transpersonal recognition of universal patterns.

Despite the trust I had in my analysis, I lived with the disquieting, sometimes brooding sense that I had lost a world of vibrancy, depth, and profundity. While all psychoanalytic theorists would agree that we cannot live always in dream fantasies that are divorced from everyday reality, I still found myself feeling uneasy at the loss of my "fantasy" world. Was this a kind of nostalgia for childhood, a loss of manic energies used to defend a desolate and lonely past? Or was my present state of health achieved at the loss of a genuine connection that had to be left behind so that I could "get real"? In trying to answer this conundrum, I have been drawn to explore both the similarities and the differences between Jung's and Kohut's ideas about dreams to see if there might be a way of integrating them.

Jaegerstaetter's dream

Both Jung and Kohut believed that the primary drive or impulse in the human psyche is to strive toward the full realization of a self that is already determined as a nucleus within the infant. Jung calls this process individuation, and Kohut refers to it as the nuclear program of the self. Both figures emphasize a striving for the development of the self toward wholeness. But how, clinically, does the self achieve its wholeness—its sense of coherence in space and continuity in time? It is in this respect, particularly in relation to dreaming, that Jung's and Kohut's ideas diverge. Jung focuses on the dream in its relation to the collective unconscious as a way to engage the individuation process. Kohut, by contrast, considers the dream as indicative of self-states, such as to portray the self–selfobject relationship manifesting at present in the analysis. Kohut's primary tool in discovering and treating patients is empathy, which he refers to as the process of "vicarious introspection." The patient and analyst are engaged in a relationship wherein the analyst's empathy enables the patient to restore lines of development that were thwarted in childhood. Kohutian analysts respond empathically to these needs by working through what Kohut terms the narcissistic transferences, as reflected most centrally in the need for mirroring, idealizing, and twinship (Kohut, 1966). This focus on empathy and the sensitive nature of the transference are primary reasons why the attention self psychologists give to dreams is always to understand and respond empathically to the micro-processes of the patient.

Prior to my self psychological analysis, I found myself buoyed by the creativity of my more "archetypal" dreams—of being in the numinous presence of the objective psyche. Jung is more explicitly receptive to the ways in which dreams can express a form of spirituality that touches on the transpersonal. While Kohut does not explore this theme directly himself, it can seem in reading him that he is perhaps not unsympathetic to the role of the numinous in the search for meaning and authenticity. An example in point is Kohut's approach to a dream reported by Franz Jaegerstaetter. Jaegerstaetter was an Austrian Catholic who refused to serve in the German army during World War II. An uneducated peasant, he describes the journey he underwent before finally deciding, in 1938, to accept death at the hands of the Nazis at the time of their invasion of Austria. During this period, he recorded a dream:

> I was shown a beautiful railroad train which circled around a mountain. Not only the grownups but even the children streamed toward this train and it was almost impossible to hold them back. I hate to tell how very few of the grownups there were who resisted being carried along by this occasion. But then I heard a voice which spoke to me and said: "This train is going to hell."
> *(Kohut, 1985, p. 14)*

Jaegerstaetter's dream helped him to consolidate his decision to face death rather than destroy his ideals. He considered the dream to be directly concerned with the Nazi invasion of Austria. Kohut depicts this dream as

> a thought sequence occurring during an altered state of consciousness, expressed through visual and auditory experiences of near hallucinatory vividness [...] The mental activity involved here strains the psychic apparatus to the utmost [...] we should give these phenomena a name which acknowledges that a hard task is joined by the depth of a psyche.
> *(Kohut, 1985, p. 14)*

A Jungian approach might consider Jaegerstaetter's report as an example of how dreams can have a prospective function. Jaegerstaetter's dream is distinctly reminiscent of Jung's visions of Europe bathed in blood, which he experienced prior to the onset of World War I. The profound effect that this dramatic imagery had on him led Jung to fear that he might be on the brink of a psychotic break until, with the outbreak of war, he concluded that he was dreaming about the state of the world and not just the state of his psyche.

Kohut recognizes that Jaegerstaetter's powerful experience of hearing a voice that announces "these people are going to hell" brings him the energy and information he needs to act with his conscience by going against the flow of the Nazi occupation and the social pressure to "get on the train." Rather than speaking in archetypal terms, however, Kohut speaks of this dream as acting in the service of the nuclear self:

> Such heroic individuals are therefore not psychotic. Nor are the hallucinations and delusional commands which the hero experiences as the motivators of his courageous actions and attitudes the manifestations of a dissolution of self. The true motivator which propels the hero toward the heroic deed is his nuclear self; the hallucinated commands are merely temporary auxiliary mechanisms, secondarily created to serve the purposes of the hero.
>
> *(Kohut, 1985, p. 15)*

Kohut is at pains to validate his position here by showing that after Jaegerstaetter's decision has been made, he exhibits the characteristics of a fully developed nuclear self, insofar as Jaegerstaetter is able to demonstrate humor and to respond with "a subtle empathy even when the agonizing consequences have to be faced" (1985, p. 15). For Kohut, humor and empathy are two of the five attributes of the mature self, the others being creativity, wisdom, and the acceptance of transience (Kohut, 1966). Through the achievement of these characteristics of mature narcissism, Kohut reaches toward the idea of a cosmic narcissism—a transcendent state enabling us to rise above our mortal condition toward eternal ideals: "the genuine shift of the cathexes toward a cosmic narcissism is the enduring creative result of the steadfast activities of an autonomous ego, and only very few are able to attain it" (Kohut, 1966, p. 120).

In his efforts to prove that Jaegerstaetter's voice hearing is not psychotic, Kohut moves close to Jung by seeing Jaegerstaetter's dream as a forward-looking message from the personal unconscious that helps to instantiate through its embodiment in imagery his convictions and ideals. Jung would agree that the unconscious is always in some respect seemingly drawn toward the future, but because he believes that the personal unconscious is undergirded by collective, archetypal processes, he would also emphasize the role of the numinous and the transcendent in supporting Jaegerstaetter's individuation process.

Ideals and idealization in transference and in the archetypal field

Both Jung and Kohut recognize the power of idealization to generate affect and bring about transformation. When the idealized images of the archetypes connect with the individual's psyche, they can elicit a movement toward wholeness. Idealization of the analyst is one way in which this affective power can be evoked. Lionel Corbett, in his attempt to show correspondences between Kohut and Jung, argues that idealizing transferences within a Kohutian frame can be seen as equivalent to the emergence of archetypal forces within a Jungian model (1989, p. 41). While it is true that analysts can hold parts of the patient's psyche transferred on to them through idealization in a fashion similar to the emotional power of archetypal manifestations in dreams, Jung's language makes it clear that the psychic creative material emerges through a third space that is contained within the alchemical vessel of the transference. It is this transformative field that contains the analytic dyad. As Miller (2004) states, "Jung conceived of fantasy as that terrain of psyche where the shackles of preconceived limits could be discarded and psyche could actually transform itself" (p. 43).

How is it possible for the numinous world of the archetypes to impact the psyche in such a way as to lead to genuine transformation? For Jung, as we have seen, the symbolism of dreams has a creative function in bringing together conscious and unconscious into a third realm. This third realm opens the psyche to the primordial archetypes of myths and religions, thus suggesting a form of experience that depends on the primacy of symbolic language. Archetypal psychologist Stephen Aizenstat suggests that with an approach of this kind we need to "Ask not what dream did I have?" but "Who's visiting now?" (personal communication, September 2016, and see Aizenstat, 2009). The sense of being visited by such forces can be accompanied by a sense of being held by something greater. Such an experience evokes what Christopher Bollas (1987) refers to as the "maternal" or "aesthetic" idiom:

> In adult life the quest is not to possess the object; rather the object is pursued in order to surrender to it as a medium that alters the self, where the subject-as-supplicant now feels himself to be the recipient of envirosomatic caring, identified with metamorphoses of the self. [...] Since it begins before the mother is mentally represented as another, it is an object relation that emerges not from desire, but from a perceptual identification of the object with its function: the object as envirosomatic transformer of the subject. The memory of this early object relation manifests itself in the person's search for an object [...] that promises to transform the self.
>
> *(p. 14)*

Compare this with Kohut's (1966) earlier statement:

> Just as a child's *primary empathy* with the mother is the precursor of the adult's ability to be empathic, so his *primary identity* with her must be considered as the precursor of an expansion of the self, late in life when the finiteness of individual existence is acknowledged.
>
> *(p. 119, italics in original)*

In order to demonstrate the power of archetypal dreaming and the necessity of holding the tension of the symbol in the transformation of psychic process, I will now relate a dream that I experienced long before my self psychological analysis. I experienced this dream as placing me in touch with a resonating and numinous dimension that creates the possibility for self-transformation, *seemingly without the need of the therapeutic dyad*. The dream can perhaps be read as an envirosomatic transformer of the self. My relation with the dream was felt at the time as one of fusion, perhaps recalling Bollas's maternal/aesthetic idiom.

> I am on a large ship in the middle of a small river. Suddenly, to my left, I see a fishing line in the water held by a male figure who is all blue. The line jerks down and a large fish about two or three feet long appears on it. It is cerulean blue, with flashing golden scales and scintillated dark gold/blue eyes. Looking into them is like looking into a swirling kaleidoscope. Excited as a small child, I ask the man for it. The man hands me the line, which then vanishes as I find myself holding the fish itself. The fish still has a hook in its mouth. I walk with the fish to my therapist's office. I wish to give it to him as a gift, but he is not there, so I lay down the fish, which is still quite alive, on a table. Suddenly, the fish takes on a personality. It gets off the hook, but I am afraid its stomach has been gouged out. I can see its internal organs. Despite this, it flips off the table and starts eating from a bowl filled with warm milk on the floor, as if it is a kitten. I am glad the fish is still alive. Knowing that it is now safe to do so, I leave to attend a lecture being given by my dance teacher titled "The End of Nazism."

Because consciousness has often been described in terms of light, a Jungian approach might see these multiple luminosities as reflecting "tiny conscious phenomena" (Jung, 1947, p. 199). These scintillae appear as the "star-strewn heavens, as stars reflected in dark water, as nuggets of gold or golden sand scattered in black earth, as a solitary eye in the depths of the sea or earth, and so on" (ibid.). The dream perhaps suggests a sense of being led deeper into the unconscious, as the images become "less anthropomorphic, losing their individual uniqueness" (Jung, 1969, p. 173).

Stated briefly, I understand the dream to be saying something about my unconscious relationship to a therapist who might threaten to disembowel me, and that it indicates the possibility for an emergent self that is no longer dependent upon external authorities. The sense of inspiration this dream offered enabled me to feel a new vitality through a sense of participation in the transpersonal. I believe that this is what Jung means by the objective world of the psyche, which allows for the possibility of an empathic and aesthetic connection that has, in itself, the capacity to transform. If this dream were to be interpreted simply as a reflection of the present self-state of the dreamer, such an interpretation would do a disservice to the numinous power it held.

The dream of a former patient opens itself to being read from both a self-state perspective and a transpersonal one, perhaps demonstrating the importance of holding both views in the therapeutic transference. Sally brought the following dream from the mid-point in her therapy with me:

> I saw a flower outside your therapy office, but I didn't know whether it was a flower or a butterfly. It was raining. I knew that if it was a flower, the rain would help it to grow, but if it were a butterfly, it would die. I didn't know whether or not to bring it inside.

Sally was obsessed with butterflies—so much so that she would visit butterfly farms and places in Mexico where the Monarch butterflies gather every year. While this dream could be understood as a self-state dream, perhaps suggestive of Sally's ambivalence concerning the treatment or her own state of doubt as to her ability to emerge from her chrysalis, I suggest that understanding the dream only in this way would deprive it of a crucial psychic function: not, as Kohut might suggest, because of the fragile state of her psyche, but because the image of the butterfly/flower offers a means of mediating opposites and thus the possibility of an emergent meaning.

Conclusion: Empathy and transcendence

Empathy, for Kohut, is a means to reach the deepest and most fragile parts of the psyche and to offer the possibility of establishing a coherent self. For Jung (1946), "This bond is often of such intensity that we could almost speak of it as a 'combination.' When two chemical substances combine, both are altered. This is precisely what happens in the transference" (para. 358). In this experience, there is a sense of participation in a supraordinate dimension of being that grants the self a feeling of meaning not explicable through everyday experience. Both Jungian archetypal experiences that come through dreams and become part of the archetypal field in the analysis, and Kohut's empathic immersion that is experienced in the consulting room, have a feeling of the numinous, of two becoming one in the empathic surround. While Kohut is clearly more cautious than Jung in the way in which he portrays empathy, there are moments where the overlap between the two men is more apparent. Kohut (1966) goes so far as to state: "I have little doubt that those who are able to achieve this ultimate attitude toward life do so on the strength of a new, expanded, transformed narcissism: a cosmic narcissism which has transcended the bounds of the individual" (p. 119).

Contemporary self psychologists have expanded upon Kohut's cosmic ideals, perhaps sensing the unspoken in Kohut's thought and developing it. Kulka (2012) states:

> Emergence and dissolving embody the two dimensions of human existence. Whereas emergence is the expression of an individual's ontology—a commitment to the actuality of the personal self, dissolving is an expression of the individual's *ethics*—namely, a committed dedication to the world and to everything in it [...] like any other self-need, they cannot be materialized, except in an empathic matrix of self-objects [...] empathy is the unique matrix of an *inter-being* system from which one can achieve both the emergence of the phenomenal dimension of one's self and the dissolving toward the spiritual dimension of one's cosmic selfhood.
>
> *(p. 275)*

In speaking of a similar experience, Jung writes:

> The impact of an archetype [...] stirs us because it summons up a voice that is stronger than our own. Whoever speaks in primordial images speaks with a thousand voices; he enthralls and overpowers, while at the same time he

lifts the idea he is seeking express out of the occasional and transitory into the realm of the ever-enduring. He transmutes our personal destiny into the destiny of mankind, and evokes in us all those beneficent forces that ever and anon have enabled humanity to find a refuge from every peril, and to outlive the longest night.

(1966, para. 129)

In respect to my own self psychological analysis and the discomfort I felt at somehow having to renounce my attachment to imagination and the archetypal world, I am now more at peace with my Kohutian analyst's refusal to interpret the opening dream of the analytic work and his subsequent interpretation of dreams within the analysis as reflective of self-states. I have come to appreciate that the grounded sensitivity expressed in this approach is essential for the achievement of a cohesive sense of self. Kohut's outlook on dreams as expressing the transference relationship between analyst and patient has much to offer. Kohut adds a crucial developmental trajectory to Jung's emphasis on the archetypal. Despite the numinous power of my dreams, I wasn't able to fully internalize them in my own development. Dreams were safe harbors for me—a means to retreat from the experience of trauma. Despite my initial sense of loss in the analysis, the experience-near analytic approach ultimately allowed me to more effectively integrate my experience of the transpersonal.

Note

1   For a more extensive review of Fosshage's thinking on dreams, see Giannoni (2003, pp. 611–612).

References

Aizenstat, S. (2009). *Dream tending: Awakening to the healing power of dreams*. New Orleans: Spring Journal.

Bollas, C. (1987). *The shadow of the object: Psychoanalysis of the unthought known*. New York: Columbia University Press.

Corbett, L. (1989). Kohut and Jung: A comparison of theory and therapy. In D.W. Detrick and S. P. Detrick (Eds.), *Self psychology: Comparisons and contrasts*. Hillsdale: Analytic Press.

Fosshage, J. (1983). The psychological functions of dreams: A revised psychoanalytic perspective. *Psychoanalysis and contemporary thought*, *6*, 641–669.

Fosshage, J. (2000). The organizing functions of dreaming: A contemporary psychoanalytic model: Commentary on a paper by Hazel Ipp. *Psychoanalytic Dialogues*, *10*, 605–621.

Giannoni, M. (2003). Jung's theory of dream and the relational debate. *Psychoanalytic Dialogues*, *13*, 605–621.

Jung, C. G. (1946). The psychology of the transference. In G. Adler and R. F. C. Hull (Eds.), *The collected works of C.G. Jung* (Vol. *16*, pp. 353–537). Princeton: Princeton University Press.

Jung, C. G. (1947). On the nature of the psyche. In G. Adler and R. F. C. Hull (Eds. and Trans.), *The collected works of C.G. Jung* (Vol. *8*, pp. 159–236). Princeton: Princeton University Press.

Jung, C. G. (1966). On the relation of analytical psychology to poetry. In R. F. C. Hull (Trans.), *The collected works of C.G. Jung* (Vol. 15) (2nd ed.). Princeton: Princeton University Press.

Jung, C. G. (1969). The archetypes and the collective unconscious. In R. F. C. Hull (Trans.), (Vol. *9i*) (2nd ed.). Princeton: Princeton University Press.

Kohut, H. (1966). Forms and transformations of narcissism. In A. Morrison (Ed.), *The essential papers on narcissism*. New York: New York University Press.

Kohut, H. (1974). Lecture 10. October 25th. In M. Tolpin and P. Tolpin (Eds.), *The Chicago Institute lectures*. Hillsdale: Analytic Press.

Kohut, H. (1977). *The restoration of the self*. New York: International Universities Press.

Kohut, H. (1985). On courage. In C. B. Strozier (Ed.), *Self psychology and the humanities: Reflections on a new psychoanalytic approach*. New York and London: W.W. Norton & Company.

Kulka, R. (2012). Between emergence and dissolving: Contemporary reflections on greatness and ideals in Kohut's legacy. *International Journal of Psychoanalytic Self Psychology*, *7.2*, 264–285.

Miller, J.C. (2004). *The transcendent function: Jung's model of psychological growth through dialogue with the unconscious*. New York: SUNY Press.

Ornstein, P. (1986). On self-state dreams in the psychoanalytic treatment process. In A. Rothstein (Ed.), *The interpretation of dreams in clinical work. Workshop series of the American Psychoanalytic Association, Monograph Three*. Madison: International Universities Press.

Stolorow, R. (1992). Dreams and the subjective world. In M. R. Lansky (Ed.), *Essential papers on dreams*. New York: New York University Press.

Winnicott, D. W. (1971). *Playing and reality*. New York: Routledge.

PART V
The relational turn

8

BRINGING IT ALL BACK HOME

How I became a relational analyst[1]

Warren Colman

When Bob Dylan "went electric" in 1965, he was met with a storm of protest from his erstwhile traditional folk music fans. For Dylan, though, the kind of music he was now playing was just as rooted in the traditions of American music as the "protest" folk songs that had made him famous. To indicate this, he called his first electric album *Bringing It All Back Home* in a subtle reference to the overwhelming influence of American music on the music of the Beatles, who were currently all the rage in America.

For psychoanalysis, however, the trajectory of travel has been in the opposite direction. Relational analysis was created in the 1980s primarily out of the influence of the British object relations school on a new generation of analysts in New York, amongst them Stephen Mitchell, Phillip Bromberg, Jessica Benjamin and Lewis Aron (Aron, 1996). Unfortunately, the British have been slow to acknowledge this, and relational analysis is still regarded as a slightly dubious minority influence amongst the majority of mainstream British analysts.[2] Yet a great deal of creative work has been going on in the United States over the past 20 years, and it is high time that the British became more familiar with it. It is time for us to "bring it all back home".

My aim in this chapter is to bring together these two streams of thinking by tracing the history of my own influences and professional development over the past 40 years. In this way, I hope to demonstrate by example that a relational/inter-subjective approach is as firmly rooted in the British object relations and Jungian traditions as *Blonde on Blonde* was rooted in the American tradition of country music and the blues.

Themes of relational and intersubjective analysis

The social context of mind

For relational analysts, the social aspect of our being is fundamental to psychological life – it is not an "add on" or a separate domain of our existence. This leads to a critique of what Stolorow and Atwood (1992) call "the myth of the isolated mind". Or, as Sullivan expressed it, "A personality can never be isolated from the complex of interpersonal relationship in which the person lives and has his being" (Sullivan, 1940, p. 90). It is not simply that the mind *develops* in a social context of relationships with others; there is a more fundamental idea here that mind itself is social and that the private subjective self, the intrapsychic "inner world", is subsequent to and contingent upon the relational context in which it is embedded.[3]

While the object relational views of Fairbairn and Winnicott already recognised the relational context of early development, the distinctive feature of the relational group concerns the implications of these ideas of inherent relationality for psychotherapeutic practice. The analyst can no longer be regarded as an impartial observer who is capable of acting as an objective arbiter of what is real and what is not. It is not possible for the analyst to "know" what is in the patient's unconscious and interpret on that basis; rather, interpretation becomes a matter of negotiation between analyst and patient, resulting in the co-creation of meaning arising out of the uniquely shared reality that the analytic dyad co-construct between them.

Infant research and dyadic systems theory

A second strand in the relational perspective arises from decades of infant development research, first summarised by Daniel Stern in *The Interpersonal World of the Infant* in 1985 and leading on to the formulation of dyadic systems theory in the work of Beebe and Lachmann (2002, 2003). A key influence here is Louis Sander, who introduced systems theory into infant research, particularly the idea of mutual bi-directional regulation between mother and infant alongside each partner's self-regulation. He suggested that "exchanges between interacting components in a system, through mutual modification reach a harmonious co-ordination" (Sander, 1977, p. 138. Quoted in Beebe and Lachmann, 2003, p. 385). Since most of what goes on in the interactive regulatory dance between mother and infant is implicit and occurring at a pre-symbolic level – i.e. below the threshold of conscious representational form – the extrapolation of these fundamental relational strategies to the interaction between patient and analyst has led to an increased emphasis on the implicit, out-of-awareness dimensions of what the Boston Change Process Study Group (BCPSG) has called "implicit relational knowing". In 1998, the group applied these ideas to a rationale for the role of the relationship in the therapeutic action of psychoanalysis, the "something more than interpretation" of which relational analysts had long been aware but which they had been unable to formulate in such a research-based empirical way (Stern *et al.*, 1998).

Interpretation or relationship

The emphasis on relationship rather than interpretation as the key to therapeutic change is another defining element of the relational approach. This derives from both the interpersonal school and the object relations school. From the interpersonal school comes the focus on the real interaction between two persons, while from the object relations school comes the belief in fostering a "new experience" of relating that allows an experience to occur through the opportunities for regression to dependence presented by the analytic situation (Balint, 1968). This opens up the possibility of what Balint called a "new beginning" that can heal the "basic fault" in the personality derived from an early mismatch in the mother/infant relationship – a view that seems to anticipate the notion of misalignment and lack of attunement in the findings of the infant researchers.

Personal engagement, spontaneity, and boundaries

The centrality of relationship leads to two further features of relational analysis – an emphasis on the personal engagement of the analyst and a reconsideration of the role of analytic boundaries. The analyst as a person brings to the analytic encounter their own unique qualities, which are expressed in everything they say and do. Lewis Aron expresses the importance of the analyst as a real person with passionate eloquence:

> Unless patients can feel that they have reached their analysts, moved them, changed them, discomforted them, angered them, hurt them, healed, known them in some profound way, they themselves may not be able to benefit from their analyses. From this perspective, psychoanalysis is a profound emotional encounter, an interpersonal engagement, an intersubjective dialogue, a relational integration, a meeting of minds.
>
> *(Aron, 1996, p. 136)*

The idea of a meeting of minds echoes Stern *et al.*'s (1998) concept of "moments of meeting" between analyst and patient that may have a transformative impact on the patient's patterns of "implicit relational knowing", especially where there is an experience of being "met" in relation to aspects of themselves that have not found acknowledgement before.

Recognition

A further aspect of the attention given to the analyst's subjectivity is the importance of experiences of *recognition*, a key theme in the work of Jessica Benjamin. Benjamin (1990) states:

> Intersubjective theory postulates that the other must be recognized as another subject in order for the self to fully experience his or her subjectivity in the

other's presence. This means that we have a need for recognition and that we have a capacity to recognize others in return, thus making mutual recognition possible.

(1990, p. 35)

Benjamin's starting point is Winnicott's late, controversial paper on "The use of an object" (1968), wherein she sees Winnicott's distinction between object relating and object usage as referring to the difference between an "object" and an "other". In this paper, Winnicott was pushing at the boundaries of object relations theory by posing a question rarely broached by analysts – what is reality? Winnicott saw that a theory that remains in the realm of internal objects avoids facing this crucial question, and his answer was that "the feeling of real" can only be established through discovering the reality of another. Reality is thus shared reality.

R.D. Laing: Ontological insecurity and interpersonal perception

This brings me back to my own early concerns with the nature of reality in the context of 1960s counter-culture and its critique of the "taken for granted" reality of the everyday world. During my first year at university, I discovered the work of R.D. Laing, whose book *The Politics of Experience* (1967) had turned him into a celebrity guru a couple of years earlier. Laing's intellectual roots were in existentialism and phenomenology, and although he was interested in psychoanalytic ideas, he took a critical stance from the outset. In his first and, arguably, his best book, *The Divided Self*, he wrote:

> Instead of the original bond of *I* and *You*, we take a single man in isolation and conceptualize his various aspects into "the ego," "the superego," and "the id." The other becomes either an internal or external object or a fusion of both. This difficulty faces not only classical Freudian metapsychology but equally any theory that begins with man or a part of man abstracted from his relation with the other in his world.
>
> *(Laing, 1959, p. 19)*

The Divided Self analysed the experience of schizoid and psychotic individuals as problems of being a self or a person. Anticipating many relational and intersubjective ideas, Laing argued that being a self is dependent on feeling recognised by another. He introduced the concept of *ontological insecurity* to describe the experience of those who do not feel that they are alive and real, who lack temporal continuity, consistency and cohesiveness. Referencing the work of Sullivan and Fromm-Reichmann, he argued that, for the ontologically insecure person, "the ordinary circumstances of living threaten his low threshold of security" (1959, p. 42). Lacking a sense of integral selfhood and personal identity, such persons are continually preoccupied with preserving their own existence.

Drawing on the phenomenological idea of mind as embedded in its socio-environmental context, Laing was able to show how psychotic symptoms might constitute a reasonable response to a mad environment. He pointed out that the "symptoms" of psychosis that patients show in a typical psychiatric investigation may in fact be due to the patient being treated as a scientific object rather than engaged as a person. Such "symptoms" may represent the ontologically insecure person's attempt to preserve themselves in the face of threats of engulfment and impingement by the alienating other (1959, pp. 43–44).

This is a profoundly revealing insight that extends far beyond psychiatric investigations of psychotics to include all of the ways in which the therapist and their environment affect the patient. Later, Laing used game theory to create a model of interpersonal perception that saw the behaviour of one person in relation to the behaviour of the other. For example, in traditional psychiatry (or psychoanalysis), one person's behaviour may be taken out of context, and direct links may be made between a sequence of their behaviour (e.g. p1 → p2 → p3 etc.) without considering the effect of the other person's contribution, which would create a very different sequence of interaction (e.g. p1 → o1 → p2 → o2 → p3 → o3 etc.) (Laing, 1967, p. 43). Laing's argument explains why intersubjective and relational analysts pay so much attention to exploring how their actual behaviour is affecting their patients. This leads to a stance I would describe as *the self-reflexive analyst.* For example, how are patients affected by analysts' refusal to engage in ordinary social conversation, especially those analysts who greet and dismiss their patients in silence? How far do interpretations that insist on the patient's aggression towards the therapist *induce* aggression in the same way that "objective" psychiatric investigation induces psychotic symptoms? Thus, my early reading of Laing forever sensitised me towards the idea that there is no "neutrality", since neutrality is itself a highly powerful stance that has a massive impact on the patient. This means that I need to think about the significance of everything I say and do – and everything I do not say and do – not merely in terms of the patient's "fantasies" but, as the interpersonalists argue, in terms of a real interaction that is having a real effect on the patient.

The Tavistock and the Institute of Marital Studies

From 1956 to 1964, Laing worked at the Tavistock Centre in London, initially in the Tavistock Clinic, a psychoanalytically oriented training centre for adult, child and family psychotherapy and latterly at the Tavistock Institute of Human Relations (TIHR), a pioneering unit formed in the post-war heyday of the British welfare state that sought to extend psychoanalytic thinking to wider social systems. At the Tavistock Clinic he would have encountered John Bowlby, Wilfred Bion and J.D. (Jock) Sutherland, a fellow Scot who introduced him there (Miller, 2004, p. 84). Sutherland is an important figure in the history of relational analysis, as he was annual visiting professor at the Menninger Foundation in Kansas. According to an obituary in *Psychoanalytic Dialogues* in 1992, "Interest in object relations theory in the United States and, in particular, in the work of W.R.D. Fairbairn, was unquestionably due to Jock's influence" (Corrigan, 1992, p. 277).

Sutherland was also involved with TIHR, which brought together staff from different disciplines to find ways to apply psychoanalytic and open systems concepts to group and organisational life. In many ways, the kind of creative intellectual atmosphere at the Tavistock would have been similar to Robert Stolorow's account of his clinical psychotherapy training at Harvard:

> It was set in the Department of Social Relations, which had been formed by leading scholars from four disciplines – sociology, cultural anthropology, social psychology, and personality psychology – all of whom had a common interest and background in psychoanalysis.
>
> *(Stolorow, 2004, p. 543)*

One of the units within TIHR was the Institute of Marital Studies (IMS), where I trained and worked from 1982 to 1997. The IMS had been founded after the Second World War by Enid Balint and Lily Pincus and was a world leader in the development of a psychoanalytic approach to couple therapy for several decades. By the time I joined the unit, it had developed a model of couple interaction in which the couple itself (rather than separate individuals) was the focus of intervention.

I felt this was just the combination of psychoanalytic and systemic thinking I was looking for. A psychoanalytic approach to couples that focused on interaction offered me the best of both worlds, since it addressed the way the inner world of each partner's experience was expressed in the interactional dynamics of the marital system they created between them. It was, in its essence, a dyadic systems theory that, like Benjamin's approach to intersubjectivity, took cognisance of the intrapsychic as well as the interpersonal. Psychotherapy with couples provides the ideal opportunity to study how dyadic systems work in adult life, and this has had a foundational influence on my work as an analyst. It is hardly surprising that I take an intersubjective relational view of analysis, considering that, as a couples therapist, I've been working with intersubjective interaction for over 30 years.

Working with couples inevitably sensitises the therapist to the way each partner is affected by the behaviour of the other, resulting in a pattern of mutual regulation that becomes the characteristic interactional style of the couple. For example, the detailed observation of mother and infant couples engaged in "chase and dodge" is very reminiscent of the concept of "distance regulation" in couple and family therapy – a typical pattern found in couples in which as one retreats, the other pursues (Byng-Hall & Campbell, 1981).

Situated as it was within TIHR, the IMS became the nexus of a very rich confluence of ideas. Primarily, its thinking developed out of an object relations model, in which Kleinian influence was originally quite limited. Laing and Sutherland were both closely associated with the IMS, as was John Bowlby, who still gave occasional seminars while I worked there. This led to the use of attachment theory as one of the main theoretical themes underlying Mattinson and Sinclair's study of working with the couple relationship in multi-problem families presenting to a social service department, published as *Mate and Stalemate* in 1982.

In contrast to the criticism levelled against Winnicott and Guntrip by Stephen Mitchell that they imagined an ideal conflict-free state of "perpetual internal harmony and equilibrium" (Mitchell, 1988, p. 159), the IMS approach espoused the idea that "conflict is inherent in relatedness", as Mitchell puts it (ibid., p. 160), as evidenced by the first book produced by the IMS in 1960, called *Marriage: Studies in Emotional Conflict and Growth* (Pincus, 1960). Similarly, the tension inherent in couple relations epitomises Mitchell's (1997) depiction of a dialectic between being oneself and being influenced by others. Furthermore, Benjamin's use of Hegel's "master/slave" relationship to describe "how the self's wish for absolute independence conflicts with the self's need for recognition" (Benjamin, 1990, p. 39) is redolent of one of the main themes in couple interaction – the tension between autonomy and dependence. This is well expressed in the question posed by Mattinson and Lyons (1993) in their paper on "Individuation in marriage": "Can a person be a fully committed partner and at the same time develop his own wholeness and capacity for individuation?" (p. 104).

The IMS also included a strong Jungian influence. Mattinson and Lyons were both Jungian analysts as well as marital psychotherapists, and the Jungian influence is clearly apparent in the way they brought together Bion's idea of containment with Jung's (1925) notion of marriage partners "containing" each other to create the idea of marriage itself as a container, a theme I later developed in a paper of my own (Colman, 1993). In another paper I suggested that the idea of "resonance" in the interactive field provided a better metaphor for many aspects of couple relating than the over-used notion of projective identification (Colman, 1995).

In these papers I was trying to move beyond the object relations perspective of an ego that relates to objects to one that conceptualised interaction in terms of "self and other", an indication of Laing's continuing influence. In an unpublished paper written in 1985, I had already attempted to tackle the same issues Jessica Benjamin was to address a few years later in her paper on the importance of recognition in the development of the self (Benjamin, 1990, 1995). Like Benjamin, this took me to Winnicott's account of the emergence of a sense of shared reality. Although I was writing at the same time as the relational and intersubjective groups were developing their ideas on the other side of the Atlantic, I was entirely unaware of these developments, yet wrote in very similar terms:

> The self does not, indeed cannot exist in isolation. It can only be discovered in and through relation to something or someone other [...] The recognition of the other as truly external to the self, i.e. existing in objective reality, is the only basis for the establishment of a truly personal individual relationship where both self and other can be seen and known for what they are.
>
> *(Colman, 1985)*

Despite these influences, my view of individual therapy/analysis at that time was entirely conventional. It was to be another decade or so before I began to modify my clinical approach as an analyst. During this time, the prevailing climate at the IMS had begun to shift away from the ecumenical approach of TIHR towards the more Kleinian culture of the Tavistock Clinic.[4] The Kleinians were making exciting innovations at that time, and two of their most prominent figures, John Steiner and Ron Britton, were teaching and working at the Tavistock Clinic. I had become a lone Jungian and could only make myself heard through my fluent grasp of the Kleinian language. Frustratingly, there was a great deal of Jungian thinking that seemed entirely unspeakable in that language. Nevertheless, it seemed to me that this was how psychoanalysis was supposed to be done, and this seemed to be the prevailing view even at the Society of Analytical Psychology (SAP), where I had recently completed my analytic training.

It was a watershed revelation for me when, shortly before leaving the Tavistock in 1997, I discovered Victoria Hamilton's book on *The Analyst's Pre-Conscious* (1996). Hamilton conducted a survey of British and American analysts trained in different times, places and schools of thought, asking them their views on a range of controversial technical issues such as psychic reality, objective reality and the "real relationship", holding and containment, counter-transference and the analyst's model of change. She found that, whatever their rationale, analysts' views tended to depend on where and when they trained. This seemed to me far more like the operation of local craft schools than the practice of a scientific discipline. It was liberating to discover that analysts in different parts of the world operated quite differently from the increasingly dominant British Kleinian approach I had come to take for granted. I realised that there was indeed more than one way to do analysis and that other schools of analysis were engaged in equally valid debates about concepts that some British analysts seemed either unaware of or dismissed, such as the notion of therapeutic alliance. So it was a further ironic twist when I began to read the relational analysts and discovered that many of their ideas came from the British! As I have shown, these ideas were embedded in my own history, yet I had not realised many of their clinical implications. I now began to see why my own practice did not conform to the model in which I had been trained and why I needed to go ahead and develop my own approach.

The Jungian connection

This also enabled me to deepen my connection to the Jungian element in the hybrid psychoanalytic Jungian orientation of my analytic training at the SAP. Many of Jung's statements about the practice of psychotherapy find an almost uncanny echo in the statements of the relational point of view made 50 or 60 years later, especially as few relationalists seem to have actually read Jung. Consider, for example, Jung's remarks in a lecture given in 1935. He describes psychotherapy as "a dialogue or discussion between two persons" (Jung, 1935, para. 1) and as "a dialectical

procedure consisting in a comparison of our mutual findings" in which the psychotherapist "must give up all pretension to superior knowledge" (ibid., para. 2).
In this process, he says, "the therapist is no longer the agent of the treatment but a
fellow participant in a process of individual development" (ibid., para. 7). One of
the reasons for this is the need for multiple theories, and another is "the multiple
significance of symbolic contents" (para. 9), a statement of his view that symbols
are necessarily multiple and indeterminate in their meaning, since they express
unknown factors.

Compare all this with Lewis Aron's opening statement of the relational view in
his book *A Meeting of Minds*:

> The relational view [...] abandons the idea that the analyst has *superior
> knowledge* of the patient's psyche or psychodynamics [...] *meaning is seen as
> relative, multiple and indeterminate*, with each interpretation subject to con-
> tinual and unending *interpretation by both analyst and analysand*. Meaning is
> generated relationally and *dialogically* which is to say that *meaning is negotiated
> and co-constructed*. Meaning is arrived at through a meeting of minds.
>
> *(Aron, 1996, p. xii, italics added)*[5]

Jung's emphasis on the importance of the analyst's personal engagement in the
work beyond his professional role resonated deeply with my own belief that the
relationship was the primary factor in therapeutic change. In a paper written a
couple of years after leaving the Tavistock, I contrasted this view with the popular
Kleinian concept of "the total transference", in which all events within the analytic
relationship, including counter-transference and enactments, are seen as manifestations of the patient's inner world, thus maintaining a curiously non-relational view
of relating in which intrapsychic insight remains the goal of analysis and the means
of therapeutic change (Colman, 2003).

The clinical example I gave concerned a largely silent patient, who felt intensely
threatened by me in a way that made being in the room with each other excruciat-
ingly painful for both of us. Despite the fact that she felt unable to have any impact
on me, I was actually struggling with the same excruciating pain of feeling that I was
unable to have an impact on her. In one of those situations where it is impossible
to say who is doing what to whom, both of us felt trapped in a near-unendurable
impasse, where each felt the other was trying to control them. However, I also
brought to the encounter a kind of "heroic" determination not to give up hope that
enabled me to endure the excruciating pain and to go on believing in her and the
value of the analysis. Eventually, the analysis came to an apparent end without very
much having changed, and this felt like a disappointing outcome until a few years
later, when the patient returned and the therapy was resumed on a once-weekly
basis. Only then could she express her appreciation that I had "hung on in there"
and showed that I could stand her hatred and despair and that, as she said, "it was
alright with you for me to be not alright". And only then did I understand the mean-

ing of my determined endurance. This was what she had called forth from my own inner being in response to the kind of paralysing anxieties which she had suffered.

As I now understand it, the analyst's availability fosters the development of an interactive field in which the patient expresses her difficulty through her way of being in the analytic situation. This creates a resonance in the analyst of the kind that Jung called a "psychic infection". The patient's difficulty is transferred to the analyst, and the analyst has to struggle with it in themselves in the hope of finding a way of dealing with it that is more successful – or at least *different* – from the way the patient has been dealing with it. As Jung puts it, following on from his well-known remarks about the analyst needing to be subject to influence,

> The effects [of the counter-transference] can best be conveyed by the old idea of the *demon of sickness*. According to this, a sufferer can transmit his disease to a healthy person whose powers then subject the demon – but not without impairing the well-being of the subduer.
>
> *(Jung, 1929, para. 163)*

Thus, my capacity to maintain hope while enduring the patient's hatred and despair altered the interactive field in which she was used to living and provided her with a new experience of being with someone for whom it was alright for her not to be alright. This may be described as being "internalised" by the patient, but I think it has more to do with the long-term effect of living with and through a sustained encounter with a new kind of personal relatedness.

Spontaneity, intrusiveness, and collusion

In response to my paper, the Kleinian analyst Robert Caper argued that it is only by interpreting that the analyst can convey to the patient that he is able to remain interested and thoughtful in the face of the patient's "attacks" (Caper, 2003, p. 363). This view throws a valuable light on the tension that arises in both Jungian and relational analysis around the vexed question of whether and when there may need to be a relaxation of ordinary analytic boundaries to allow for "extra-analytic" interventions. Jung proudly claimed to be "unsystematic by intention", eschewed technique and valorised spontaneity. The same attitudes can be found among relational analysts, and for very much the same reasons. Here is Lewis Aron again:

> as a group, relational analysts are more likely than other analysts to advocate a high degree of freedom of expression and spontaneity on the part of the analyst. [...] If what is thought to be transformative is not only insight but new forms of engagement, [...] if what matters most is the patient's meeting with an authentic response from the analyst ... then why limit our interventions only to formal interpretations?
>
> *(Aron, 1996, pp. 213–214)*

For the first generation of London Jungians who were engaging with psycho-analysis in the 1950s, the same issues arose, but in reverse. Thus, Michael Fordham was keen to point out the pitfalls of the traditional Jungian emphasis on the analyst's subjectivity. He warned that this could lead to "intrusive displays of his personality or acting out the counter-transference" (Fordham, 1969, p. 268). He cautioned that the tendency of many Jungians to justify giving personal information about themselves on the grounds of "mutuality" risked ignoring the transference, in which how the analyst saw themselves might be very different from how they were seen by their patients (Astor, 1995, p. 127). While strongly maintaining Jung's view that the analyst was as much in the analysis as the patient (Jung, 1929, para. 166), Fordham argued that "it was not so much the qualities of the analyst *per se* which were therapeutic as his abilities to manage them" (Astor, 1995, p. 126).

Many of Fordham's criticisms of traditional Jungians also apply to some of the more excessive examples of "freedom and spontaneity" displayed in the relational literature, a tendency that Jay Greenberg warned against in a paper on "The ana-lyst's participation" in 2001. Greenberg argued that the over-reliance on "throwing away the book", as Hoffman (1994) calls it, leads analysts away from focusing on the patient's own experience, "inflames the analyst's desire to be a good analyst or even a good person" (op. cit., p. 372) and encourages them to avoid those moments that are unbearable because they attack the analyst's desire to help and to heal (Caper, 1992). As Casement says in his response to Greenberg, "an analytic good object [...] is that which can tolerate being used to represent the worst in a patient's experience" (Casement, 2001, p. 384).

Nevertheless, for me, this remains one of the most consistently difficult and anxiety-provoking aspects of analytic work, as I strive to steer a course between the Scylla of technical rigidity and the Charybdis of collusion. For, as well as the danger of giving in to the temptation of being benevolent and attempting to cure through suggestion and kindness (Carmeli & Blass, 2010, p. 224), there is the opposite danger that "staying firm" in the face of patients' attempts to get the analyst to collude in their defences can result in becoming deaf to the patient's genuine needs for a personal response adapted to their par-ticular needs. This may lead to iatrogenically produced reactions in the patient that are then interpreted as "intrapsychic" impulses, just as Laing described in his studies of interpersonal perception. The point is well made by Stolorow and Atwood:

> "Negative therapeutic reactions" are most often produced by prolonged unrecognized intersubjective disjunctions wherein the patient's emotional needs are consistently misunderstood and thereby relentlessly rejected by the therapist. Such misunderstandings typically take the form of erroneously interpreting the revival of an unmet developmental longing as if it were an expression of malignant, pathological resistance.
>
> *(1992, p. 106)*

Bringing Jungians together: Patterns of relating

One of the great benefits of the relational perspective is that it offers a bridge that brings together differing orientations within the Jungian world. There is an important difference here between Jungian practice and Jungian theory. Despite the strong relational implications of Jung's dialectical model of psychotherapy as a personal encounter, most of his theoretical assumptions are more like those of drive theory in viewing mental life as "the expression of preformed forces or pressures", as Mitchell puts it (1988, p. 5). For Jung, the preformed forces are the archetypal forms conceived as the a priori organising principles which drive psychic life.

In one respect, though, Jung's "organising principles" lend themselves to an intersubjective approach much more readily than Freudian drives. Once they are stripped of their a priori essentialist assumptions, they start to look very much like the models of psychic organisation and mental structure proposed by relational and intersubjective analysts. Jean Knox's work played a central role in this reformulation, replacing the linkage between archetypes and unconscious phantasy with a model of archetypes as "image schemas" (drawing on cognitive science and developmental psychology) and "internal working models" (drawing on attachment theory) (Knox, 1997, 2003).

This reformulation links Jungian thinking with intersubjective concepts such as "patterns of experience" (Beebe and Lachmann), "scripts" (Lichtenberg), "relationship patterns" (Emde) (see Stolorow and Atwood 1992, p. 23) built out of Stern's concept of "representations of interactions which have been generalized" RIGs (Stern, 1985), and Stolorow and Atwood's "invariant principles that unconsciously organise the child's subsequent experiences" (op. cit., p. 24). These are all concepts of implicit models that are pre-reflective and not normally subject to conscious awareness. These models are also related to the reformulated idea of "shared unconscious phantasy" used by couple therapists, which really refers to unconscious *beliefs* about relationships rather than the "wish-fulfilling expressions of instinctual drives" (Knox, 1997, 657–658) intended by the original Kleinian use of the term. It is these implicit patterns of relating that couple and family therapists look for by focusing their attention on what the family's shared assumptions of relating seem to be like.

In the context of family relationships, then, so-called unconscious phantasies refer to the crystallisation of patterns of experience that shape how things are said and done within the family and what can and cannot be expressed. In turn, this provides a model for thinking about and working with the relational matrix the individual patient brings to therapy and re-enacts there. There is nothing intentional about this, defensive or otherwise – it is simply the way that the patient has learnt to relate to themselves and others and implicitly assumes that others think and feel this way too. As patients often say to me, "But that's normal, isn't it?" This provides one of the most powerful opportunities for the analytic process to slowly alter the patient's "relational matrix" via what Bromberg calls the "relational gestalt of experience that is constantly being repatterned as relative roles are being redefined" (Bromberg, 1991, p. 298).

Clinical example

I would like to give an example of this process that gives some indication of the way I now work. I have a patient who apparently related to the analytic set-up in a very casual way that did not acknowledge the normal boundaries. He would frequently arrive late and would sometimes fail to turn up at all. On these occasions he would not contact me to let me know why he had not come, but would simply turn up to the next session and continue from there. Initially, I would attempt to interpret his behaviour as a defence against a dependence on me that would arouse his terror of abandonment. This was probably true, but was completely ineffective. It made him feel he was "getting it wrong" and reinforced his feeling that he was not worthy of having an analysis. Furthermore, interpretations along these lines led him to become stubbornly and exasperatingly concrete in rebutting them. It took me some time to realise that this was a defence against his feelings of being "invalid" and "not knowing how to be", which made him experience my interpretations as threats to his existence. Eventually, I more or less gave up attempting to interpret his lateness, but I was still curious about why he didn't contact me when he failed to turn up at all. I explained that this was not a matter of wanting him to comply with my expectations but of trying to understand what was going on in his mind. What emerged from this was that he had no notion that I would be concerned about his absence in any way, and that this was part of a larger picture in which he had no notion about being cared about. He could neither care nor be cared for. Instead, he had an unformulated sense of "lacking something" from his childhood that he was unable to name.

He described the dominant way of relating in his family in terms of an unspoken requirement of "pleasantness" or "blandisation", which effectively meant that nothing of any import could be discussed and anything painful was minimised in expressions like "mustn't grumble" and "not too bad". Gradually, I was able to piece together an impression of a mother who was chronically anxious and probably suffering from an undiagnosed agitated depression. The injunction of "pleasantness" was probably one of the ways the family had learnt to manage the mother's illness, but it certainly meant that my patient could never risk challenging her. This was instanced in two early memories. In one of these, when he was probably under five years old, his mother took him to see a pantomime but forgot to bring his glasses. Although he was unable to see, he knew that he must not mention this to his mother. The second memory concerned a painting he did at school, which was chosen to be shown in a high-profile exhibition of children's work. His parents showed no interest in this and did not take him to see the exhibition. Again, nothing was said about it.

I began to see that when he didn't think to let me know why he had gone missing, he was behaving just in the way he had learnt in his family – this was the procedural "*modus vivendi*", the implicit relational knowing or unconscious organising principle that structured his way of being and feeling. It was *not* projective identification, in that there was no intentionality involved, so it was not, for example, a way of getting me to feel the way he felt, nor was there anything being evacuated. It was, for him, simply the way he did things, and wasn't that the way everyone did things?

By talking to him about this, I was implicitly teaching him about seeing things from another point of view, such as pointing out that it didn't occur to him that, for example, I might wonder where he was or even be worried about him. I linked this up to his childhood experience of being forgotten or ignored, but made it clear that it was not that I felt he was doing this to me but that it was an expression of what he obscurely felt he lacked. This way of talking also showed him that it was possible to challenge another without attacking them or precipitating a collapse, as he feared with his mother. Sometimes, though, he did collapse in panic and shame, defensively warding off the threat of being seen to be invalid. These occasions provided an opportunity for him to discover how these states of mind could be recovered from through patient efforts to maintain communication in a mutually respectful and caring manner. And when I did occasionally react to his defensiveness with exasperation, I would acknowledge this. For example, I once said that I was indeed irritated with him but that I didn't mind being irritated. In this way, he began to understand what it meant to be cared about and to care for others. Eventually, this bore fruit in reliable phone calls when he missed sessions, for which there was actually always a good reason. But I was particularly pleased when he phoned me one day in the middle of one of his anxious panics and asked for my help and advice. In the context of his history, this had nothing to do with "boundary-breaking" – rather, it was an indication that I had arrived in his mind as a potentially helpful figure to whom he could turn. It represented the emergence of a new relational gestalt.

Conclusion

I hope this brief example gives an indication of at least some of the influences I have traced through this chapter and why I think my approach can best be described as "relational Jungian psychoanalysis". The idea of a relational matrix of beliefs, assumptions and ways of doing things is rooted in my experience of couple interaction, while my Jungian training has given me a freedom to relate directly to the patient in an interactive way that does not privilege interpretation as an exclusive form of intervention and may sometimes include elements of personal disclosure. With this patient, I have also needed to be alive to the threat that my more substantial presence may pose to someone whom the early Laing would have recognised as a schizoid personality suffering from ontological insecurity.

Perhaps most important of all, though, is the maintenance of a self-reflexive attitude that includes not only my counter-transference but a consideration of the total impact of what I say and do and how the analytic relationship is structured. It is this stance that enables the analyst not only to relate to the patient where he or she is, but to learn from the patient how they are experiencing the analytic situation and themselves as an analyst. In this way, the analyst can develop their own working practice, or, as Jung would put it, this creates a combination in which both parties are transformed.

Notes

1 This chapter, in slightly different form, was first published in the *Journal of Analytical Psychology*, 2013, 58.4, 570–590.
2 Notable exceptions that prove the rule include Susie Orbach and Andrew Samuels.
3 See Zinkin (1991/2008) for a similar relational-constructivist view in which the experience of a private self is contingent on a prior intersubjective and "public" interaction with the (m)other.
4 An exception to this was the systemic family therapy team in the Child and Family Department, although even this seemed to disappear from view during the 1990s.
5 Similar overlaps were pointed out in a symposium in *Psychoanalytic Dialogues* in which several Jungian analysts were asked to comment on a piece of clinical material by Stephen Mitchell (Fosshage and Davies, 2000).

References

Aron, L. (1996). *A meeting of minds. Mutuality in psychoanalysis*. New Jersey: Analytic. Reprinted New York: Routledge (2009).

Astor, J. (1995). *Michael Fordham. Innovations in analytical psychology*. London and New York: Routledge.

Balint, M. (1968). *The basic fault. Therapeutic aspects of regression*. London: Tavistock.

Beebe, B. and Lachmann, F. (2002). *Infant research and adult treatment. Co-constructing interactions*. New Jersey: Analytic.

Beebe, B., & Lachmann, F. (2003). The relational turn in psychoanalysis: A dyadic systems view from infant research. *Contemporary Psychoanalysis*, *39*(3), 379–409.

Benjamin, J. (1990). An outline of intersubjectivity: The development of recognition. *Psychoanalytic Psychology* , 7 (Supplement), 33–46.

Benjamin, J. (1995). Recognition and destruction: An outline of intersubjectivity. In *Like subjects, love objects: Essays on recognition and sexual difference*. New Haven: Yale University Press.

Bromberg, P. M. (1991). Artist and analyst. *Contemporary Psychoanalysis*, *27*, 289–299.

Byng-Hall, J., & Campbell, D. (1981). Resolving conflicts in family distance regulation: An integrative approach. *Journal of Marital and Family Therapy*, *7*(3), 321–330.

Caper, R. (1992). Does psychoanalysis heal? A contribution to the theory of psychoanalytic technique. *International Journal of Psychoanalysis*, *73*, 283–292.

Caper, R. (2003). Response to Colman. In R. Withers (Ed.) *Controversies in analytical psychology and psychoanalysis*. Hove and New York: Brunner-Routledge.

Carmeli, Z., & Blass, R. B. (2010). The relational turn in psychoanalysis: Revolution or regression? *European Journal of Psychotherapy and Counselling*, *12*(3), 217–224.

Casement, P. (2001). Commentaries [on Greenberg's "The analyst's participation"]. *Journal of the American Psychoanalytic Association*, *49*, 381–386.

Colman, W. (1985). Self and other in marital interaction. Unpublished.

Colman, W. (1993). Marriage as a psychological container. In S. Ruszczynski (Ed.) *Psychotherapy with couples: Theory and practice at the Tavistock Institute of Marital Studies*. London: Karnac.

Colman, W. (1995). Gesture and recognition: An alternative model to projective identification as a basis for couple relationships. In Ruszczynski, S. and Fisher, J. (Eds), *Intrusiveness and intimacy in the couple*. London: Karnac.

Colman, W. (2003). Interpretation and relationship: Ends or means? A commentary on Robert Caper's "Does psychoanalysis heal?" In R. Withers (Ed.), *Controversies in analytical psychology and psychoanalysis*. Hove and New York: Brunner-Routledge.

Corrigan, E. G. (1992). J. D. Sutherland in memoriam. *Psychoanalytic Dialogues, 2,* 277.

Fordham, M. (1969). Technique and counter-transference. *Journal of Analytical Psychology, 14* (2), 95–118. Reprinted in M. Fordham, R. Gordon, J. Hubback and K. Lambert (Eds), *Technique in Jungian analysis*. London: Heinemann, 1974.

Fosshage, J. L., & Davies, J. M. (2000). Analytical psychology after Jung with clinical case material from Stephen Mitchell's *Influence and autonomy in psychoanalysis. Psychoanalytic Dialogues, 10,* 377–388.

Greenberg, J. (2001). The analyst's participation: A new look. *Journal of the American Psychoanalytic Association, 49,* 359–381.

Hamilton, V. (1996) *The analyst's pre-conscious*. Hillsdale: Analytic.

Hoffman, I. (1994). Dialectical thinking and therapeutic action in the psychoanalytic process. *Psychoanalytic Quarterly, 63,* 187–218.

Jung, C. G. (1925). Marriage as a psychological relationship. In *The Development of Personality, CW17*.

Jung, C. G. (1929). Problems of modern psychotherapy. In *The Practice of Psychotherapy, CW16*.

Jung, C. G. (1935). Principles of practical psychotherapy. In *The Practice of Psychotherapy, CW16*.

Knox, J. (1997). Internal objects: A theoretical analysis of Jungian and Kleinian models. *Journal of Analytical Psychology, 42*(4), 653–666.

Knox, J. (2003) *Archetype, attachment, analysis. Jungian psychology and the emergent mind*. Hove and New York: Brunner-Routledge.

Laing, R. D. (1959). *The divided self. An existential study in sanity and madness*. London: Tavistock. Reprinted, Harmondsworth: Penguin, 1965.

Laing, R. D. (1967). *The politics of experience and the bird of paradise*. Harmondsworth: Penguin.

Mattinson, J., & Lyons, A. (1993). Individuation in marriage. In S. Ruszczynski (Ed.) *Psychotherapy with couples: Theory and practice at the Tavistock Institute of Marital Studies*. London: Karnac.

Mattinson, J., & Sinclair, I. (1982). *Mate and stalemate. Working with marital problems in a social services department*. Oxford: Blackwell.

Miller, G. (2004). *R.D. Laing*. Edinburgh: Edinburgh University Press.

Mitchell, S. A. (1988). *Relational concepts in psychoanalysis. An integration*. Cambridge: Harvard University Press.

Mitchell, S. A. (1997). *Influence and autonomy in psychoanalysis*. Hillsdale: Analytic.

Pincus, L. (Ed.) (1960). *Marriage: Studies in emotional conflict and growth*. London: Methuen. Reprinted London: Institute of Marital Studies, 1973.

Sander, L. (1977). The regulation of exchange in the infant-caretaker system and some aspects of the context-content relationship. In M. Lewis and L. Rosenblum (Eds), *Interaction, conversation, and the development of language*. New York: Wiley.

Stern, D. N. (1985). *The interpersonal world of the infant: A view from psychoanalysis and developmental psychology*. New York: Basic.

Stern, D. N., Sander, L., Nahum, J., Harrison, A., Lyons-Ruth, K., Morgan, A., Bruschweiler-Stern, N., & Tronick, E. (1998). Non-interpretive mechanisms in psychoanalytic therapy. The "something more" than interpretation. *International Journal of Psychoanalysis, 79*, 903–921.

Stolorow, R. D. (2004). Autobiographical reflections on the intersubjective history of an intersubjective perspective in psychoanalysis. *Psychoanalytic Inquiry, 24*, 542–557.

Stolorow, R. D., & Atwood, G. E. (1992). *Contexts of being. The intersubjective foundations of psychological life*. New Jersey: Analytic.

Sullivan, H. S. (1940). *Conceptions of modern psychiatry*. New York: Norton.

Winnicott, D. W. (1968). The use of an object and relating through identifications. In *Playing and reality*. London: Tavistock, 1971.

Zinkin, L. (1991/2008). Your self: Did you find it or did you make it? *Journal of Analytical Psychology, 53*(3), 389–406.

9

TO THE BEGINNING AND BACK AGAIN

Trauma, splits, and confluences

Marcus West

In this chapter, I will cast a fresh eye on the split between Jung and Freud, particularly in relation to their respectively moving away from considering trauma as the foundation stone of psychopathology. In doing so, I will draw from contemporary research on infant development, trauma, and attachment. I will outline a position focused on early relational trauma and highlight how developments in the two streams of theory complement each other.

In the United States, the relational psychoanalytic movement has developed many ideas that are familiar to Jungians—an appreciation for the equality of analyst and patient, an interest in challenging traditional views of the analyst's authority and privileged access to knowledge, the recognition of intersubjectivity, the affirmation of different self-states in the individual, and the espousal of real world trauma as central to the origins of psychopathology—all suggest good grounds for rapprochement. Within the Jungian field, meanwhile, many analysts, particularly within the London developmental school, turned to object relations theory (and Kleinian theory in particular) for help with their clinical work with more disturbed, borderline patients. Michael Fordham, a founding figure of the London School, espoused what has been called a Jung–Klein hybrid (Fordham, 1993).

The early relational trauma position I will outline, derived from clinical experience rather than from adherence to a fixed theoretical stance, offers a critique of both the Jung–Klein hybrid (primarily in terms of the Kleinian omission of trauma) and of certain aspects of the relational psychoanalytic movement. It also shows how the different theory streams complement each other. This is, inevitably, a very personal understanding. While Jung himself moved away from his early interest in trauma and was, at times, critical of "everlastingly reducing all the finest strivings of the soul back to the womb" (Jung, 1921/1928, para. 279), he bequeathed us his rich understanding of the complex, which serves as an ideal vehicle for integrating recent developments in trauma research and acts as a bridge between contemporary Jungian and psychoanalytic positions.

★ ★ ★

In writing the chapter in *Symbols of Transformation* (Jung, 1911/1912) which he knew "would cost [him his] friendship with Freud" (Jung, 1963, p. 191), Jung stated:

> Christ's teaching [on the necessity of a spiritual rebirth[1]] means ruthlessly separating a man from his family […] freeing a man from his family fixations, from his weakness and uncontrolled infantile feelings. For if he allows his libido to get stuck in a childish milieu, and does not free it for higher purposes, he falls under the spell of unconscious compulsion. Wherever he may be, the unconscious will then recreate the infantile milieu by projecting his complexes, thus reproducing all over again, and in defiance of his vital interests, the same dependence and lack of freedom which formerly characterized his relations with his parents.
>
> *(Jung, 1911/1912, para. 644)*

I have argued elsewhere (West, 2016a, chapter 19) that Jung was himself entrapped in "recreating his own infantile milieu," which included an apparent independence from his parents, self-isolation, and annihilation/defeat of the ego. What I mean by this latter term will, I hope, become clear, and I will be describing the potential that he found through these experiences below.

Regarding his break from Freud, as he was to put it later, Jung was "unable to feel that all neuroses were caused by repression or sexual traumata" (Jung, 1963, p. 171); additionally, he felt that "Freud's attitude to the spirit seemed highly questionable," with Freud insinuating that any expression of spirituality "was repressed sexuality" (ibid., p. 172). Jung felt that he had found a means of resolving the individual's tendency to get stuck in the repetition of their infantile traumas and complexes (which both Freud and Jung had learned about from Charcot and Janet) by recognizing the narrowness of the ego and moving beyond it toward the broader "wisdom" held in the unconscious or, as he was later to term it, "the self." This is the "rebirth" to which Jung refers in the block quote above. In this way, Jung introduced one of his most significant contributions to psychology, but also cut himself off from mainstream psychoanalysis. Furthermore, he bequeathed a problem to those of us who have followed his line: Jung himself preferred to work with those patients with whom there was only a mild transference, and in particular with those whose ego was strong enough to make use of, and integrate, what emerged from the unconscious. Consequently, he referred his more borderline patients, and those that he felt needed a reductive (i.e., "Freudian") analysis of their infantile material, to colleagues (Wiener, 2009). Many post-Jungian practitioners who have wanted to work with a broader patient population have thus frequently turned to psychoanalysis for help.

I do not believe that Jung's proposed resolution of the problem of repetition compulsion was wholly successful, even if his critique of Freud's over-emphasis on infantile sexuality had substance (not least because not all trauma is of a sexual nature). I believe that Jung set up a false dichotomy between infantile neurosis, embodied in the traumatic complex, and the broader vision of the self. Specifically, I would argue that the "infantile complexes" need to be worked through in order to successfully and stably achieve the expanded, broader sense of self (held by the ego) and more fluid contact with, and use of, what emerges from the unconscious self. Even though there are times when Jung appeared to appreciate that it was not *either* addressing the complexes *or* recognizing the spirit, he didn't always proceed as if that was the case. I think this is because he took the problem to be due to the "narrowness" of the ego itself, a position that I have previously argued against (West, 2008), rather than the traumatic experiences that cause the ego to operate narrowly until they are worked through. It was likely Jung's selective choice of patients that allowed him to maintain this split, as the neurotic individual can, for a while, get around their complexes, while the borderline patient is inextricably bound to their early traumatic experience. Furthermore, I believe it is Jung's attitude toward the ego (including his relative lack of interest in it) that lies at the heart of the ongoing split from psychoanalysis, as it has sometimes led to his psychology seeming otherworldly and less well-suited to addressing certain psychopathologies. Having said that, I will here offer a way of looking at Jung's contributions regarding the spirit that will hopefully make his approach more comprehensible and accessible.

Fundamentally, I understand psychoanalytic practitioners to be working through the individual's early traumatic experience (embodied in their traumatic complexes) in the context of the analytic relationship,[2] and I believe that this approach can potentially lead to the same release from narrow ego-functioning, the same fluid relationship with the unconscious, the same openness for the individual to be guided by the unconscious/self as can be achieved in Jungian analysis; viz. the work of Ogden (2009) or Bion (1965, 1970). I would argue, therefore, that the dichotomy is, at least potentially, a false one.

Irreconcilable language?

A number of Jungian theorists (e.g., Haule, 1984; Astor, 2002; Shamdasani, 2003; Morey, 2005; Saban, 2016) have pointed out the fundamental differences in the way that Freud and Jung considered the ego and the psyche, focusing particularly on whether dissociated elements of the psyche are necessarily pathological, as some psychoanalysts appear to have held (Freud, Klein, Winnicott), or whether a measure of dissociation is to be found in the normal psyche (Myers, 1888; Jung, 1934, para 218). As Jung put it, these are a natural phenomenon of the psyche, which could be considered as "attempts of the future personality to break through" (1902/1957, para. 136).

While it is significant whether dissociation is considered inherently pathological, all clinicians would presumably agree that it is helpful to work toward integration of dissociated parts of the personality. Jung (1921/1928) certainly held that this was to be aimed for, even if he recognized that the process was interminable and that the ego would always be subject to the individual's complexes. He held that integration of the dissociated elements of the personality was one of the characteristics that distinguished his attitude to trauma from that of Freud, whom he characterized as recommending abreaction (ibid.).

I do not believe that this different attitude to dissociation makes a rapprochement impossible, and, in their respective papers, Morey (2005) and Saban (2016) simply argue for this difference to be taken into account. Their objection is focused on Winnicott's pathologizing of Jung's "split personality" and Winnicott's consequent dismissal of analytical psychology, a position I have also challenged (West, 2016a, chapter 19).[3] In this light, it might be noted that while Winnicott (1960) theorizes that the infant needs to bring their early experience into their sphere of omnipotence, Jung stresses the significance of experiences of powerlessness and the "defeat of the ego," famously stating that "the experience of the self is always a defeat for the ego" (1955–1956, para. 778). Of course, it might be argued that by embracing this defeat, the individual in a sense brings it into their sphere of omnipotence, although there will now be a difference in the way the individual considers, experiences, and constellates their sense of agency; for example, whether they consider that they should guide their lives by conscious control, or whether they rely on intuition and a deep sense of what is congruent. This, perhaps, represents a key difference between analytical psychology and psychoanalysis, or rather, between the individuals who are attracted to the practice of each.

The loss of the trauma perspective

It is commonly understood that in abandoning the seduction theory, Freud became convinced that the individual's infantile sexuality played the key role, and that in most cases no sexual violation had occurred. Krystal (1978) has argued, however, that in fact Freud continued to hold two theories—the "unbearable situation" model, which stresses the role of actual trauma, and the "unacceptable impulse" model, which emphasizes the way that the child's sexual and aggressive wishes threaten the ego. Despite the co-existence of these two models, it was the latter model that became the dominant theory strain in the early development of psychoanalysis. Melanie Klein is particularly well known for focusing on the pathogenic nature of the individual's innate envy and destructiveness. While recognizing that traumatic experience might play a part, she argued that it was a minor one, and specifically disagreed with Fairbairn on the significance of the bad (traumatizing) object (Klein, 1946, p. 3 ff.).

Similarly, while Jung began his clinical work studying trauma through his word association experiments, he, too, became more interested in other phenomena, writing in *The Symbols of Transformation*:

A person sinks into his childhood memories and vanishes from the existing world. He finds himself apparently in deepest darkness, but then has unexpected visions of a world beyond. The "mystery" he beholds represents the stock of primordial images which everybody brings with him as his human birthright, the sum total of inborn forms peculiar to the instincts. I have called this "potential" psyche the collective unconscious.

(Jung, 1911/1912, para. 631)

The Jung–Klein hybrid

What, then, of the role of trauma in subsequent Jungian thinking? While post-Jungian analysis has developed in many different ways and directions, the so-called London School, led by such figures as Michael Fordham, Louis Zinkin, Fred Plaut, Rosemary Gordon, Kenneth Lambert, and Joe Redfearn at the Society of Analytical Psychology, were particularly interested in two overlapping strands of theory and clinical experience: first, understanding how Klein's work and Jung's ideas of the self and individuation apply to the early years of development, and second, applying Kleinian ideas on the transference, countertransference, and projective identification to working with borderline states of mind. Fordham pointed out that Jung and Klein shared a similar perception of the significance of unconscious phantasy, which he linked to Jung's concept of archetypes (Fordham, 1993). Building on Fordham's work, and interested in exploring the similarities and differences between analytical psychology and psychoanalytic ways of thinking, Astor noted the centrality of "certain patterns in the development of the individual," which he thus related to the collective, as a link between the two fields (2002, p. 608). Many contemporary colleagues have found this kind of integration helpful and have often drawn from this line of thinking when working with more borderline or narcissistic patients. Fordham considered that such patients were demonstrating "defences of the self" (Fordham, 1974) and, linking his position to Herbert Rosenfeld's in *Impasse and Interpretation*, suggested that they "struggle with a monstrously destructive demon, the death instinct" (Fordham, 1993, p. 236).

While this integration of Kleinian ways of thinking has offered a fertile approach for many Jungians to work with more disturbed patients, Jean Knox has pointed out that "the Kleinian model proposes innate complex psychic imagery arising directly from instinctual drives with very little contribution from the external world" (1999, p. 524). If real world traumatic experience is considered to be pathogenically fundamental, then this calls into question the Kleinian position and thus, the Jung–Klein hybrid.

An early relational perspective

Empirical studies of the interaction between mothers and infants (e.g., Bowlby, 1969; Ainsworth *et al.*, 1978; Stern, 1985/1998; Beebe & Lachmann, 2002, 2013; Tronick, 2007; Boston Change Process Study Group, 2010) have allowed us to

understand in more detail the way that early parent–infant interactions can be traumatic, and how these interactions can become embedded in the individual's implicit
behavior and internal working models (Bowlby, 1969), their "ways of being with
others" (Stern, 1985/1998), or their implicit relational knowing (Lyons-Ruth,
1998). Thus, while an individual who is nihilistic, suicidal, despairing, and angry
might be understood to be making an oral- or anal-sadistic attack on the analyst
(Klein, 1946), through the lens of early relational trauma we can now understand
how such a person is staying true to, and is bound to, their negative affective core
(Tronick & Gianino, 1986), born of repeated failures to positively engage with
and repair mismatches with a parent. Attempts to move away from such experience before it has been properly worked through in the analytic relationship are
unrealistic and will be resisted by the patient, leading to the phenomena that Freud
described under the rubric of a negative therapeutic reaction, particularly when this
early experience forms the core of the individual's identity.

We can see how such early traumatic experience disrupts the development of the
individual's ego-functioning,[4] and how the person is, in the analysis, re-enacting
their implicit, early relational patterns; for example, of not being responded to and
having hope and connection extinguished by a depressed parent (these are the
trauma-related internal working models that structure the child's future behavior
and understanding). This re-enactment can be understood as a co-construction
whereby the patient, in an unconscious identification with the aggressor, negates
the analyst's attempts to communicate and connect, while the patient experiences
the analyst as insufficiently responsive and as inhibiting the patient's attempt to
establish a connection. The patient's negative perception of the analyst will doubt-
less have some basis in the reality of the analytic exchanges, perhaps because the
analyst gives up trying to connect on some key occasions, feeling that they are
being continually frustrated in their attempts to make positive contact.[5] It is these
ways of being that are "slouching towards Bethlehem," as Nina Coltart (1986)
described the way that problematic patterns of relationship make themselves manifest in the analytic relationship. The analyst being open to, rather than resisting
and frustrating, these emerging patterns is a key element in analysis. Thus, rather
than being seen as being manifestly destructive or enviously wishing to destroy the
analyst's healthy functioning (which they may, of course, nonetheless wish to do),
the patient can be understood to be enactively demonstrating their early relational
experience as held in procedural memory.

This is where Jung's concept of the complex comes into its own in integrating
recent advances in trauma theory and offering a bridge between analytical psychology and psychoanalysis. The feeling-toned complex "embodies" both the powerful
affective-somatic reactions consequent upon the trauma that disrupts ego-functioning, as well as the trauma-related internal working models and the primitive, talion
response to the aggressor/bad object. As Jung described, the complex contains
"the opposites," or, as I have outlined (West, 2016a), the trauma-related internal
working models operate in direct and reversed forms; for example, the patient
experiences their attempts to connect as negated (the direct form) while negating

others' attempts to connect (the reversed form).[6] In addition to the disruption of ego-functioning due to powerful affects, this conflict makes it extremely difficult for the individual to develop coherent, effective ego-functioning. This is because it is, initially, hard to reconcile being subject to traumatizing ways of being with subjecting others to them (Liotti, 2004). As a result, the individual is held in thrall to the bad object, which is in some way currently "causing" re-traumatization. To say that the patient has simply projected an unwanted part of themselves into the object through projective identification leaves out both the traumatic roots and the interactive detail of the process, in both historical and immediate terms.

It has been my experience that the analyst falls in with these ways of being precisely because they are implicit, deeply held, and powerfully enacted. The analyst seeks to avoid becoming the traumatizing, bad object, while all the while being experienced incipiently as such. Of course, the analyst's own personality and experiences play a large part here; for example, analysts can rarely bear to expose others to what they cannot themselves bear, so they may make unrealistic, unhelpful, heroic efforts to remain good (Davies & Frawley, 1992). Alternatively, if the analyst cannot bear or, importantly, understand this dynamic, they are likely to blame the patient and simply label them as unanalyzable (see West, 2016b). Additionally, the analyst frequently re-enacts their own early relational patterns, perhaps trying to rescue the patient/parent they had not been able to make better in their childhood (see Harris, 2009).

My criticism of some relational psychoanalytic practitioners is that their approach makes it more difficult for them to embody the bad object (e.g., Benjamin, 2004), or that they sometimes try to disconfirm the patient's experience of seeing themselves as, for example, bad, unlovable, or unattractive (e.g., Davies, 1994), or guiltily "confess" to harboring "bad"/destructive feelings toward the patient (e.g., Davies, 2004), which are, in fact, natural responses to the original traumatic experience that are inevitably co-constructed in the analytic relationship (where they can be usefully explored). If the analyst feels that they are bad or destructive for feeling hatred, how is the patient to come to terms with their own hatred? As Casement says, "an analytic good object [...] is that which can tolerate being used to represent the worst in the patient's experience" (2001, p. 384).

Role responsiveness and projective identification

Understanding the patient–analyst interactions in this way is akin to what Sandler (1993) would call role responsiveness, although I would suggest that the power and intensity in the interaction are almost always due to the fact that the original traumatic experiences were, by definition, unbearable. The analyst therefore senses that they are exposing the patient to extreme and unbearable distress (West, 2016a, chapter 11), even if it may sometimes seem that the patient is chronically "turning molehills into mountains" (Bollas, 2000, p. 9). Furthermore, experiences of, for example, not being responded to frequently feel annihilatory to the individual (see, for example, Bromberg, 2011), so that, rather than these experiences being related to *phantasies* of being killed, the annihilation is experienced as real. I understand these experiences to be related, in part, to the collapse response initiated by extreme threat (see, for example, Porges, 2011), whereby the individual (ego) experiences being "killed off" and the person dissociates; an archetypal example being the antelope that collapses and dissociates just before the lion strikes (which, of course, can equally occur when a person is assaulted or otherwise overwhelmingly threatened). Experiences of murderousness or suicidality can follow directly, either as a talion response to the aggressor, or in order to bring the experience of dying directly into the individual's sphere of omnipotence (Winnicott, 1974).

This is an alternate model to projective identification and its different forms and functions (as fantasy, defense, object relationship, or mode of communication), which I have found to better fit clinical experience; as I have described above, Jung's concept of the complex plays a central role in this understanding. This model has the benefit of putting any question of "destructiveness" (aggression, murderousness, suicidality) in a comprehensible context for both patient and analyst, thereby lessening the sense of shame and blame.

Relating these recent developments in the field back to Freud and Jung's movement away from considering trauma foundational, we can recognize that precisely the characteristics that made Freud doubt some of his patients—their lack of a coherent narrative and exaggerated sexualized reactions—are now recognized to be characteristic of traumatic experience (van der Kolk, 1996). Jung was similarly disillusioned, writing that the impulse to "create the impression that the neurosis is caused by some trauma or other" is based upon "unimportant and secondary occurrences [...] given an artificial prominence for the sake of the theory" (Jung 1921/1928, para. 257). Jung was not then cognizant of how early relational experience can be profoundly traumatic and have a foundational effect on the individual. However, his appreciation of the significance of real world experience and the functioning of the complex throws important light onto this area of work. Knox (1999) has pointed out that trauma has also slowly made a reappearance in psychoanalytic theory through the recognition of, and focus on, anxiety aroused by traumatic events, as well as in extending the understanding of trauma to include attachment and separation issues. The relational movement in psychoanalysis is founded on a recognition of the significance of real world (traumatic) experience (Mitchell & Aron, 1999).

Jung's contribution and the development of the ego

So why did Jung think that the individual has to leave their "family fixations [...] and uncontrolled infantile feelings" behind (1911/1912, para. 644), and where does the spiritual vertex come in? While Jung, like Freud and Janet, recognized that the individual can get stuck in the repetition of their traumatic experiences, he felt that the problem lay, in part, with the nature of the ego itself, and that a spiritual response was called for. This can be understood in terms of the developmental pathway of the ego and Jung's conceptualization of the self.

In healthy development, the individual is able to expand and broaden the way they see themselves to include experiences of, for example, failure, loss, success, triumph, aggression, hate, and so on. Each expansion represents a shift, and sometimes a seismic, category shift, from the way the person saw themselves before, and will usually require a disidentification from the previous, narrower way of seeing themselves. Thus, the person who perceives themselves to be "wholly good" will have to disidentify from that self-image in order to recognize their hatred or envy; the person who sees themselves as uniformly successful will have to disidentify from that picture in order to integrate experiences of failure; and the person who sees themselves as unlovable will have to sufficiently disidentify from this image to accept experiences of being loved. These self-perceptions will likely have been reinforced by relationally traumatic experiences of, for example, a critical parent who demanded good behavior, proscribed failure, or left the person feeling unlovable. Experiences of this kind establish complexes that will need working through in the analytic relationship before there can be a shift in self-perception. While there may be some loss associated with each of these changes, there is also the potential for gain, as the resulting organization is more realistic and thus more easily maintained.[7] This alleviates the pressure on the immature, narrowly functioning ego to attempt to control the self (in the everyday sense of the word) and the world.

While the individual (ego) suffers the defeat of realizing that he or she is not wholly in control of their environment, a further vertex opens up, and the individual may, over time, discover that they can to some extent trust their psyche: that whatever emerges from the unconscious has a meaning, purpose, and place, that they can allow themselves to be guided by intuition and, to some extent, to hand themselves over and be led by what Jung called the self.[8] This process tends to be incremental in nature, with the individual slowly relinquishing conscious control and trusting more in unconscious processes and the core self. This change recognizes the depth and sophistication of unconscious functioning and represents a shift in the center of gravity from cognitive functioning and control, an embracing of "not knowing" and of allowing oneself to be flexibly in touch with the unconscious.[9] This is perhaps similar to what Bion (1965, 1970) was referring to when he talked of Faith and the experience of O. This process need not be understood in terms of relinquishing the ego, but rather, as allowing ego-functioning to operate more broadly, including being flexibly in touch with the unconscious (West, 2008, 2016a).[10] Jungian analysis has conceptualized this in terms of the ego–self relationship (Edinger, 1972).

The process of relaxing the ego's attempts to be in control can also be more radical, whereby the individual takes what Kierkegaard called "a leap of faith" and puts themselves in the hands of God, the universe, or however else the person may envisage it. As Jung puts it, "there are things greater than the ego's will and to these we must bow" (1963, p. 181); for Jung, this is the self, which represents the inner empirical deity (see Edinger, 1972) with which the ego must be careful not to identify (lest inflation follow), yet to which the ego is subject and can come to form a vital relationship through the process of individuation. To give a clinical example, this view is enshrined in the 12-step Alcoholics Anonymous program (in the inception of which Jung and his work played a role[11]), the first three steps of which state:

1   We admitted we were powerless over alcohol—that our lives had become unmanageable.
2   Came to believe that a Power greater than ourselves could restore us to sanity.
3   Made a decision to turn our will and our lives over to the care of God as we understood Him.

(Wilson, 2001)

A person in the grip of an alcoholic addiction attempts to control their experience through the use of a substance, and thus to avoid the traumatic complexes and harsh realities which beset their lives. Addiction is rarely overcome through willpower alone, but rather through establishing a connection with the whole psyche and the reality-orienting functions that reside therein; for example, the deep knowing that you have taken a wrong turn in life. These functions "demand" that the individual face their difficulties and put aside the ego's misguided attempts to control through the use of alcohol. The more radical process of "experiencing a conversion" is not a direct aspect of the analytical psychologist's work, but those who seek out Jungian analysis have often had such experiences or seek psychological help from someone who will be sympathetic to those experiences.

In addition to relaxing control and trusting in their unconscious processes and the core self, it is the process of disidentification, which I outlined earlier, that relates most directly to Jung's previously cited claim that the person needs to separate from their "family fixations and uncontrolled infantile feelings." The process of disidentification is uncanny, and essentially spiritual in nature. In relinquishing a particular identification and recognizing that I am "not that," the individual enters a liminal space in which they are particularly open to the functioning of the core self. Specifically, they can experience the unconscious functioning that recognizes the sameness between one thing and another. Matte Blanco (1975) called this "symmetrization." It is fundamental to our functioning from an early age, since, in order to recognize that "this is mother," the infant has to recognize her similarity to previously held senses of her. Similarly, our experience of what is good or bad, safe or dangerous, is built up through the similarity to previous good or bad, safe or dangerous experiences. Bowlby described how we are all the time unconsciously "appraising" the value and quality of experience, which relies on just this primitive functioning.[12]

This sameness-recognizing function lies behind the experience of connectedness that an individual might feel when they are, for example, out walking in nature, or in any situation when the individual's ego-identifications are lowered. Such an experience might occur spontaneously when the individual has become absorbed in what they are doing, or more intentionally through the practice of meditation or mindfulness techniques that enable the practitioner to disidentify with the contents of consciousness. This is not without risk, as, without stable identifications, the individual can easily be taken over by their traumatic complexes and swallowed up in reliving experiences of loss, rejection, or abuse, or in making manic-omnipotent attempts to avoid such experiences.[13] Alternatively, through spiritual practice, an individual may continue the process of disidentification and come to question or reject all identifications: "if I am not that, nor that, nor that, then perhaps I am nothing." Of course, if someone chooses to live in a wholly "spiritual" frame divorced from all ego-identifications, then that is their prerogative. However, I would suggest that disidentification is a natural, passing state in the process of broadening identifications; this might include the experience of being no-thing, or, as I have put it previously, recognizing that "the not-I is also who I am" (West, 2008). It can, of course, be that seeking spiritual experience serves as an avoidance of traumatic experience and the traumatic complex (which tend to have an angry, "egocentric" component). This is unlikely to be successful in the long term however, since, to the extent that early traumatic experiences have not been integrated with ego experience, the associated complexes will likely reassert themselves at some other point.

Conclusion

Working through the individual's early relational traumatic experience, as embodied in their complexes, makes the complexes less powerful and allows those experiences to be integrated so that the ego can function more broadly and less defensively (West, 2016a). Addressing infantile experience and recognizing the role of the spiritual vertex in the development of the ego are two necessary aspects of the process of development that Jung called individuation. I cannot know what elements, if any, post-Jungian, post-Freudian, post-Kleinian, or relational psychoanalytic practitioners would recognize or accept (although I suspect that much of the clinical section would be familiar to a Middle School Freudian or a relational psychoanalyst). I can only hope that, as well as demystifying Jung's position, what I have outlined will demonstrate how the different theoretical trajectories can complement and contribute to each other.

Notes

1   Jung quotes Jesus in his response to Nicodemus, who had asked, "How can a man be born when he is old? Can he enter the second time into his mother's womb, and be born?" to which Jesus replied, "Except a man be born of water and of the Spirit, he cannot enter into the kingdom of God" (Jung, 1911/1912, para. 333).

2   This working through in the analytic relationship involves the "whole person" of the analyst, as recommended and described by Jung as early as 1921 (see Jung, 1921/1928, para. 269 ff.).

3   I suggest that Jung's split between his number 1 and number 2 personalities, besides being rooted in his early infantile trauma (the early "defeat" of his ego), also reflects a split between an everyday ego perspective (personality no. 1) and a perspective open to the unconscious/self (personality no. 2). Jung could, with some justification, claim that these different aspects of the personality are "played out in every individual" (Jung, 1963, p. 52), even if most people do not have discrete personality complexes centered on them. This split lies at the heart of what Jungians think of in terms of the ego–self axis.

4 Herman (1992) would class this as an element of complex post-traumatic stress disorder, while van der Kolk would describe it as developmental trauma.

5 The relational psychoanalytic movement describes such interactions particularly well; see, for example, Davies and Frawley (1992), although this intersubjective view was presaged by Jung (1921/1928) and Winnicott (1974).

6 See also Perry (1970) and Meares (2012).

7 This also goes on unconsciously, partly through dreaming, and is a key element in the process of individuation (see West, 2011; Wilkinson, 2006).

8 I use the term "core self" rather than "self" to denote that the experiences I am describing follow from fundamental and often primitive, yet sophisticated, functions of the psyche that go on unconsciously (see below), as well as to counter an idealized view of the unconscious/self that sometimes prevails in Jungian circles. See West (2007) for further discussion.

9 As Morey put it, "It is my contention that as Jungian analysts our essential target is our effort to understand, reflect upon and connect with the living psyche, a notion that includes more than Winnicott's unconscious" (2005, p. 348).

10 The processes of defensive control and narrow identification are not, therefore, intrinsic to the ego.

11 Jung suggested to a former patient, Roland Hazard, who had had an alcoholic relapse, that he should "put himself in a position to experience a conversion." Hazard went on to experience just such a conversion, with this experience being influential in the beginnings of AA (Addenbrooke, 2011, pp. 8–9).

12 This suggests further confluences between Jungian, attachment theory, infant developmental, and psychoanalytic ways of thinking.

13 While Jung saw the self as over and above such personal experience, my embodied conceptualization of the core self recognizes that, through traumatization, the individual can experience "soul murder" and loss of contact with the (core) self, which is only re-established securely by working through the traumatic complex, as I have described.

References

Addenbrooke, M. (2011). *Survivors of addiction: Narratives of recovery*. Hove: Routledge.

Ainsworth, M., Blehar, M., Waters, E., & Wall, S. (1978). *Patterns of attachment: Assessed in the strange situation and at home*. Hillsdale: Erlbaum.

Astor, J. (2002). Analytical psychology and its relation to psychoanalysis. *Journal of Analytical Psychology, 47*, 599–612.

Beebe, B., & Lachmann, F. (2002). *Infant research and adult treatment: Co-constructing interactions*. Hillsdale: Analytic.

Beebe, B., & Lachmann, F. (2013). *The origins of attachment: Infant research and adult treatment*. Abingdon: Taylor & Francis.

Benjamin, J. (2004). Beyond doer and done to: An intersubjective view of thirdness. *Psychoanalytic Quarterly, 73*, 5–46.

Bion, W. R. (1965). *Transformations: Change from learning to growth*. London: Tavistock.

Bion, W. R. (1970). *Attention and interpretation*. London: Routledge.

Bollas, C. (2000). *Hysteria*. Abingdon: Taylor & Francis.

Boston Change Process Study Group (BCPSG) (Stern, D. N., Sander, L. W., Nahum, J.P., Harrison, A. M., Lyons-Ruth, K., Morgan, A. C., Bruschweilerstern, N., & Tronick, E. Z.) (2010). *Change in psychotherapy: A unifying paradigm*. New York: Norton.

Bowlby, J. (1969). *Attachment and loss, volume 1: Attachment*. Harmondsworth: Penguin.

Bromberg, P. (2011). *The shadow of the tsunami: And the growth of the relational mind*. New York: Routledge.

Casement, P. J. (2001). Commentaries. *Journal of the American Psychoanalytic Association, 49,* 381–386.

Coltart, N. (1986). Slouching towards Bethlehem … or thinking the unthinkable in psychoanalysis. In Coltart, N. (Ed.), *Slouching towards Bethlehem … and further psychoanalytic Explorations* (pp. 1–14). London: Free Association, 1993.

Davies, J. M. (1994). Love in the afternoon: A relational reconsideration of desire and dread. *Psychoanalytic Dialogues, 4,* 153–170.

Davies, J. M. (2004). Whose bad objects are we anyway? *Psychoanalytic Dialogues, 14,* 711–732.

Davies, J. M., & Frawley, M. G. (1992). Dissociative processes and transference-countertransference paradigms in the psychoanalytically oriented treatment of adult survivors of childhood sexual abuse. *Psychoanalytic Dialogues, 2,* 5–36.

Edinger, E. (1972). *Ego and archetype: Individuation and the religious function of the psyche.* Boston: Shambhala.

Fordham, M. (1974). Defences of the self. *Journal of Analytical Psychology, 19,* 192–199.

Fordham, M. (1993). The Jung–Klein hybrid. *Free Associations, 3,* 631–641.

Harris, A. (2009). You must remember this. *Psychoanalytic Dialogues, 19,* 2–21.

Haule, J. (1984). From somnambulism to the archetypes: The French roots of Jung's split with Freud. *The Psychoanalytic Review, 71,* 635–659.

Herman, J. L. (1992). *Trauma and recovery: The aftermath of violence – from domestic abuse to political terror.* New York: Basic.

Jung, C. G. (1902/1957). On the psychology of so-called occult phenomena. *CW 1.* London: Routledge & Kegan Paul.

Jung, C. G. (1911–12). *Symbols of transformation. CW 5.* London: Routledge & Kegan Paul.

Jung, C. G. (1921/1928). The therapeutic value of abreaction. In: *The practice of psychotherapy. CW 16.* London: Routledge & Kegan Paul.

Jung, C. G. (1934). A review of the complex theory. In: *The structure and dynamics of the psyche. CW 8.* London: Routledge & Kegan Paul.

Jung, C. G. (1955–1956). *Mysterium coniunctionis. CW 14.* London: Routledge & Kegan Paul.

Jung, C. G. (1963). *Memories, dreams, reflections,* A. Jaffé (Ed.). New York: Random House.

Klein, M. (1946). Notes on some schizoid mechanisms. In: *Envy and gratitude and other works, 1946–1963* (pp. 1–24). London: Virago.

Knox, J. (1999). The relevance of attachment theory to a contemporary Jungian view of the internal world. *Journal of Analytical Psychology, 44,* 511–530.

Krystal, H. (1978). Trauma and affects. *Psychoanalytic study of the child, 33,* 81–116.

Liotti, G. (2004). Trauma, dissociation, and disorganized attachment: Three strands of a single braid. *Psychotherapy: Theory, Research, Practice, Training, 41,* 472–486.

Lyons-Ruth, K. (1998). Implicit relational knowing: Its role in development and psychoanalytic treatment. *Infant Mental Health Journal, 19,* 282–289.

Matte Blanco, I. (1975). *The unconscious as infinite sets.* London: Karnac.

Meares, R. (2012). *A dissociation model of borderline personality disorder.* New York: Norton.

Mitchell, S., & Aron, L. (1999). *Relational psychoanalysis: The emergence of a tradition.* Hillsdale: Analytic.

Morey, J. R. (2005). Winnicott's splitting headache: Considering the gap between Jungian and object relations concepts. *Journal of Analytical Psychology, 5,* 333–350.

Myers, F. W. H. (1888). French experiments in strata of personality. *Proceedings of the Society of Psychical Research, 5,* 374–397.

Ogden, T. (2009). *Rediscovering psychoanalysis: Thinking and dreaming, learning and forgetting.* Hove: Routledge.

Perry, J. W. (1970). Emotions and object relations. *Journal of Analytical Psychology, 15*, 1–12.

Porges, S. W. (2011). *The polyvagal theory: Neurophysiological foundations of emotions, attachment, communication, and self-regulation.* New York: Norton.

Saban, M. (2016). Jung, Winnicott and the divided psyche. *Journal of Analytical Psychology, 61*, 329–349.

Sandler, J. (1993). On communication from patient to analyst: Not everything is projective identification. *International Journal of Psychoanalysis, 74*, 1097–1107.

Shamdasani, S. (2003). *Jung and the making of modern psychology: The dream of a science.* Cambridge: Cambridge University Press.

Stern, D. N. (1985/1998). *The interpersonal world of the infant: A view from psychoanalysis and developmental psychology.* London: Karnac.

Tronick, E. Z. (2007). *The neurobehavioural and social-emotional development of infants and children* (pp. 402–411). New York: Norton.

Tronick, E. Z., & Gianino, A. (1986). Interactive mismatch and repair: Challenges to the coping infant. *Zero to Three, Bulletin of the National Center for Clinical Infant Programs, 5*, 1–6.

van der Kolk, B. (1996). Trauma and memory. In: A.C. McFarlane, L. Weisaeth, & B. Van der Kolk (Eds), *Traumatic stress: The effects of overwhelming experience on mind, body, and society* (pp. 279–302). New York: Guilford.

West, M. (2007). *Feeling, being and the sense of self: A new perspective on identity, affect and narcissistic disorders.* London: Karnac.

West, M. (2008). The narrow use of the term ego in analytical psychology: The "not-I" is also who I am. *Journal of Analytical Psychology, 53*, 367–388.

West, M. (2011). *Understanding dreams in clinical practice.* London: Karnac.

West, M. (2016a). *Into the darkest places: Early relational trauma and borderline states of mind.* London and New York: Karnac.

West, M. (2016b). Working in the borderland: Early relational trauma and Fordham's analysis of "K". *Journal of Analytical Psychology, 61*, 44–62.

Wiener, J. (2009). *The therapeutic relationship: Transference, countertransference, and the making of meaning.* College Station: Texas A & M University Press.

Wilkinson, M. (2006) *Coming into mind: The mind-brain relationship: A jungian clinical perspective.* New York: Taylor & Francis.

Wilson, B. (2001). *Alcoholics Anonymous* (PDF) (4th ed.). Alcoholics Anonymous World Services. ISBN 1-893007-16-2. OCLC 32014950; www.aa.org/pages/en_US/alcoholics-anonymous.

Winnicott, D. W. (1960). The theory of the parent-infant relationship. *International Journal of Psychoanalysis, 41*, 585–595.

Winnicott, D. W. (1974). Fear of breakdown. *International Review of Psychoanalysis, 1*, 103–107.

10

WHERE DO MINDS MEET?

Mutual recognition in light of Jung

Robin S. Brown

TALK TO YOUR BABY   THEIR BRAIN DEPENDS ON IT

Thus ran the slogan for a recent New York City public health campaign (nyc.gov, 2015). Alarming though it is that parents might require encouragement to communicate with their newborn children, a more insidious danger is perhaps reflected in the justification given—that the lived experience of the child (or parent) would be deemed a less persuasive basis for argument than the health of a bodily organ is, I feel, a less readily acknowledged concern than might be warranted. For people to be valued first and foremost as material objects has alarming implications. In so far as the human subject is interpreted on the assumption of an objective recognition of his or her physical nature (whether in terms of neuroanatomy or, more simply, physical appearance), a gesture is made such as to disempower the individual. For this reason, it may be considered significant that the relational turn in psychoanalysis has placed considerable emphasis on the role of subjectivity. But to what extent have contemporary analysts succeeded in challenging the fundamentally totalitarian assumption of the subject's one-sided dependence on the object?

The question is complicated, for while relational analysts have emphasized the clinician's irreducible subjectivity (Renik, 1993), the thrust of contemporary discourse has concerned itself not with championing subjectivity *per se*, but more with recognizing the role played by the *analyst's* subjectivity in terms of clinical technique. In fact, the constructivist leanings of some relational thinkers have sometimes threatened to reduce subjectivity itself to a depthless and purely social phenomenon (Brown, 2017b). But while relational conceptions of the individual are thus prone to implicitly legitimize systemic power, this tendency is seemingly counterbalanced by the fashion in which relationalists have sought to destabilize clinical authority. Correspondingly, the notion of subjectivity has often been raised only in the context of a different kind of conversation concerning *inter*subjectivity, with shifting assumptions concerning the former only emerging through careful engagement with the latter. Thinking again of our brainy babies, we might ask to what extent psychoanalytic conceptions of intersubjectivity offer a less reductive means of interpreting the encounter with another person.

This chapter will argue that, despite appearances, relational conceptions of intersubjectivity often imply a fundamentally isolated model of mind, resulting in lingering implications of biological and/or linguistic reductionism. In seeking to challenge this tendency, it will be suggested that Jungian thinking has much to offer. Jung's transpersonal approach to the psyche has sometimes been understood to reinforce classical conceptions of the self as fundamentally alienated from others—this being reflected in the implication of the other being treated merely as a "screen" for archetypal projections. I will suggest that readings of this kind fail to acknowledge that Jung's notion of the collective unconscious moves beyond reductive conceptions of spiritual a prioris to express a radically communal approach to the psyche. How might post-Jungian notions of intersubjectivity challenge and supplement mainstream psychoanalytic ideas about relationship? With particular attention to the work of Jessica Benjamin and Thomas Ogden, I argue that a transpersonal conception of the third is theoretically necessary if the notion of mutual recognition is to be considered meaningful.

An equivalent center of being

As is often acknowledged, the term "intersubjectivity" has been adopted by analysts to encompass a range of theoretical perspectives so diverse as to render casual use of the term problematic. Nevertheless, that the term itself has been adopted so broadly suggests that it exhibits a connotative appeal which appears to express something of the recent psychoanalytic zeitgeist. In the present context, I am concerned to emphasize the fashion in which this notion has come to suggest the possibility of what Lewis Aron (1996), following Loewald (1980), refers to as a "meeting of minds." It should be noted that this use of the word is at odds with the intersubjectivist thinking associated with Robert Stolorow and his colleagues. While Stolorow, Atwood, and Ross (1978) are widely regarded as having introduced the term "intersubjectivity" to American psychoanalysis, they adopt it to signify "any psychological field formed by interacting worlds of experience" (Stolorow & Atwood, 1992, p. 3). This definition has been criticized by Jessica Benjamin for failing to differentiate the intersubjective from the interpersonal. Benjamin (1999a) suggests that the term should be reserved for "the specific matter of recognizing the other as an equivalent center of being" (p. 201). For Benjamin, intersubjectivity thus expresses a relationship of "mutual recognition" such that each participant acknowledges the other as an equivalent yet distinct center of consciousness.

Benjamin conceptualizes mutual recognition in terms of the emergence of *thirdness*. The third is a notion that has frequently been invoked to signify a point of reference existing outside of the relational dyad, such as to enable the creation of triangular space and the recognition of bi-directionality. This notion is given early expression by Lacan, for whom the third is considered necessary so as to prevent relationship from becoming a fight to the death. Benjamin objects to the emphasis common to both Lacanians and Kleinians on perceiving the oedipal father as emblematic of the third. Drawing from infant attachment studies, she argues that a latent form of non-verbal thirdness is established from the outset within the maternal situation. In this connection, Benjamin's conceptualization of intersubjectivity is significantly influenced by Daniel Stern, who in turn draws his own definition from Trevarthan and Hubley (1978): "a deliberately sought sharing of experiences about events and things" (p. 213). Trevarthan (1979) elsewhere posits a condition of "primary intersubjectivity." Similarly, while Stern contends that intersubjectivity proper does not emerge until 9–12 months, he nevertheless asserts that "beginning at birth the infant enters into an intersubjective matrix" (2004, p. 90). Benjamin (1988) wishes to supplement this line of thought by drawing attention to the role played by conflict. While emphasizing the notion of primary intersubjectivity, Benjamin also seeks to accommodate Margaret Mahler's notion of separation-individuation. Drawing from Winnicott's (1971) ideas concerning the destruction of an object, Benjamin argues that the object's negation and subsequent survival are what enables mutual recognition—a developmental accomplishment that she links to Winnicott's potential space. Although a basic condition of intersubjectivity is given to the infant from the outset, the other person only comes to exist for them in their own right having been able to withstand the infant's omnipotent attacks. In coming to recognize the existence of other people, we thus come to realize that our own existence is contingent upon their recognition of us. The stark contrast experienced between the needs of self-assertion and those of recognition results in a conflict of interests that is, in Benjamin's view, best resolved by maintaining a constant tension between object-relational and intersubjective positions.

The paradoxical nature of recognition expresses the extent to which Benjamin's reading of Winnicott is informed by Hegel's master-slave dialectic. But for Benjamin, intersubjectivity is about more than the clash of wills and the mirroring function of the other. Essential to her approach is what she postulates as our inherent need for recognition of others *as* others. This need is considered additional to those of object relating, and is posited to operate alongside of them. Aron (2000) emphasizes that both patient and analyst are pulled back and forth between intersubjective and intrapsychic modes of relating, and that the triangular space of recognition must inevitably make way for perceiving the other as an object of needs and wishes. As Benjamin (2004) states, "This collapse can take the form of merger (oneness), eliminating difference, or of a two-ness that splits the differences—the polarized opposition of the power struggle" (p. 12). These dynamics can be seen at play in the clinical situation, in which context the recognition of the analyst as a distinct subject plays a central role in enabling the emergence of reflective space in the patient.

The notion of mutual recognition clearly suggests a major challenge to earlier psychoanalytic conceptions of relationship. While in classical terms the concept of cathexis has given expression to the idea that individuals are not directly invested in other people but merely in their representations of them, Benjamin (1990) boldly states: "where objects were, subjects must be" (p. 34). The nature of this intersubjective recognition, however, remains somewhat enigmatic. While the notion of "the real relationship" has historically served as a means of signifying the interaction between individuals in the absence of the distorting influence of transference, the relational shift has indicated a rather complicated challenge to this—recognition of the other person has been empowered as a basis for change, yet the notion that we might speak of any relationship on essentially objective terms has been thrown into doubt. Benjamin surely doesn't intend mutual recognition in such a light. Intersubjectivity is essentially described as the capacity to *imagine* the possibility of difference—this does not seem equivalent to a concern for directly encountering it. Benjamin's lack of engagement with what we might term the "substance" of intersubjective experience is reflected in her approach to thirdness—for Benjamin (2004), the third is defined as "anything one holds in mind that creates another point of reference outside the dyad" (p. 7). As such, thirdness is posited as a mental space which creates room for the other person, thus enabling surrender of the need to coerce or control. Benjamin therefore professes not to be concerned with the different kinds of third that might be postulated (examples of which would include the Oedipal father, speech/language, the analyst's theory, or the professional community), but rather with the emergence of the mental space that seemingly allows for such a notion to be held in the first place.

While Benjamin explicitly acknowledges the interdependence of the intrapsychic and intersubjective domains, she nevertheless conceptualizes them in relative independence. An alternative approach might seek to locate intersubjectivity more directly within the structure of object relations. Doing so, however, clearly jeopardizes the explicit conscious recognition of the other which Benjamin posits as the essential feature of an intersubjective position. Following Freud's claim that the analyst should "turn his own unconscious like a receptive organ towards the transmitting unconscious of the patient" (1912, p. 115), and reflecting his contention that "the Ucs. of one human being can react upon that of another, without passing through the Cs." (1915, p. 194), such an approach has been particularly associated with the Kleinian lineage, and has been exemplified in North America by the work of Thomas Ogden. It is this strand of thinking that also bears most direct comparison to Jung.

Projective identification and *participation mystique*

In distinction to Benjamin's emphasis on mutual recognition, Ogden's approach to intersubjectivity focuses on the communication of unconscious affect. His notion of thirdness is fundamentally informed by the clinical experience of projective identification. Benjamin (2004) differentiates her understanding of the third from Ogden's (1994) "subjugating third" by pointing out that Ogden's approach doesn't have to do with the creation of space but rather with the consumption of it—she thus suggests that we would be more correct to speak of Ogden's third as "the negative third" (p. 10). While for Benjamin the third is conscious and enables relief from the merger versus kill-or-be-killed dynamics of the dyad, for Ogden the third is largely unconscious and is experienced as imposing on freedom. Ogden (1994) describes the third as follows:

> The analytic process reflects the interplay of three subjectivities: the subjectivity of the analyst, of the analysand, and of the analytic third. The analytic third is the creation of the analyst and analysand, and at the same time the analyst and analysand (qua analyst and analysand) are created by the analytic third. (There is no analyst, no analysand, no analysis in the absence of the third.)
>
> *(p. 93)*

Drawing from the work of Bion, Ogden emphasizes the use of reverie as a means of accessing a third area that is co-constructed by both partners in the relationship. Entering into a mild hypnogogic state, the analyst is encouraged to attend to their fleeting thoughts and somatic experiences so as to intuitively recover unconscious elements of the patient's experience. Expanding on the work of Klein and Bion, Ogden (1986) argues that projective identification shouldn't be understood simply in terms of the caregiver metabolizing experiences for the infant, since a definition of this nature fails to explain how the infant's capacity to process experience is itself transformed in the process. Ogden therefore argues that only by recognizing the caregiver–infant relationship as an entity does the possibility emerge for new forms of experience. This would appear to move projective identification beyond the kind of symbolic exchange potentially implied in weaker readings of this idea. In fact, Ogden goes so far as to state that projective identification "bridges the intrapsychic and the interpersonal" (p. 39).

Ogden's conclusions find extensive support in the Jungian literature. Drawing attention to shifting conceptions of countertransference during the mid-twentieth century, Gordon (1965) provides an early recognition of the importance that Jung's thinking may have in terms of understanding projective identification as a transpersonal phenomenon:

> it is probably a process which, if it is sufficiently primitive and elemental, may really break down the boundaries between persons and lead to truly shared experiences. Admittedly, some of the emotional sharing may be the result of conscious or pre-conscious and subliminal perceptions. But some of these so-called perceptions, when they are described, seem almost more truly *post hoc* than *propter hoc*. [...] However, in order to account for projective identification as a fact rather than as merely a phantasy, we must have recourse to Jung's own concepts, such as *participation mystique*, the collective unconscious, and his conception of the psychoid.
>
> *(p. 145)*

Some 50 years ago, Gordon had already recognized that Jung's psychology might provide a suitable vocabulary to give voice to emerging psychoanalytic concerns pertaining to the nature of relationship. Nevertheless, Jung's own thinking in this respect remains inconclusive and at times contradictory. The fashion in which he deploys the notion of *participation mystique*[1] demonstrates the ways in which his approach might appear to align with conventional psychoanalytic assumptions concerning disenchantment. In *Psychological Types*, he defines "identity" as an unconscious phenomenon:

> It is a characteristic of the primitive mentality, and is the actual basis of *participation mystique*, which in reality is merely a relic of the original psychological non-differentiation of subject and object, and hence of the primordial unconscious state. It is also a characteristic of the mental state of early infancy, and, finally, of the unconscious of the civilized adult, which, in so far as it has not become a content of consciousness, remains in a permanent state of identity with objects.
>
> *(Jung, 1921, p. 441)*

Ironically, from a contemporary vantage point, it seems that Jung's approach to *participation mystique* might suffer from its own lack of differentiation—the experience of the newborn child, "the primitive," the neurotic, and the mob are all interpreted in terms of the same underlying phenomenon, and in a fashion that is liable to seem reductive. Segal (2007) has claimed that Jung's approach to this notion in fact reflects a misreading: "by *participation mystique* Lévy-Bruhl means the ascription to others of what we recognize, not what we deny, in ourselves. He means the assumption of outright identity between us and others" (p. 645). With the emphasis that Jung's understanding of *participation mystique* places on projection, a sense emerges that the process of individuation entails an increasing awareness of fundamental alienation—a sense that seems to be reinforced by the nature of the term itself. Objecting to this tendency in Jung, Schwartz-Salant (1988) draws attention to the way in which Jung emphasizes the negative aspects of projective identification, as reflected in his explicit emphasis on psychotherapy being concerned with the dissolution of *participation mystique* (Jung, 1967, p. 45).

Nevertheless, in "The Psychology of the Transference" Jung (1946) is at pains to emphasize the shared nature of the analytic relationship. This is reflected both in his well-known analogy of transformation in chemical substances and in his claim that the analyst must take on the sufferings of his patient so that they become his own. Jung's illustrative use of the alchemical woodcuts of the *Rosarium Philosophorum* further underscores the theme of intimacy. As Stevens (1986) observes,

> The image of the king and queen meeting, uniting, and being mutually transformed in the process, is a double image of the essential nature of any therapeutic relationship that works. On the one hand, it is an image of the individual patient's intrapsychic experience in which his conscious self meets

and unites with some portion of his unconscious self, releasing a fresh current of energy for life. On the other hand, it is an image of the patient's union with the analyst, a highly charged emotional experience within which the patient is transformed.

(p. 188)

According to this reading, Jung is effectively suggesting that the desire to be whole is the flipside of the desire to merge with the other. As Jung (1946) himself puts it: "wholeness is the product of an intrapsychic process which depends essentially on the relationship of one individual to another" (p. 245). Stevens emphasizes that where the transference has been fully constellated, the central therapeutic factor is, in Jung's view, the analyst's willingness to enter as far as possible into the experience. This fundamentally relational model of clinical action appears to suggest that, by virtue of the shared experience of the archetypal material activated in the transference, the analyst is able to access something of the patient's subjective world. Yet to what extent this line of thinking can be thought to reflect a direct apprehension of the other remains open to question; the shared quality of the analytic encounter is seemingly given by virtue of a relationship to the archetype as a third entity. Whether this shared state of participation constitutes a direct relationship between partners may seem unclear. In fact, Jung conceptualizes the potential for an enduring quality of the relationship that remains subsequent to the retraction of projections—the development of "kinship libido" (1946, p. 233), which expresses a communal feeling that has its original basis in *participation mystique*. Confusingly, however, this notion is defined as the "instinct" underlying the transference. While, for Jung, self and other are ultimately to be understood as parts of a transcendent unity (p. 245), it isn't clear to what extent the development of kinship libido constitutes a direct apprehension of this.

Change in the third

For Jung, the central therapeutic factor in the archetypal transference is expressed by the analyst's capacity to immerse himself in the analytic encounter while abstaining from acting out. This approach thus recalls the problem raised by Ogden in seeking to account for the fashion in which the analyst's role as a container enables structural change in the patient—a problem that Ogden seeks to resolve by considering the analytic couple as an entity formed of the subjugating dynamics of the third. As has already been touched upon, however, this approach is far removed from Benjamin's notion of mutual recognition defined as the *conscious* acknowledgement of the other person as an equivalent center of being. Yet, if mutual recognition is to be considered most fundamentally reflective of a shift in the relationship itself (and not merely a solipsistic achievement of the respective partners), then it seems necessary to ground this position in a collective dimension of the psyche; one that would presumably be considered otherwise inaccessible by virtue of its being unconscious. If such a notion is to be linked with mutual recognition, however, then the unconscious as third must be considered to be in some respect accessible to consciousness. Thus, while Jung and Ogden both have significant recourse to defining the third as unconscious, it should be noted that without some question of challenging one's relationship to this third, the analyst would presumably be barred from upholding therapeutic agency. That the patient must, in Jung's (1946) view, become "a problem" for the analyst clearly indicates a question of conscious engagement. This is equally apparent in Ogden's use of reverie, for in lowering the threshold of consciousness Ogden is suggesting that the analytic third can be made in some respect more accessible to the conscious mind. The concept of reverie clearly bears comparison with Jung's technique of active imagination where, with the notion of a "confrontation with the unconscious," the meaning of "unconscious" has likewise seemingly been stretched beyond its natural capacity. But while the technique of active imagination was developed by Jung as a means to self-analysis and stresses direct engagement with one's own imagery (by establishing an internal dialogue), the notion of reverie is essentially passive and was developed in the clinical setting as a means of working with projective identification. It is perhaps owing to these fundamental differences that while reverie has come to occupy a central role in post-Kleinian technique, the clinical uses of active imagination have been less centrally emphasized. Von Franz (1980) reports that Jung usually warned against doing active imagination with living persons, since "The borderline between active imagination and magic is sometimes very subtle" (p. 132). Such a statement indicates that Jung went so far as to assert that the patient can be directly influenced by means of a conscious engagement with the imagery of the unconscious. Clearly, however, the specifically *active* quality of this practice raises ethical questions.

Reflecting the conceptual difficulties that arise in speaking of "the unconscious," James Hillman (1972) suggests that this term obscures Jung's emphasis on image. In seeking to challenge the conscious/unconscious dichotomy, Hillman draws from the French philosopher and theologian Henry Corbin, who refers to an order of reality which he terms the *mundus imaginalis*. Corbin (1977) observes that Islamic mysticism makes a distinction between three metaphysical worlds: the intellectual world (*Jabarut*), the imaginal world (*Malakut*), and the sensible world (*Molk*). In emphasizing the notion of the psyche as a third term serving to connect body and mind, Hillman's approach to Jung underscores the notion that therapy is fundamentally concerned with developing the capacity to imagine. The imaginal thus bears comparison with Winnicott's notion of transitional space, yet with the notable difference that the former is postulated to correspond with a pre-existent dimension of reality while the latter is co-created. Similar implications attend Ogden's work—Cwik (2006, 2011) observes that Ogden's outlook is in keeping with an imaginal approach to the clinical situation, but that it lacks an underlying theoretical basis. While Ogden (2004) speaks of the "subjugating third" and thus acknowledges how the intersubjective field can subsume the personalities of analyst and analysand, he nevertheless posits that this field is a joint creation of the two individuals. While acknowledging the need for a directly shared experience if reverie is to bring about a change in the other person, Ogden abstains from exploring further. Samuels (1985) observes that Corbin's notion of the *mundus imaginalis* offers a basis from which to understand the functioning of projective identification. In this frame of reference, projective identificatory processes correspond with a particular dimension of reality—one that pre-exists the participation of analyst and patient.

Corbin's notion of the *mundus imaginalis* provides an ontological grounding for Jung's archetypes. Significantly, the conception of the collective unconscious thus offered potentially disrupts the assumption that archetypes should be considered as though existing in distinction from human participation. Among Jungians, clinical interest in imaginal insight has therefore led to an increasing emphasis on mutual understanding in preference to self-understanding (Reed, 1996). Schwartz-Salant (1988) suggests:

> projective identification has the goal of transforming the structure and dynamics of processes in the third area, and, with this, one's perception of these processes. One may often refer to this area as 'in between' two people, for it can be experienced in this way, especially as an interactive field that is structured by images that have a strong effect upon the conscious personalities. But the more deeply it is entered, the more spatial metaphors vanish.
>
> *(p. 43)*

This position leads Schwartz-Salant to emphasize that it is not things that are transformed in the context of this kind of therapeutic work, so much as the relationship between them.[2] He recommends thinking of the analytic situation as an interactive field, the dynamics of which are best understood by conceptualizing projective identification in terms of the aspects of an unconscious couple that structure the third—"For then one moves out of a sphere of omnipotence [...] and into a domain in which both people can discover how they have, so to speak, been acting out a mutual dream, or how they have been being dreamed" (p. 50). Such an approach is fostered by refraining from interpreting in terms of projection, and instead focusing on the quality of the field itself.

Although this approach seems to clearly complement recent psychoanalytic conceptions of intersubjectivity, the more explicitly metaphysical nature of the claims thus made is liable to be challenging. Yet it might be argued that the Jungian approach is merely drawing attention to theoretical problems that others have alluded to without directly addressing them. Reflecting this claim, Gerson (2004) objects to speaking of a "third" precisely because he feels that this language tends to foster what he perceives to be a mistaken sense of the intersubjective process as a "force beyond the dyad" (p. 80). Alongside the work of Ogden, Gerson cites Green's (1975) notion of intersubjective processes as an *analytic object*, the Barangers' (1993) *analytic field*, Bollas's (1987) *third intermediate object*, and Orange's (1995) *intersubjective triad*. Similarly, in outlining her conceptualization of a general psychoanalytic field theory, Katz (2013) objects to the fashion in which many theorists appear to endorse notions of the third as a distinct entity. She states: "A third, independent nonhuman entity with its own unconscious process is not necessary for general psychoanalytic field theory" (p. 285). It is precisely as a consequence of having taken this position, however, that Katz subsequently asserts an extreme dualism in stating that "just as there is no direct contact with the unconscious, neither is there with humans, couches, or other items purported to be in the world" (p. 286). Should such a position be allowed to stand, then the notion of mutual recognition would appear fundamentally deluded and, in keeping with a more Lacanian perspective, perhaps even unjustifiably coercive.[3]

Mutual recognition re-visited

If the notion of recognition described by Benjamin is to be considered as more than an adaptive illusion, then a medium has to be posited through which this process takes place. In so far as adopting an intersubjective position in the sense Benjamin intends is to be regarded as a capacity of the imagination, then a conception of the imagination is required such as to enable a meeting of minds. Yet pursuing this question in earnest readily invites accusations of wooly thinking. Responding to the notion of recognition, Orange (2010a) writes:

> Is there really any such thing as being "out of the fly-bottle"? Is there really enlightenment, Buddhist-style? Is there really, as in the politics and psychoanalysis of recognition, an almost magical mutual process that creates the other in subject–subject relating? I think not, and do not believe Wittgenstein did either. But, allusions in the psychoanalytic literature to the incompletely analyzed patient, and descriptions of putatively recognition-creating enactments, suggest that we still seek a path to Nirvana.
>
> *(p. 241)*

Although Orange (2010b) subsequently expresses regret for what she would retrospectively perceive to be her unnecessarily harsh wording, perhaps she is getting at something here—surely there *is* something altogether fantastical about the existence of other people. It is a testament to Benjamin's careful scholarship that she has been able to introduce this notion of mutual recognition in such a way as to retain intellectual respectability. Yet this accomplishment has required some deft juggling and a sense that the crux of the matter may have been left unaddressed.

It has been observed that Hegel's master-slave dialectic does not in and of itself constitute a refutation of solipsism (R. Stern, 2012). In keeping with this observation, Reis (1999) argues that grounding a relational approach to intersubjectivity in Hegel can only be expected to result in a restrictive definition of subjectivity considered merely as an operation of thinking. In Benjamin's Winnicottian take on Hegel, it may seem that the existence of the other person is essentially an intellectual inference gained through the other's capacity to survive omnipotent attacks. As Varga (2011) observes, however, Winnicott's notion that the infant's recognition of the other is dependent on an initial frustration caused by the disjunction between what they want and what they get appears to require that the child is already aware of the distinction between self and other—in sum, frustration could never arise without prior acknowledgement of a reason to become frustrated.

Both Reis (1999) and Varga (2011) turn to the work of Merleau-Ponty in search of an alternative position. Recognizing that any question of comparing oneself to the other already seems to entail an intersubjective relationship, Merleau-Ponty argues that recognition of self and other should be considered ontologically co-primordial. If there is to be any question of comparison between self and other, such as is indicated in a clash of wills, then intersubjectivity must already have been achieved (Welsh, 2007). Intersubjectivity is thus considered an originary given rather than posited to evolve out of solipsism. Merleau-Ponty grounds this claim in the notion of a body-subject. As Reis explains:

> bodily perception is our primordial experience of or in the world, and so the world first appears to us by way of perception. Primordial perception is not conscious reflection (i.e., thinking) but the immediacy of prereflective experience mediated by the relation of the body to the world.
>
> *(p. 384)*

Reis claims that this perspective is uniquely reflected in the work of Ogden, suggesting that Ogden's adoption of reverie is best understood not along the lines of Bionian containment but rather, in terms of Merleau-Ponty's notion of *milieu*—"as a medium for the appearance of the world from which he is not separated" (p. 390). He positively compares this outlook with Benjamin's claim that "all fantasy is the negation of the real other"; a statement which suggests the extent to which Benjamin's theorizing can seem to have divorced her conception of the intersubjective from the intrapsychic.

In response to Reis, Benjamin (1999b) underscores that her thinking embraces both Winnicottian omnipotence and the primary intersubjectivity of Trevarthen and Stern—a fundamental contradiction that she readily acknowledges. While indicating the possibility that this seeming tension may itself be worth preserving (the path effectively taken by Merleau-Ponty in establishing both self and other as given from the outset), Benjamin nevertheless suggests an approach to resolution—she seeks to define two different intersubjective phases, the first emphasizing the notion of a gradual differentiation out of primary intersubjectivity, and the second reflecting the developmental emergence of omnipotence and (simultaneously) confrontation with the independent other. Elsewhere, Benjamin (1999a) posits the notion of a nascent third in order to emphasize her belief that intersubjectivity originates in non-verbal experiences of shared interaction. Benjamin (2004) explicitly connects this notion with infancy research. She states:

> I consider this early exchange to be a form of thirdness, and suggest that we call the principle of affective resonance or union that underlies it the *one in the third*—literally, the part of the third that is constituted by oneness.
>
> *(p. 17)*[4]

Benjamin seemingly requires this notion so as (1) to prevent her theory of intersubjectivity from becoming excessively rational and (2) to provide a foundational awareness of the other such as to enable reflective recognition. It might be noted, however, that these are strange expectations to have of infancy research thinking. The notion of an originary form of intersubjectivity points to a foundational claim about the nature of reality itself, yet Trevarthan (1998) is content to portray primary intersubjectivity as a form of "protoconversation." This notion is also reflected in Stern, for whom the infant is able to discern a mental state in the other on the basis of the intensity, timing, and shape of the partner's behavior (Beebe *et al.*, 2003). It should be noted that this is *not* equivalent to intersubjectivity considered as an originary principle. If primary intersubjectivity is merely a form of protoconversation, this doesn't address how the conversation comes to be established in the first place. At this point, there seems to be a temptation to fall back on biology. Trevarthan (1998) and Stern (2007) both explicitly link their ideas about intersubjectivity with the nature of the brain, and Benjamin (2004) herself states that mirror-neurons may offer the "basis for appreciating this *intention* to align and to accommodate" (p. 19). However, if primary intersubjectivity is postulated to emerge from brain activity, surely we conflate subjective and objective ontologies and only reinforce the very disjunction between mind and body out of which the problem of other minds arises. Furthermore, in the notion of primary intersubjectivity as a form of protoconversation considered developmentally prior to thought *per se*, it seems that the charge of excessive rationality must still stand.

Because Benjamin enlists infancy research as a basis from which to theorize early forms of subjectivity, this approach is handicapped by the limitations attending engagement with what Daniel Stern (1985) has termed *the observed infant*.[5] Trevarthan and Stern both rely on the microanalysis of baby–mother interactions. When the basis for talking about early forms of intersubjectivity is behavioral observation, however, it goes without saying that the nature of the interaction will be interpreted in terms of protolanguage—this is merely to conclude what was already assumed in the design of the study. Since subjective experience is being inferred by means of observed behavior, the mother's and child's subjectivities are in fact excluded from direct consideration altogether—such studies seek to achieve the false impression of having eliminated subjectivity from the conditions of the experiment, so as to then claim to have discovered it again in observed behavior. The danger thus arises of confusing Merleau-Ponty's body-subject with the body considered as a material entity. In this light, intersubjectivity comes to be grounded in an objective ontology and conceptualized merely in terms of brain functioning. Such an approach therefore misses the notion of subjectivity altogether. The activity of the body comes to be interpreted as the function of a biological organism instinctually expressing an early form of language. Subsequently, an awkward transition is negotiated in seeking to explain intersubjectivity first as a product of the relationship between objects in space, and later as an operation of linguistic reflection. But neither of these positions offers a basis from which mutual recognition might be understood in such a way that the experience of intimacy can be considered more than illusion.

In emphasizing that the body-mind should be treated as fundamentally paradoxical, Dimen (2000) observes that psychoanalytic thinking tends more towards "indecision and contradiction" (p. 15). The transition between the two moments of subjectivity Benjamin suggests are liable to be reflective of this claim, and do a disservice to her own commitment to paradox (Benjamin, 2005). Starr (2008) argues that "the analytic relationship is embedded in and potentiates a transcendent Third" (p. 217). She suggests this claim is what Benjamin (2004) is angling for in her conceptualization of thirdness as "a deeper law of reality" (p. 18). This certainly seems to be reflected where Benjamin (1988) speaks of the mother attributing to the newborn child "a knowledge beyond ordinary knowing" (p. 13). But while Benjamin breaks new ground in seeking to draw attention to the role of the mother's subjectivity, the perspective she takes in negotiating this theme continues to emphasize the infant—that is, the relevance for psychoanalytic theorizing of the mother's subjectivity is explored only in terms of the mother differing from her child. While this particular avenue of inquiry has borne much fruit, what of those elements of the mother's experience not associated with this question of divergence? Might we not also seek to learn from the mother's participatory experiences of belonging and merger?

In support of her opposition to the notion that mother and child ever exist in a state of unity, Benjamin (2004) invokes Lacan's objection to Balint's "primary love"—that if a recognition of difference weren't present in the nursing mother from the outset then there would be nothing to prevent her, upon becoming hungry, from turning the tables and eating the baby. Amusing though this line of thinking might be, it also seems a little hastily dismissive. In failing to more fully explore mothers' experiences of union with their newborns, a danger emerges that we are liable to recapitulate Winnicott's (1956) potentially reductive understanding of primary maternal preoccupation as a state of identification engendered in the mother purely to serve the baby's needs. In this light, the mother's subjectivity comes to be implicitly defined in terms of the extent to which she succeeds in breaking free of the state of maternal preoccupation. We thus come to value the mother's subjectivity as a marking phenomenon indicating the question of difference such as to enable mutual recognition, but fail to attend more seriously to experiences of unity and merger. While Benjamin (1995) acknowledges the significance of the mother's subjectivity in terms of the pleasure that she feels in contacting her child's mind and in being recognized by her baby to have her own "rights" and "feelings" (p. 32), she appears (2000) to dismiss the experience of primary maternal preoccupation as merely a product of Winnicott's romantic idealization of motherhood. It seems conceivable, however, that seeking to eliminate such a notion from the conceptualization of maternal subjectivity could be subtly linked with the societal pressure placed on women to pursue a career alongside of motherhood and the widespread implication that this state of affairs is by definition reflective of female empowerment. Motherhood thus increasingly comes to be perceived as a "sacrifice" (the broader psychodynamics of which needn't concern us here) preventing women from serving their "own needs"—i.e., taking up a position in the working world.

While for many women there may be a great deal of legitimacy in this narrative, we might note the extent to which this position has come to be assumed to be true by definition and at the expense of a more direct valuation of motherhood itself. It is this state of affairs that leads Fraser (2013) to argue that women have become the "handmaidens" of neoliberal capitalism, and it may also be this line of thinking that has significantly informed relational ideas about maternal subjectivity such as to shore up secular assumptions.

If primary maternal preoccupation is to be taken seriously as a phenomenon without reducing this experience to one concerned only with serving the needs of the infant, then the sense thus emerging raises questions of self-transcendence and spirituality[6]—something that Winnicott himself may quietly have been alluding to in speaking of a tendency in mothers to subsequently repress their memories of this experience. Owing to the ways in which the field of psychology has historically sought to retain a rigid adherence to secular values, attending to the prevalence of this theme in the experiences of mothers is perhaps only now emerging as a possibility.[7] In this light, we might consider Winnicott's claim that, in the absence of a child, the state of primary maternal preoccupation would qualify as a form of illness. If such a claim is allowed to stand, then we might recall Ellenberger's (1970) notion of "creative illness"—examples of which include Fechner's nervous breakdown, Freud's period of self-analysis, and Jung's confrontation with the unconscious.

Concluding thoughts

While objects in the material world are conventionally understood to relate to each other owing to their respective positions in space, relationships between subjects are less clearly defined. Loewald (1979) writes:

> There are kinds off relatedness between what conventionally we call self and object, that call into question the universal validity of these very terms. We have come to see that there are levels of mental functioning and experience where these distinctions are not made, or made only fleetingly and in rudimentary form. These are deep unconscious layers showing modes of interpsychic relatedness, of emotional ties that are active under the surface in both analysand and analyst, and thus in their relatedness, forming ingredients of therapeutic potential. [...] These layers of experience, too, coexist with the more advanced levels of mental functioning and organization of mental content, and continue to exert their influence throughout life.
>
> *(p. 376)*

In the present chapter I have sought to demonstrate that should the notion of mutual recognition be accepted in the spirit with which it is seemingly intended, then Benjamin's (1999a) claim that "the third appears only in the relationship of recognition" (p. 204) is in need of revision. Benjamin (2016) has recently stated that mutual recognition should not be confused with empathy—that it goes beyond this to reflect an acknowledgement that something is "real." For an achievement of the imagination to be concerned with the recognition of "reality" surely registers Benjamin's thinking as more compatible with Jung than may have been supposed. The experience described by Benjamin in terms of "mutual recognition" appears to reflect the operation of what Jung terms *the transcendent function*. But where Benjamin limits her definition of recognition to the perception of the other as an equivalent center of being, Jung's notion of the transcendent function is concerned with the creation of meaning more broadly:

> It is an account of the meaning-making function of the psyche that suggests meaning to be the outcome of a process of opposition between two or more opposing elements that are somehow transcended in the creation of a third with a new level of complexity.
>
> *(Colman, 2007)*

For Jung, the transference relationship constitutes a struggle to effectuate a change in the collective, the byproduct of which is a feeling of participation not only between individuals but in the life process itself. This feeling of correspondence between microcosm and macrocosm is the crux of his notion of synchronicity—a concept Jung developed in an apparent effort to reconcile the relationship between inner and outer (see Brown, 2014), thus potentially challenging his earlier emphasis on retracting projections in an effort to overcome *participation mystique*.

In her earlier work, Benjamin was already expressing an interest in how intersubjective and intrapsychic approaches might be synthesized: "The problem is that each focuses on different aspects of psychic experience which are too interdependent to be simply severed from one another" (Benjamin, 1988, p. 21n). For Jung (1946), both positions are interpreted as aspects of individuation:

> in the first place it is an internal and subjective process of integration, and in the second it is an equally indispensable process of objective relationship. Neither can exist without the other, although sometimes the one and sometimes the other predominates. This double aspect has two corresponding dangers. The first is the danger of the patient's using the opportunities for spiritual development arising out of the analysis of the unconscious as a pretext for evading the deeper human responsibilities, and for affecting a certain "spirituality" which cannot stand up to moral criticism: the second is the danger that atavistic tendencies may gain the ascendency and drag the relationship down to a primitive level.
>
> *(p. 234)*

Jung was surely speaking from experience: his relationship to the rise of Nazism perhaps suggested in the former danger, and his sexual indiscretions with female patients in the case of the latter. Needless to say, in the early history of psychoanalysis (and, to some extent, perhaps even still), Jung's susceptibility to these all-too-human dangers has been exploited relentlessly in seeking to discredit his work.

Just as Jung draws attention to the shifting emphasis between integration and what he terms "objective relationship," we might recall Aron's (2000) claim that the analytic couple is necessarily pulled between intrapsychic and intersubjective positions. In a related sense, Edinger (1985) makes a distinction between what he terms the "lesser" and "greater" aspects of the *coniunctio*—in so far as the lesser aspect predominates, the union consists of substances that have yet to be fully discriminated. This lesser dimension of the *coniunctio* occurs as a consequence of the individual coming to identify with material emerging from the unconscious, thus signifying the need for dissolution and further discrimination. Both the lesser and greater aspects of the *coniunctio* are reflected in all experiences of union, with the task of individuation being conceived as an interminable refinement of relations between the ego and the unconscious. While moments of recognition are always colored by elements of the lesser *coniunctio*, this in no way undermines those elements of the *coniunctio* reflecting a less confused condition of union. Ulanov (2004) thus emphasizes that a relatively fused state is nevertheless an achievement of trust:

> Heretofore this partner had remained mute, filled with a noxious suspicion. To assume, now, that the other follows along with one implicitly is an achievement. Some bit of ego trusts that it is held in attention by an unconscious inner matrix and by the receptive listening of the other person.
>
> *(p. 134)*

Clinical challenges are associated not only with entering this state, but also in leaving it. It might be suggested, therefore, that the analyst's role in the transference is to mediate between the needs of immersing himself in the subjugating third and creating psychic space for the other (and himself) via the careful use of self-disclosure—in this connection, it seems noteworthy that Kalsched (2013) refers to the lesser *coniunctio* as "a rescue from without" (p. 310). The relational literature has been of inestimable value in exploring how such a rescue might be effectuated. Post-Kleinians, meanwhile, have demonstrated the ways in which an emphasis on phantasy can enrich and deepen practice. In the present context, I have sought to show that both approaches might benefit from a more direct engagement with Jung.

Notes

1   A term adopted by Lévy-Bruhl (1926) to signify a state of non-differentiation from the wider world that is postulated to reflect the psychology of indigenous peoples.

2   "In the deepest sense we all dream not out of ourselves but out of what lies between us and the other" (Jung, 1973, p. 172).

3   Furthermore, once such a position is assumed, any question of uncanny or telepathic relatedness can only be dismissed out of hand. It has been widely observed that counter-transferential reactions can sometimes elicit feelings so discrepant with the patient's presentation that it is difficult to credit the idea that non-verbal cues would be sufficient to trigger the experience. Field (1991) offers the example of a patient who is relating a dramatic story in animated fashion while the analyst experiences deep sleepiness. Without a conception of a transpersonal third, such clinical experiences can only be accounted for dismissively—Renik (1993) complains that the notion of unconscious communication tends to assume an unwarranted cast of mysticism, and argues that when the analyst is unaware of the basis for their responses, it is merely because the analyst is motivated to keep them unconscious. For some clinicians, however, such a position remains unconvincing (e.g., Bass, 2001; de Peyer, 2016; Mayer, 2001; Suchet, 2004; Tennes, 2007). While the notion of the imaginal may readily be dismissed as far-fetched, to some this idea may seem no less fanciful than a claim that the full range of projective identificatory experiences can be explained purely in terms of implicit communication and the analyst's defensively motivated unconsciousness.

4   The idea of positing two different kinds of intersubjectivity corresponding to different phases of early development is also forwarded by Beebe *et al.* (2003).

5   See the conclusion of Brown (2017b) for further discussion.

6   In an article drawing attention to the paucity of literature addressing motherhood as an opportunity for spiritual awakening, Athan and Miller (2013) identify six interrelated themes in the reports of new mothers: the emergence of unconditional love and interdependence, a sense of transcending ego or self-centeredness, the awakening of compassion and empathy, experiences associated with an attitude of mindfulness and heightened awareness, a heightened sense of meaning and purpose, and a tendency towards examining questions of faith and the existence of a higher power.

7   See Brown (2015, 2016, 2017a, 2017b) for reflections on the clinical challenges of cultural diversity and the increasingly apparent need for a more extensive engagement among clinicians with the theme of spirituality.

References

Aron, L. (1996). *A meeting of minds: Mutuality in psychoanalysis*. Hillsdale, NJ: Analytic.

Aron, L. (2000). Self-reflexivity and the therapeutic action of psychoanalysis. *Psychoanalytic Psychology, 17*(4), 667–689.

Athan, A. M., & Miller, L. (2013). Motherhood as opportunity to learn spiritual values: Experiences and insights of new mothers. *Journal of Prenatal and Perinatal Psychology and Health, 27*(4), 220–253.

Baranger, M. (1993). The mind of the analyst: From listening to interpretation. *International Journal of Psychoanalysis, 74*, 15–24.

Bass, A. (2001). It takes one to know one; or, whose unconscious is it anyway? *Psychoanalytic Dialogues, 11*(5), 683–702.

Beebe, B., Knoblauch, S., Rustin, J., & Sorter, D. (2003). A comparison of Meltzoff, Trevarthen, and Stern. *Psychoanalytic Dialogues, 13*, 809–836.

Benjamin, J. (1988). *The bonds of love: Psychoanalysis, feminism, & the problem of domination*. New York: Pantheon.

Benjamin, J. (1990). An outline of intersubjectivity: The development of recognition. *Psychoanalytic Psychology, 7*, 33–46.

Benjamin, J. (1995). *Like subjects, love objects: Essays on recognition and sexual difference*. New Haven: Yale University Press.

Benjamin, J. (1999a). Afterword. In S. A. Mitchell & L. Aron (Eds.), *Relational psychoanalysis: The emergence of a tradition* (pp. 201–210). New York: Routledge.

Benjamin, J. (1999b). A note on the dialectic: Commentary on paper by Bruce E. Reis. *Psychoanalytic Dialogues, 9*(3), 395–399.

Benjamin, J. (2000). Response to commentaries by Mitchell and by Butler. *Studies in Gender and Sexuality, 1*, 291–308.

Benjamin, J. (2004). Beyond doer and done to: An intersubjective view of thirdness. *Psychoanalytic Quarterly, 73*, 5–46.

Benjamin, J. (2005). From many into one: Attention, energy, and the containing of multitudes. *Psychoanalytic Dialogues, 15*(2), 185–201.

Benjamin, J. (2016). *Panel discussion.* Paper presented at the Celebrating Two New Developments from Beatrice Beebe's Lab—Book Release and Film Screening, Ferenczi Center, New School, NYC.

Bollas, C. (1987). *The shadow of the object.* New York: Columbia University.

Brown, R. S. (2014). Evolving attitudes. *International Journal of Jungian Studies, 6*(3), 243–253.

Brown, R. S. (2015). An opening: Trauma and transcendence. *Psychosis: Psychological, Social and Integrative Approaches, 7*(1), 72–80.

Brown, R. S. (2016). Spirituality and the challenge of clinical pluralism: Participatory thinking in psychotherapeutic context. *Spirituality in Clinical Practice, 3*(3), 187–195.

Brown, R. S. (2017a). Bridging worlds: Participatory thinking in Jungian context. *Journal of Analytical Psychology, 62*(2), 187–207.

Brown, R. S. (2017b). *Psychoanalysis beyond the end of metaphysics: Thinking towards the postrelational.* London: Routledge.

Colman, W. (2007). Symbolic conceptions: The idea of the third. *Journal of Analytical Psychology, 52*, 565–583.

Corbin, H. (1977). *Spiritual body and celestial earth: From Mazdean Iran to Shi'ite Iran* (N. Pearson, Trans., 2nd ed.). Princeton: Princeton University Press.

Cwik, A. J. (2006). The art of the tincture: Analytical supervision. *Journal of Analytical Psychology, 51*, 209–225.

Cwik, A. J. (2011). Associative dreaming: Reverie and active imagination. *Journal of Analytical Psychology, 56*, 14–36.

de Peyer, J. (2016). Uncanny communication and the porous mind. *Psychoanalytic Dialogues, 26*(2), 156–174.

Dimen, M. (2000). The body as Rorschach. *Studies in Gender and Sexuality, 1*, 9–39.

Edinger, E. F. (1985). *Anatomy of the psyche: Alchemical symbolism in psychotherapy.* Peru: Open Court.

Ellenberger, H. F. (1970). *The discovery of the unconscious: The history and evolution of dynamic psychiatry.* New York: Basic.

Field, N. (1991). Projective identification: Mechanism or mystery? *Journal of Analytical Psychology, 36*, 93–109.

Fraser, N. (2013, October 14). How feminism became capitalism's handmaiden—and how to reclaim it. *The Guardian.* Retrieved from www.theguardian.com/commentisfree/2013/oct/14/feminism-capitalist-handmaiden-neoliberal (accessed 31 January 2017).

Freud, S. (1912). Recommendations to physicians practising psycho-analysis. *The standard edition of the complete psychological works of Sigmund Freud* (Vol. 12, pp. 109–120). London: Hogarth.

Freud, S. (1915). The unconscious. In J. Strachey (Ed.), *The standard edition of the complete psychological works of Sigmund Freud* (Vol. 14, pp. 159–215). London: Hogarth.

Gerson, S. (2004). The relational unconscious: A core element of intersubjectivity, thirdness, and clinical process. *The Psychoanalytic Quarterly, 73*, 63–98.

Gordon, R. (1965). The concept of projective identification: An evaluation. *Journal of Analytical Psychology, 10*(2), 127–149.

Green, A. (1975). The analyst, symbolization and absence in the analytic setting. *International Journal of Psychoanalysis, 56*, 1–21.

Hillman, J. (1972). *The myth of analysis: Three essays in archetypal psychology*. Evanston: North Western University Press.

Jung, C. G. (1921). Psychological types. In G. Adler & R. F. C. Hull (Eds), *Collected works* (Vol. 6). Princeton: Princeton University Press.

Jung, C. G. (1946). The psychology of the transference. In G. Adler & R. F. C. Hull (Eds), *Collected works* (Vol. 16, pp. 353–537). Princeton: Princeton University Press.

Jung, C. G. (1967). Commentary on "The secret of the golden flower" (R. F. C. Hull, Trans.). In G. Adler & R. F. C. Hull (Eds), *Collected works* (Vol. 13, pp. 1–56). Princeton: Princeton University Press.

Jung, C. G. (1973). *Letters [volume 1]* (R. F. C. Hull, Trans.). Princeton: Princeton University Press.

Kalsched, D. (2013). *Trauma and the soul: A psycho-spiritual approach to human development and its interruption*. Hove and New York: Routledge.

Katz, S. M. (2013). General psychoanalytic field theory: Its structure and applications to psychoanalytic perspectives. *Psychoanalytic Inquiry, 33*(3), 277–292.

Lévy-Bruhl, L. (1926). *How natives think* (L. A. Clare, Trans.). London: G. Allen & Unwin Ltd.

Loewald, H. W. (1979). Reflections on the psychoanalytic process and its therapeutic potential. *The essential Loewald: Collected papers and monographs* (pp. 372–383). Hagerstown: University Publishing Group.

Loewald, H. W. (1980). *Papers on psychoanalysis*. New Haven: Yale University Press.

Mayer, E. L. (2001). On "telepathic dreams?": An unpublished paper by Robert J. Stoller. *Journal of the American Psychoanalytic Association, 49*, 629–657.

nyc.gov. (2015). Talk to your baby. Retrieved from www1.nyc.gov/site/talktoyourbaby/index.page.

Ogden, T. H. (1986). *The matrix of the mind: Object relations and the psychoanalytic dialogue*. Northvale: Jason Aronson.

Ogden, T. H. (1994). *Subjects of analysis*. Northvale: Jason Aronson.

Ogden, T. H. (2004). The analytic third: Implications for psychoanalytic theory and technique. *Psychoanalytic Quarterly, 73*, 167–195.

Orange, D. M. (1995). *Emotional understanding*. New York: Guilford.

Orange, D. M. (2010a). Recognition as: Intersubjective vulnerability in the psychoanalytic dialogue. *International Journal of Psychoanalytic Self Psychology, 3*, 227–243.

Orange, D. M. (2010b). Revisiting mutual recognition: Responding to Ringstrom, Benjamin, and Slavin. *International Journal of Psychoanalytic Self Psychology, 5*(3), 293–306.

Reed, H. (1996). Close encounters in the liminal zone: Experiments in imaginal communication Part I. *Journal of Analytical Psychology, 41*, 81–116.

Reis, B. (1999). Thomas Ogden's phenomenological turn. *Psychoanalytic Dialogues, 9*(3), 371–393.

Renik, O. (1993). Analytic interaction: Conceptualizing technique in light of the analyst's irreducible subjectivity. *The Psychoanalytic Quarterly, 62*, 553–571.

Samuels, A. (1985). Countertransference, the "mundus imaginalis" and a research project. *Journal of Analytical Psychology, 30*, 47–71.

Schwartz-Salant, N. (1988). Archetypal foundations of projective identification. *Journal of Analytical Psychology, 33*, 39–64.

Segal, R. A. (2007). Jung and Levy-Bruhl. *Journal of Analytical Psychology, 52*, 635–658.

Starr, K. E. (2008). Faith as the fulcrum of psychic change: Metaphors of transformation in Jewish mysticism and psychoanalysis. *Psychoanalytic Dialogues, 18*, 203–229.

Stern, D. N. (1985). *The interpersonal world of the infant: A view from psychoanalysis and developmental psychology*. New York: Basic.

Stern, D. N. (2004). *The present moment in psychotherapy and everyday life*. New York: Norton.

Stern, D. N. (2007). Applying developmental and neuroscience findings on other-centred participation to the process of change in psychotherapy. In S. Bråten (Ed.), *On being moved: From mirror neurons to empathy* (pp. 35–47). Amsterdam: John Benjamins.

Stern, R. (2012). Is Hegel's master–slave dialectic a refutation of solipsism? *British Journal for the History of Philosophy, 20*(2), 333–361.

Stevens, B. (1986). A Jungian perspective on transference and countertransference. *Contemporary Psychoanalysis, 22*, 185–200.

Stolorow, R. D. & Atwood, G. E. (1992). *Contexts of being: The intersubjective foundations of psychological life*. New York: Routledge.

Stolorow, R. D., Atwood, G. E., & Ross, J. M. (1978). The representational world in psychoanalytic therapy. *International Review of Psycho-Analysis, 5*, 247–256.

Suchet, M. (2004). Whose mind is it anyway? *Studies in Gender and Sexuality, 5*, 259–287.

Tennes, M. (2007). Beyond intersubjectivity. *Contemporary Psychoanalysis, 43*, 505–525.

Trevarthan, C. (1979). Communication and cooperation in early infancy: A description of primary intersubjectivity. In M. Bullowa (Ed.), *Before speech*. Cambridge: Cambridge University Press.

Trevarthan, C. (1998). The concept and foundations of infant intersubjectivity. In S. Braten (Ed.), *Intersubjective communication and emotion in early ontogeny* (pp. 15–46). Cambridge: Cambridge University Press.

Trevarthan, C. & Hubley, P. (1978). Secondary intersubjectivity: Confidence, confiders and acts of meaning in the first year. In A. Lock (Ed.), *Action, gesture and symbol*. New York: Academic.

Ulanov, A. B. (2004). *Spiritual aspects of clinical work*. Einsiedeln: Daimon Verlag.

Varga, S. (2011). Winnicott, symbolic play, and other minds. *Philosophical Psychology, 24*(5), 625–637.

von Franz, M.-L. (1980). *Projection and re-collection in Jungian psychology: Reflections of the soul* (W. H. Kennedy, Trans.). La Salle: Open Court.

Welsh, T. (2007). Primal experience in Merleau-Ponty's philosophy and psychology. *Radical Psychology, 6*(1).

Winnicott, D. W. (1956). Primary maternal preoccupation. *Through paediatrics to psychoanalysis: Collected papers* (pp. 300–305). New York: Brunner/Mazel.

Winnicott, D. W. (1971). *Playing and reality*. New York: Basic.

PART VI

The Lacanian
(non-)connection

11

STAYING ALIVE

Anima and *objet a*

David Henderson

> It is something that lives of itself, that makes us live.
>
> *(Jung, 1971a, para. 57)*

When someone comes to analysis, they are usually confused and in pain. One way of thinking about this confusion and pain is that they have had an inchoate experience of disenchantment. Something has been lost. A link has been severed. A container is broken. An attachment has withered. A projection has been unconsciously withdrawn.

One response to this is to attempt to cling to the previous state of affairs and to deny the loss. Another is to try manically to leap over the debris to an imagined future. It is difficult to dwell in the land of disenchantment, disillusionment, and dissolution. Something has drawn the person into this predicament, and something is calling them out of it. In this chapter I will use Jung's concept of *anima* and Lacan's concept of *objet a* to think about this something. These elusive concepts are fundamental to the theory and practice of Jungian and Lacanian psychoanalysis. For Jung, "The anima is the archetype of life itself" (1971a, para. 66). According to Lacan:

> the interest the subject takes in his own split is bound up with that which determines it—namely, a privileged object, which has emerged from some primal separation, from some self-mutilation induced by the very approach of the real, whose name, in our algebra, is the *objet a*.
>
> *(1987, p. 83)*

The exploration of *anima* and *objet a* is part of an emerging Jung/Lacan dialogue. Lacan visited Jung at Kusnacht in 1954, but we know nothing about their discussions (Falzender, 2015, p. 319). The fact that Lacan introduced his theory of the three registers—the Imaginary, the Symbolic, and the Real—after his meeting with Jung remains a tantalizing stimulus for speculation. There are no references to Lacan in Jung's *Collected Works* or the *C.G. Jung Letters*. There are ten references to Jung in Lacan's *Ecrits* (Lacan, 2006), as well as a number of oblique statements that can be taken to refer to Jung. Lacan mentions *Study of the Transformations and Symbolisms of the Libido*, but he does not provide references to any of Jung's works, and the tone of his comments is uniformly negative.

Until recently, there has been little comparative work done at the interface between analytical psychology and Lacanian theory and practice (Joseph, 1987; Quintaes, 2001; Dunlap, 2008; Kantza, 2008; Julien, 2008, 2010; Gullatz, 2010; Stebbins, 2010; McGrath, 2010; Chabaud, 2012; Augusto, 2013; Manzi, 2015; Gildersleeve, 2015a, 2015b, 2016a, 2016b, 2016c, 2016d). I recall with amusement the comment of an eminent Lacanian analyst when I surmised that it would be interesting to compare Jung's self and Lacan's subject. He shot back, "I don't do comparative." This echoes Lacan's (2006) view that with respect to a dialogue between Freudian and Jungian approaches, "In fact, there is nothing more different than the reading that these two schools apply to the same object" (p. 370). According to Leupin, "Jungian psychoanalysis is but an avatar of mythological (or primitive) thinking, a model that cannot be inscribed in the realm of modern science and one that gives birth to a series of deleterious confusions" (2004, p. 17).

Nevertheless, efforts at dialogue are being made. For instance, a joint Jung/Lacan conference was held at Cambridge University in 2014. Subsequently, the Jung/Lacan Research Network, based at the Centre for Psychoanalysis, Middlesex University, London, has been running public seminars to foster an on-going discussion of some of the clinical and theoretical issues at stake between the two approaches.

Barnett (1966) has addressed the problem of how to compare psychoanalytic theories:

> The history of psychoanalysis has been marked by many different approaches to theorizing about the phenomenal field of human behavior. This diversity could enrich the science, were it not for the unfortunate isolation and partisanship of the adherents of different theoretical positions.
>
> *(p. 85)*

He goes on to attempt the development of "a tool or method, however crude, that might be useful to compare and evaluate the various psychoanalytic theories" (1966, p. 86). Bernardi published a fascinating case history of how Kleinians and Lacanians in Argentina and Uruguay tried to engage in dialogue about their theoretical and clinical differences. While in many respects the dialogue was stymied by epistemological blind spots on both sides, Bernardi (2002) remains robust in his advocacy of "true controversies" in psychoanalysis:

> Controversies demand a particular intellectual and emotional effort, connected to the acceptance of the other as different. The reward we can expect

from such effort does not reside exclusively in a reduction of disagreements; indeed, controversies are also good for developing better substantiated theories, encouraging more careful examination of our clinical evidence and reminding us that there always are alternate hypotheses, whose careful consideration can both lead us to strengthen our previous convictions or see the need to revise and modify them, in both cases carrying us forward in the search for new ideas.

(p. 870)

The larger problem of a theory or methodology of comparative psychoanalysis remains in the background of this chapter, which focuses on two discrete, but fundamental, elements of Jungian and Lacanian theory—*anima* and *objet a*. If there can be said to be a method to this chapter, it is to begin the process of marking out ways in which these two concepts have similar functions within their respective theoretical frameworks. This reflects my own conviction that dialogue begins with finding at least a sliver of common ground. One similarity between *anima* and *objet a* that is immediately apparent is that the concepts both carry a wide range of often incompatible meanings within Jungian and Lacanian theory. They have both undergone significant development over time. It is beyond the scope of this chapter to chart the history of the concepts or to arrive at any definitive description of the relationship between them. In clustering my suggestions under six headings—the empty signifier, desire, trace, bridge, psychosis, and therapy—I am merely opening the door a crack to future analysis and reflection.

The empty signifier

The *objet petit a* is the little "a" or the little other, in contrast to objet *A,* the big "A" or the big Other. The English translations maintain the *a* and *A* from the French *autre* (other):

> The first type of Other is Lacan's "big Other" *qua* symbolic order, namely, the overarching "objective spirit" of trans-individual socio-linguistic structures configuring the fields of inter-subjective interactions. Relatedly, the Symbolic big Other also can refer to (often fantasmatic/fictional) ideas of anonymous authoritative power and/or knowledge (whether that of God, Nature, History, Society, State, Party, Science, or the analyst as the "subject supposed to know" [...] But, as already becomes evident in Lacan's first few annual seminars of the early 1950s, there also is a Real dimension to Otherness. This particular incarnation of the Real, about which Lacan goes into greatest detail when addressing both love and psychosis, is the provocative, perturbing enigma of the Other as an unknowable "*x*," an unfathomable abyss of withdrawn-yet-proximate alterity.
>
> *(Johnston, 2016, pp. 11–12)*

Lacan chose this oblique terminology because he did not want to specify the content of the *objet a*. According to Sheridan, Lacan claims that *objet a* has "the status of an algebraic sign" (Lacan, 1977, p. xi). Ross states that as "Absolutely unattainable, then, the *objet a* is little other than the name we give to that absence that structures signification, subjectivity and desire" (2002, p. 18). This absence, gap, or lack acts as the cause of desire. The *objet a* is an answer to the question "Who is the other?" that leaves the question open. It is "the ephemeral, unlocalizable property of an object that makes it especially desirable" (Kirshner, 2005, p. 84).

Jung described the *anima* as X: "X. is undoubtedly the anima, representing the coll. unc." (1973, p. 85) He also writes that "The anima [...] is a 'factor' in the proper sense of the word. Man cannot make it; on the contrary, it is always the *a priori* in his moods, reactions, impulses, and whatever else is spontaneous in psychic life" (1971a, para. 57). The psyche produces a plethora of *anima* images. According to Jung, "When projected, the anima always has a feminine form with definite characteristics. This empirical finding does not mean that the archetype is constituted like that *in itself*" (1971b, para. 142). Lacan's *objet a* and Jung's X refuse to specify content, but provocatively point to a space where something important is happening.

Desire

Kirschner (2005) writes: "The concept of the *objet petit a* is central to Lacan's theory of desire, which arguably represents his major contribution to psychoanalysis" (p. 83). To begin with, the *objet a* was described as the object of desire, but from 1973 Lacan stated that it was the cause of desire. In Evans's (1996) words:

> From this point on, *a* denotes the object which can never be attained, which is really the CAUSE of desire rather than that towards which desire tends ... *Objet petit a* is any object which sets desire in motion, especially the partial objects that define the drives. The drives do not seek to attain the *objet petit a*, but rather circle round it.
>
> *(p. 125)*

Nasio (1998) tells us: "Object *a* is the hole [in] the structure if you imagine it as the source of a sucking force that pulls and animates the signifiers, giving the chain consistency" (p. 80).

According to Jung (1971a),

> the soul lures into life the inertness of matter that does not want to live. She makes us believe incredible things, that life may be lived. She is full of snares and traps, in order that man should fall, should reach the earth, entangle himself there, and stay caught.
>
> *(para. 56)*

Hillman (1985) argues that "her unknownness, ignites the compulsions toward her. She bears in her belly our individualized becoming, we are drawn into soul-making" (p. 15). Jung's *anima* is at play in a proliferation of images, all of which have an unknowable quality to them. In the case of the *objet a*:

> *Object a* can take on many different guises. It may be a certain kind of look someone gives you, the timber of someone's voice, the whiteness, feel, or smell of someone's skin, the color of someone's eyes, the attitude someone manifests when he or she speaks—the list goes on and on. Whatever an individual's characteristic cause may be, it is highly specific and nothing is easily put in its place. Desire is fixated on this cause and this cause alone.
>
> *(Fink, 1997, p. 52)*

Hillman observes that "These lengthy phenomenologies of the notion of soul [...] do not have markedly erotic traits" (1985, p. 21). Jung, Lacan, and Hillman appear to suggest that the cause of desire, that which enflames eros, is not in itself erotic.

Trace

The *objet a* can be seen as the trace of the lost object discussed by Freud in *Mourning and Melancholia*, Abraham's partial object, Klein's part-object, and Winnicott's transitional phenomena. But according to Jacobus (2005), Lacan is not seeking to expand object relations theory, but to develop an alternative view:

> In Lacan's seminars of the late 1950s and early 1960s, the evolving concept of the *objet (petit) a* is viewed in the *matheme* of phantasy as the object of desire sought in the other [...] a deliberate departure from British Object Relations psychoanalysis.
>
> *(p. 26n)*

Lacan is exploring the allure of a dimension of being before the subject–object dichotomy. Johnson (2000) writes:

> For Lacan, the mother is not the primary love-object (as claimed by Freud). She is, in fact a substitutive object. In reference to *objet a*, Lacan alleges that each and every libidinal object is a substitute for something lost, for a lost form of archaic enjoyment no longer possible after the genesis of the subject–object dichotomy in the field of the individual's experience—[Lacan claims that] "this object ... is in fact simply the presence of a hollow, a void, which can be occupied, Freud tells us, by any object, and whose agency we know only in the form of the lost object, the *petit a*."
>
> *(p. 61)*

Jung (1973) differentiates between the mother complex and the *anima*. In masculine psychology, "The anima, being psychologically the female counterpart of male consciousness, is based upon the minority of genes in a masculine body" (p. 484). However, in a broader sense, *anima*, like any complex, carries the trace of earlier experience, trauma, and affect. *Anima* echoes something beyond consciousness. As Hillman (1985) states:

> Anima-consciousness favors a protective mimicry, an *attachment* to something or someone else to which it is echo [...] life, fate and death cannot become "conscious," so that with her is constellated a consciousness of our fundamental unconsciousness. In other words, consciousness of this archetypal structure is never far from unconsciousness. Its primary attachment is to the state of nature, to all things that simply are—life, fate, death—and which can only be reflected but never separated from their impenetrable opacity. Anima stays close to this field of the natural unconscious mind.
>
> *(pp. 23–25)*

One might ask whether the "hollow" or "void" that can be "occupied by any object" can be read as analogous to the self in Jungian thought. As the *objet a* functions as a trace of this lost space, the *anima* can function as a trace of the self, following the ego's differentiation from the self.

Bridge

Lacan at first placed the *objet a* close to his category of the Imaginary. Over time, however, the *objet a* became associated with the Real. For Lacan, the Real is unrepresentable and unknowable. The *objet a* is between the subject and the Real. It is the "basic fantasy of restoring the lost link to the unsymbolized 'real' " (Kirshner, 2005, pp. 82–83). It "is a fantasy attempting to bridge the gap between separate symbolic existence and the unmediated biological 'real' of harmonious mix-up with the primal other" (Kirshner, 2005, p. 89). Jung (1970b) uses the idea of bridging with reference to the *anima*: "I have defined the anima as a personification of the unconscious in general, and have taken it as a bridge to the unconscious, in other words, as a function of relationship to the unconscious" (para. 62).

Lacan and Jung use "subject" in different ways. In general, Jung uses subject to refer to the ego. Lacan's idea of subject is closer to, though not identical with, Jung's concept of self. While it would not make much sense within a Jungian context to say that the *anima* lies between the self and the collective unconscious, we can see that *objet a* and *anima* both perform bridging functions within their respective theories. The *anima* is situated between the ego and the collective unconscious. As Jung says, "The *anima* mediates between consciousness and the collective unconscious" (1970c, para. 498, n. 381). *Anima*, according to Jung, "live[s] and function[s] [...] especially in that phylogenetic substratum which I have called the collective unconscious [...] [It] bring[s] into our ephemeral consciousness an unknown psychic life belonging to a remote past. It is the mind of our unknown ancestors" (1971c, para. 518). *Anima* and *objet a* carry an echo of raw being.

Psychosis

This relation with the Real and the collective unconscious suggests that the *objet a* and *anima* are connected to psychosis. The *objet a* is not in itself psychotic. However, its link with the Real, anxiety, primitive part-objects, unattainability, and loss means that it plays a role in the development of psychosis:

> The *objet petit a*, to summarize, is a fantasy attempting to bridge the gap between separated symbolic existence and the unmediated biological "real" of the harmonious mix-up with the primal other. When a patient in analysis, for example, demonstrates a wish to actualize this fantasy through symptomatic action, signs of heightened anxiety indicate a slippage from the logic of the pleasure and reality principles toward the lure of a *jouissance* "beyond." According to Lacan, this process can lead to a dangerous situation, which he called the *passage a l'acte,* in which the subject identifies with the *objet petit a,* incarnating in fantasy the missing part object that has fallen away with separation. He then proceeds beyond the unconscious pursuit of symbolic pleasure toward a fantasy of restored wholeness and total satisfaction.
>
> *(Kirshner, 2005, p. 89)*

The *passage a l'acte* resembles Jung's notion of possession. In psychosis, the *objet a* is experienced as "a strange internal element the subject has to manage" (Vanheule, 2011, p. 137). It stimulates an excitement which might be compared to a manic dimension of *anima* possession:

> Contrary to the neurotic, who uses the object *a* in the Other as a benchmark for comprehending questions of desire, the subject in psychosis is plagued by a non-separated object. Indeed, in psychosis the object *a* is not an external element that fuels desire in the subject, but a strange internal element the subject has to manage. To characterize this Lacan says that the subject in psychosis "has its cause in its own pocket," which is to say that it is confronted with an overwhelming non-signified excitation that manifests from within. This excess excitation threatens to efface the subject's footing in the signifier, and in this respect makes up the *structural cause* of how the subject takes shape ... At a vital level, people living through a psychosis typically feel that their sentiment of life has changed. A strange force, which manifested itself as an experiential fact that cannot easily be named, seizes the subject.
>
> *(Vanheule, 2011, pp. 137–138)*

An unrepresentable something is impinging on the person. Jung observes that "Everything the anima touches becomes numinous—unconditional, dangerous, taboo, magical" (1971a, para. 59). According to Colman (2009):

> a diagnosis of "anima possession" or "excessive projective identification" could never be like a diagnosis of cancer since these are merely interpretations—there can never be any-"thing" in the psyche that can be reliably or experimentally identified beyond the material which gave rise to the interpretation in the first place.
>
> *(pp. 202–203)*

Jung explicitly links the *anima* with psychosis. The *anima*'s "irruption into consciousness often amounts to a psychosis" (1971c, para. 519). "Unlike other contents, the [*anima* and *animus*] always remain strangers to the world of consciousness, unwelcome intruders saturating the atmosphere with uncanny forebodings or even with the fear of madness" (1971c, para. 517). "They [*anima* and *animus*] undoubtedly belong to the material that comes to light in schizophrenia" (1971c, para. 519). Like the *objet a*, the *anima* wields immense hidden influence:

> Both these archetypes [the *anima* and *animus*] possess a fatality that can on occasion produce tragic results [...] It is only when we throw light into the dark depths of the psyche and explore the strange and tortuous paths of human fate that it gradually becomes clear to us how immense is the influence wielded by those two factors that complement our conscious life.
>
> *(Jung, 1970a, para. 41)*

Hillman (1985) observes that

> it is precisely this psychic unconsciousness, beyond the reach of insight and knowledge, that the anima mediates. She makes us unconscious. As she is the very craziness of life, she drives us crazy [...] Union with anima also means union with my psychosis, my fear of madness, my suicide.
>
> *(p. 135)*

By their connections with the collective unconscious and the Real, the *anima* and *objet a* have the power to drive us mad.

Therapy

Returning to the disenchanted person who has appeared in the consulting room, we are reminded of Jung's observation that "permanent loss of the anima means [...] resignation, weariness, sloppiness, irresponsibility" (1971b, para. 147). Lacan (1987) observes:

Is it not remarkable that, at the origin of the analytic experience, the real should have presented itself in the form of that which is *unassimilable* in it—in the form of the trauma, determining all that follows, and imposing on it an apparently accidental origin?

(p. 55)

The psyche is animated by something outside of consciousness that is in turns maddening and enlivening. The flirtations with disenchantment and re-enchantment can be simultaneously resistances to analysis and spurs to analysis. It is normal that through transference this something is located in the analyst. In this case, the analyst is experienced as "the cause of the analysand's desire" (Evans, 1996, p. 125). For some Lacanians, the *objet petit a* is *the* analytic object. Schneiderman (1980) observes that within Lacanian analysis:

If the analyst during the analysis will come to be this object, he will also at the end of analysis not be it. He will submit himself to the fate of any object that stands in for *a*, and that is to be discarded.

(p. 8)

For Jung (1971d), the *anima* "sums up everything that a man can never get the better of and never finishes coping with" (para. 485). The encounter with the *anima* is the "masterpiece" of individual development. The *anima* and the *objet a* are endlessly shifting:

Object a lies beyond the signifier, it cannot be expressed in signifiers but it can be distinguished as the object cause of desire precisely because desire endlessly shifts through a chain of signifiers; it never coincides with them.

(Marks et al., 2001, p. 125)

It seems to me that therapy offers neither cure nor re-enchantment. In a sense, it doesn't offer disenchantment either. Therapy is not about disenchantment and re-enchantment. It is about hearing and receiving the next word, the next thought, the next breath, the next transference. The analyst is not there to play the disenchantment/re-enchantment game, but to pay attention. Disenchantment and re-enchantment happen. The client comes and goes. With any luck, the analyst has, in Winnicott's words, been alive and awake throughout. Nasio (1998) writes:

analysis creates the conditions for the subject to become a stranger to him or her self [...] an essential loss that reorganises the psychic reality of the subject. I call this loss "exile." Rather than wishing to bring about changes in the patient, or to situate the finality of analysis in terms of a transformation or a recovery, psychoanalysis aims to create conditions for the subject to encounter that which is most intimate to its being, as if coming from the outside, and as if unfamiliar to it.

(p. 73)

These words have an uncanny echo of Jung's words in *Memories, Dreams, Reflections* at the end of his life. Reflecting on his life-long pursuit of individuation, he wrote:

> I am astonished, disappointed, pleased with myself. I am distressed, depressed, rapturous. I am all these things at once, and cannot add up the sum. I am incapable of determining ultimate worth or worthlessness; I have no judgement about myself and my life. There is nothing I am quite sure about. I know only that I was born and exist, and it seems to me that I have been carried along. I exist on the foundation of something I do not know.
>
> *(Jung, 1961, p. 358)*

Jung says of the *anima*, "She represents the longing that has always to be sacrificed" (1970d, para. 438). Every thought, dream, gesture expresses longing. Free association and active imagination involve taking up one desire at a time, only to relinquish each desire when the time is up. Alternatively, we ourselves are lifted up and carried by one desire at a time until the wave subsides. As Jung observes, *anima* "is a subtle imperceptible smoke" (1968, para. 394, n105).

The end of analysis is paradoxical. From a certain perspective, at the end of analysis we are left not with the accomplishments of the analysis, but with the detritus of analysis, the well-chewed gristle of psychic challenges, the unreachable core of the fundamental symbolic provocations in our lives and our essential psychopathology. The important question may be not "What have I achieved?" in my analysis, but "What is unachievable in my life?" Is my life itself a symbol of something that I cannot comprehend or lay claim to? And yet this incomprehensible something is singular to myself. Perhaps at the end of analysis I may arrive at a fleeting sense of the peculiar and particular demand that being makes upon me.

Conclusion

Jung and Lacan were seemingly aware of much the same territory, but there are differences in their cartographies. Boundaries are drawn in different places on their maps, although in some cases the borders of the spaces that they have named are extremely close. Often, however, on closer inspection, initial similarities melt away. At other times, concepts that appear to be completely unrelated reveal powerful affinities. This chapter has suggested that interesting functional and phenomenological resonances can be found between two such concepts: Jung's concept of *anima* and Lacan's concept of *objet a*. The notions of the empty signifier, desire, trace, bridge, psychosis, and therapy were used to stimulate and organize these reflections. One final similarity might be added to those examined above—the potential for *anima* and *objet a* to act as spurs to individuation.

References

Augusto, L. M. (2013). *Freud, Jung, Lacan: Sobre o inconsciente*, Porto: U. Porto editora.

Barnett, J. (1966). The structural analysis of theories in psychoanalysis. *Psychoanalytic Review*, *53A*, 85–98.

Bernardi, R. (2002). The need for true controversies in psychoanalysis: The debates on Melanie Klein and Jacques Lacan in the Rio de la Plata. *International Journal of Psychoanalysis*, *83*, 851–873.

Chabaud, F. (2012). "La fonction analytique: Freud, Jung, Lacan: Approche transdisciplinare," These de Doctorat, Universite Paul Valery – Montpellier III.

Colman, W. (2009). Theory as metaphor: Clinical knowledge and its communication. *The Journal of Analytical Psychology*, *54*(2), 199–215.

Dunlap, A. (2008). *Counting to four: Accessing the quaternity of C.G. Jung in the light of Lacan and sophiology*, PhD thesis, Temple University.

Evans, D. (1996). *An introductory dictionary of Lacanian psychoanalysis*. London: Routledge.

Falzender, E. (2015). *Psychoanalytic filiations: Mapping the psychoanalytic movement*. London: Karnac.

Fink, B. (1997). *A clinical introduction to Lacanian psychoanalysis: Theory and technique*. Cambridge: Harvard.

Gildersleeve, M. (2015a). Acknowledging, moving toward and transcending psychophysiological angst during a paradox of conflicting desires. *Quadrant: The Journal of the CG Jung Foundation*, *45*, 69–86.

Gildersleeve, M. (2015b). Unconcealing Jung's transcendent function with Heidegger. *The Humanistic Psychologist*, *43*, 297–309.

Gildersleeve, M. (2016a). Complexes tickling the $ubject. *Humanities*, *5*, 85.

Gildersleeve, M. (2016b). Demystifying complexes, transference, and narcissistic personality disorder with Jung and Lacan. *Indian Journal of Psychological Medicine*, *38*, 269–272.

Gildersleeve, M. (2016c). Jung's transcendent function as Nietzsche's will to power and eternal recurrence of the same. *Agathos*, *7*, 48–71.

Gildersleeve, M. (2016d). Retrieving and projecting the transcendent function with complexes and the Rosarium Philosophorum. *Cosmos and History: The Journal of Natural and Social Philosophy*, *12*, 87–106.

Gullatz, S. (2010). Constructing the collective unconscious. *Journal of Analytical Psychology*, *55*: 691–714.

Hillman, J. (1985). *Anima: An anatomy of a personified notion*. Dallas: Spring.

Jacobus, M. (2005). *The poetics of psychoanalysis*. Oxford: Oxford University Press.

Johnson, A. (2000). The driving force of lack: Objet a and Lacan's extension of the Freudian drive. *Psychoanalysis and Contemporary Thought*, *23*, 51–64.

Johnston, A. (2016). Jacques Lacan. *The Stanford encyclopedia of philosophy*. Zalta, E. N. ed., https://plato.stanford.edu/archives/win2016/entries/lacan/ (accessed 31 January 2017).

Joseph, S. M. (1987). Fetish, sign and symbol through the looking-glass: A Jungian critique of Jacques Lacan's *Ecrits*. *San Francisco Jung Institute Library Journal*, *7*(2), 1–16.

Julien, P. (2008). La psychoanalyse et le religieux: Freud, Jung, Lacan. Paris: Editions du Cerf.

Julien, P. (2010). *A psicanalise e o religioso: Freud, Jung, Lacan*. Rio de Janeiro: Zahar.

Jung, C. G. (1961). *Memories, dreams, reflections*. New York: Random House.

Jung, C. G. (1968). Psychology and alchemy (1952). *The collected works of C. G. Jung*, *volume 12*. R. F. C. Hull (trans.). Princeton: Princeton University Press.

Jung, C. G. (1970a). Aion (1950). *The collected works of C. G. Jung, volume 9ii*. R. F. C. Hull (trans.). Princeton: Princeton University Press.

Jung, C. G. (1970b). Commentary on "The secret of the golden flower" (1957). *The collected works of C.G. Jung, volume 13*. R. F. C. Hull (trans.). Princeton: Princeton University Press.

Jung, C. G. (1970c). Mysterium coniunctionis (1954). *The collected works of C. G. Jung, volume 14*. R. F. C. Hull (trans.). Princeton: Princeton University Press.

Jung, C. G. (1970d). The psychology of the transference (1946). *The collected works of C. G. Jung, volume 16*. R. F. C. Hull (trans.). Princeton: Princeton University Press.

Jung, C. G. (1971a). The archetypes of the collective unconscious (1954). *The collected works of C.G. Jung, volume 9i*. R. F. C. Hull (trans.). Princeton: Princeton University Press.

Jung, C. G. (1971b). Concerning the archetypes, with special reference to the anima concept (1936). *The collected works of C. G. Jung, volume 9i*. R. F. C. Hull (trans.). Princeton: Princeton University Press.

Jung, C. G. (1971c). Conscious, unconscious and individuation (1939). *The collected works of C. G. Jung, volume 9i*. R. F. C. Hull (trans.). Princeton: Princeton University Press.

Jung, C. G. (1971d). The psychology of the trickster-figure (1954). *The collected works of C. G. Jung, volume 9i*. R. F. C. Hull (trans.). Princeton: Princeton University Press.

Jung, C. G. (1973). *C. G. Jung letters: Volume 1, 1906–1950*. G. Adler (ed.). London: Routledge.

Kantza, G. (2008). *Il nome del padre nella psicoanalisi. Freud, Jung, Lacan*. Milano: Ares.

Kirshner, L. A. (2005). Rethinking desire: The *objet petit a* in Lacanian theory. *Journal of the American Psychoanalytic Association, 53*, 83–102.

Lacan, J. (1977). *Ecrits: A selection*. A. Sheridan (trans.). London: Routledge.

Lacan, J. (1987). *The four fundamental concepts of psycho-analysis*. J.-A. Miller (ed.). A. Sheridan (trans.). Harmondsworth: Penguin.

Lacan, J. (2006). *Ecrits*. B. Fink (trans.). New York: Norton.

Leupin, A. (2004). *Lacan today: Psychoanalysis, science, religion*. New York: Other.

McGrath, S. J. (2010). Sexuation in Jung and Lacan. *International Journal of Jungian Studies, 2*(1), 1–19.

Manzi, G. (2015). Every dream is a discourse: Lacan, Jung and the linguistic nature of the unconscious dreamscapes. *Ramify, 5*(1), 73–104.

Marks, Z. M., H. Glowinski & S. Murphy (eds). 2001. *Compendium of Lacanian terms*. New York: Free Association Books.

Nasio, J.-D. (1998). *Five lessons on the psychoanalytic theory of Jacques Lacan*. Albany: SUNY Press.

Quintaes, M. (2001). Alquimia das palavras. *Symbolon—Estudos Jungianos*. www.symbolon.com.br (accessed 31 January 2017).

Ross, S. (2002). A very brief introduction to Lacan. http://web.uvic.ca/~saross/lacan.html (accessed 31 January 2017).

Schneiderman, S. (1980). *Returning to Freud: Clinical psychoanalysis in the school of Lacan*. New Haven: Yale University Press.

Stebbins, M. (2010). Lacan for Jungians: A response to S. Gullatz. *Journal of Analytical Psychology, 55*, 715–721.

Vanheule, S. (2011). *The subject of psychosis: A Lacanian perspective*. New York: Palgrave.

12

WIE HAST DU ES MIT DER RELIGION?

Lacan, Jung, and the religious sublime

Paul Bishop

The starting-point of this chapter is the famous question posed by Gretchen in Part One of Goethe's *Faust*.[1] Here, in the scene in Martha's garden, we find the following exchange:

> MARGARET: Promise me, Heinrich!
> FAUST: What I can!
> MARGARET: Tell me, how is't with my religion, pray?
>   Thou art a good and kindly man,
>   And yet, I think, small heed thereto dost pay.
> *(Faust I, ll. 3414–3417; Goethe, 1908, Part I, p. 164)*

Gretchen's question is entirely pertinent, since Faust is a man who is in league with the devil! In this respect, Gretchen's question pushes against the theological framework of Goethe's entire text (reflected in the "Prologue in Heaven" of Part One and in the famous concluding scene, "Amid Mountain Gorges," at the end of Part Two). But Gretchen's question is also, it seems to me, a good question to put to Lacan and to Jung.

After all, an important dimension of psychoanalysis is its reactivation and revival of ancient traditions and doctrines, especially the notion of divinity. There already exists a body of scholarship in this field of enquiry: for instance, on Freud and Empedocles (Tourney, 1956) or on Jung and Heraclitus (Bodlander, 1990). The writings of Jung positively teem with references to antiquity; *Psychological Types*, for instance, is rich in references to the problem of types in the history of classical and medieval thought, including the figures of Tertullian and Origen, theological disputes of the ancient Church, the problem of transubstantiation, the Scholastic debate between nominalism and realism, and the Communion controversy between Luther and Zwingli.

For his part, Lacan also moves at ease across various epochs of intellectual history, among which his references to Plato (especially the *Symposium*) for a definition of *desire* as *lack* are particularly important. When Socrates says in the *Symposium* (200a), "Everything longs for what it lacks, and [...] nothing longs for what it doesn't lack" (Plato, 1989, p. 552), we find the central thesis of Lacanian psychoanalysis stated with eminent clarity. Then again, in his seminar of 1960–1961 on the transference, Lacan explained the *objet petit a* in terms of the *agalma* from the *Symposium*. In Greek, an *agalma* is an ornament, offering, or gift, left in a temple for the gods; for Lacan, it is above all "a precious object, a jewel, something which is inside" (cf. Lacan, 1991a, p. 167). So when, in the *Symposium* (216e–217a), Alcibiades describes how he had once seen "the little images [...] so golden, so beautiful, and so utterly amazing" inside Socrates, famed for his ugliness (Plato, 1989, p. 568), Lacan sees in this something fundamental about the dynamics of desire. As Lionel Bailly explains, desire's "ultimate but unattainable object is the *agalma* within Socrates, its subject is the castrated (symbolically—wanting, drunken, and demanding) Alcibiades, who uses as a lure for a secondary object of desire (Agathon) his own desire or neediness, which he knows makes him desirable" (Bailly, 2009, p. 131).

This chapter takes as its working assumption the belief that seeing Lacan and Jung in an intellectual-historical light can elucidate their common features as well as their differences, and help establish a framework for approaching both thinkers in a way that can open up a dialogue that is at once constructive and critical. For the common ground between Lacan and Jung is, I shall argue, larger than is often assumed to be the case, as a consideration of three topics—language, desire, and the quaternity—indicates. Yet, as I shall also suggest, there are significant differences between Jung and Lacan that emerge in their respective relations to religion and the sublime.

Affinities: Language

For Lacan, the unconscious is structured like a language. As he puts it in *The Four Fundamental Concepts of Psycho-Analysis* (1964), "if psycho-analysis is to be constituted as the science of the unconscious, one must set out from the notion that the unconscious is structured like a language" (Lacan, 1978, p. 203; cf. pp. 20–23). In fact, his entire account of psychosexual development is predicated on the subject's entrance into the realm of the visual (the imaginary) and language (the symbolic). And Lacan is interested not just in the structure of language, but in the structures within which we use language: for the use of language always implies a relationship of one kind or another to an interlocutor.

Consequently, for Lacan, language involves both a symbolic *and* an imaginary dimension. In the famous diagram he introduced in 1955 in his *Seminar*, known as "schema L," the axis A–S (from Other to S/Es, or language in its symbolic dimension) has a corresponding axis, from *a'* to *a* (from ego to other, or an imaginary axis). On this account, "the subject is separated from the Others, the true ones, by the wall of language," and hence it is, for Lacan, a mistake to see language as something fundamentally communicative or referential: on his account, "language is as much there to found us in the Other as to drastically prevent us from understanding him" (Lacan, 1991b, p. 244).

Language is a problem for Jung as well. At first glance, Jung approaches the problem from a different angle—from the problem of meaning. As he puts it in "Archetypes of the Collective Unconscious" (first published by Jung in 1934, and substantially revised in 1954), "from whatever side we approach this question"— i.e., the question of meaning (*Sinn*)—"everywhere we find ourselves confronted with the history of language, with images and motifs that lead straight back to the primitive wonder-world" (Jung, 1968a, para. 67). This is so, Jung argues, because "the forms we use for assigning meaning are historical categories that reach back into the mists of time," and hence "interpretations make use of certain linguistic matrices that are themselves derived from primordial images" (Jung, 1968a, para. 67). Jung insists on the *historical* context of language, which is a dimension absent from Lacan's structuralist (and hence synchronic) approach to language. Yet, for all his talk of "the mists of time," Jung is also appealing to a timeless (or synchronic) dimension by describing the "images" from which "linguistic matrices" derive as "primordial."

Both Lacan and Jung were aware of the importance of analogy. For Lacan, the unconscious *is* not a language; it is not structured *as* a language; it is structured *like* a language, and in this respect we might note Jung's interest, in *Symbols and Transformations of the Libido* (published in 1911/1912), in the importance of analogy in general and, in particular, the term *gleichwie* (i.e., "like"). As he puts it, citing the German philologist and philosopher Hermann (or Heymann) Steinthal (1823–1899) as his authority, "an absolutely overweening importance must be granted to the little phrase 'Gleich wie' (even as) in the history of the development of thought" (Jung, 1991, para. 236).[2] For, as Jung adds, his own central thesis will be that "the carryover of the libido to a phantastic correlate has led primitive man to a number of the most important discoveries" (Jung, 1991, para. 236).

This is why Jung—in this respect, similarly to Martin Heidegger—is interested in the way linguistic connections can alert us to the hidden dimensions of concepts or fantasies. In *The Psychology of the Unconscious*, he suggests that "Prometheus, the fire-bringer, may be a brother of the Hindu Pramantha, that is to say, of the masculine fire-rubbing piece of wood" (Jung, 1991, para. 241). After tracing a complicated etymological path, Jung concludes: "The path from Pramantha to Prometheus passes not through the word, but through the idea" (Jung, 1991, para. 241). So here lies an important difference between Lacan and Jung: over and above language, Jung asserts the dimension of the *idea*. And Jung is very much aware of the etymological implications of his own terminology: for instance, he notes in relation to the question as to whether God is an archetype that the word "type" is derived from *typos* = "blow," "imprint"; concluding that "an archetype presupposes an imprinter" (Jung, 1968b, para. 15).

Affinities: Desire

Desire is clearly a master category for Lacan, and as a concept he distinguishes it from need, or biological instinct, and demand, made in relation to the Other. Seen in this way, Lacan follows the etymology of the word "desire" as meaning to wish for, to long for, or to regret something that is absent. As well as being indebted to Plato, Lacan derives his specific concept of desire from Spinoza, for whom "desire [*cupiditas*] is the essence itself of man" (*Ethics*, Part III, "Definitions of the Affects", def. 1; Spinoza, 1928, p. 266).[3] Lacan refines his approach via Hegel, who explores how desire involves a relation to the Other, via Alexandre Kojève, who "existentializes" Hegel's thinking.[4]

In Jung's approach, we find a different understanding of desire, one perhaps reflecting the alternative etymology of the word as meaning "to await what the stars will bring" (from *de + sidere*, "from the stars"). For Jung, desire is linked to the notion of *libido*, which, in turn, in *Transformations and Symbols of the Libido* (i.e., *The Psychology of the Unconscious*), is intriguingly linked to the idea of *will*: "Originally taken from the sexual sphere, this word [i.e., *libido*] has become the most frequent technical expression of psychoanalysis, for the simple reason that its significance is wide enough to cover all the unknown and countless manifestations of the Will in the sense of Schopenhauer" (Jung, 1991, para. 212).[5] (Seen in this light, Schopenhauer appears as a highly Lacanian figure, emphasizing the constitutive function of desire, yet recognizing the impossibility of satisfying it.) In this same chapter, Jung goes on to adopt "the exact classical significance" of the word *libido* as it is used, "in a very wide sense," in such authors as Cicero, Sallust, and St Augustine.[6]

Yet Jung does not simply rely on classical texts: once again, following the hints provided by language, he notes that "this general classical application of the conception" is confirmed by "the corresponding etymological context of the word," namely, *libido* or *lubido* (with *libet*, or the older *lubet*) = "it pleases me," and *libens* or *lubens* = "gladly, willingly" (Jung, 1991, para. 218). Here Jung might also be thinking of Jakob Böhme's use of the term *lubet* in the initial chapters of his *Mysterium Magnum* to mean pleasing or pleasurable delight.[7]

In a chapter of *The Psychology of the Unconscious* entitled "The Conception and the Genetic Theory of Libido," Jung notes, with reference to Freud's *Three Contributions to the Sexual Theory* (1905), how libido is conceived here "in the original sense of sexual impulse, sexual need" (Jung, 1991, para. 219). Does this conception interpret libido as "everything sexual"? Jung thinks not, remarking that "the hypothetical idea at the basis is the symbol of the "Triebbündel" [bundle of impulses], wherein the sexual impulse figures as a partial impulse of the whole system, and its encroachment into the other realms of impulse is a fact of experience" (Jung, 1991, para. 219). As Jung goes on to write, however, "since the appearance of the *Three Contributions*, in 1905, a change has taken place in the libido conception; its field of application has been widened" (Jung, 1991, para. 219). Polemically, even provocatively, Jung associates himself with this conceptual "widening" of the notion of the libido by citing Freud again, this time from his study of Schreber,

Psycho-Analytic Notes on an Autobiographical Account of a Case of Paranoia (Dementia Paranoides) (1911). So for Freud—and for Jung, too, in his *The Psychology of Dementia Præcox* (1907)—paranoid schizophrenia reveals another aspect to libido, one that sounds remarkably proto-Lacanian:

> The fact is that in many cases [of paranoid schizophrenia] reality disappears entirely, so that not a trace of psychological adaptation or orientation can be recognized. Reality is repressed under these circumstances and replaced by the contents of the complex. One must of necessity say that not only the erotic interest but the interest in general has disappeared, that is to say, the whole adaptation to reality has ceased.
>
> *(Jung, 1991, para. 220)*

What else is the libido for Jung? Elsewhere, he says that "the conception of libido as developed in the new work of Freud and of his school has functionally the same significance in the biological territory as has the conception of energy since the time of Robert Mayer in the physical realm" (Jung, 1991, para. 218), and it is in this sense that Jung himself develops the term "psychic energy" (cf. Jung, 1991, para. 221).

But he also has recourse to mythology, and to those Neoplatonic systems that draw on the ancient cosmogonies of Hesiod and of Plato. For libido (as he conceives it) reminds Jung, or so he says, of "the cosmogenic meaning of Eros in Plato and Hesiod" (a footnote merely refers us to the *Theogony*), "and also of the Orphic figure of Phanes, the *shining one*, the first created, the 'father of Eros'" (Jung, 1991, para. 223). He goes on, via the figure of Phanes and the associated figures of Priapus and Dionysos Lysios (i.e., the Liberator or Deliverer, the god of "letting go"), to relate these representations of libido to two further traditions: first, the Indian figure of *kâma*, the god of love; and second, the Neoplatonic doctrine of Plotinus.[8]

On Jung's account of Plotinus, the "world-soul" is "the energy of the intellect" (Jung, 1991, para. 223), and seen in these Plotinian terms, libido can be conceived as the One, as "the creative primal principle" (as Jung puts it), and as "light in general": within this system, the intellect can be compared with the (masculine) sun and the world-soul with the (feminine) moon (Jung, 1991, para. 223). Elsewhere, Plotinus explains that "the world-soul has a tendency toward a divided existence and toward divisibility, the *conditio sine qua non* of all change, creation and procreation"; it is "an 'unending all of life' and wholly energy," it is "a living organism of ideas, which attain in it effectiveness" (Jung, 1991, para. 223; cf. *The Enneads*, 1956, II.5.3). For Plotinus, "the intellect is its procreator, its father, which, having conceived it, brings it to development in thought" (Jung, 1991, para. 223; cf. *The Enneads*, 1956, IV.8.3). Or, as Plotinus writes (in a passage directly cited by Jung), "What lies enclosed in the intellect, comes to development in the world-soul as logos, fills it with meaning and makes it as if intoxicated with nectar" (*The Enneads*, 1956, III.5.9; cited in Jung, 1991, para. 223).

In the course of this discussion, it becomes evident that Jung has a very clear sense of the difference between *repression* and *sublimation*. In *The Psychology of the Unconscious*, for instance, he notes:

> The process of transformation of the primal libido into secondary impulses always took place in the form of affluxes of sexual libido, that is to say, sexuality became deflected from its original destination and a portion of it turned, little by little, increasing in amount, into the phylogenetic impulse of the mechanisms of allurement and of protection of the young. This diversion of the sexual libido from the sexual territory into associated functions is still taking place. Where this operation succeeds without injury to the adaptation of the individual it is called *sublimation*. Where the attempt does not succeed it is called *repression*.
>
> *(Jung, 1991, para. 228)*

Here again, the difference between Lacan and Jung emerges along the faultline of the concept of adaptation: for Jung, adaptation to the world is a sign of success, whereas for Lacan, adaptation locks the individual into a permanent state of self-alienation.

Affinities: Quaternity

Third, curiously enough, it turns out that both Lacan and Jung have an interest in four-fold structures. In "Kant avec Sade" (1963), Lacan explains why his diagrams so frequently involve a quaternity: "A quadripartite structure has, since the introduction of the unconscious, always been required in the construction of a subjective ordering" (Lacan, 1966, p. 774); in this case, the four elements involved are the will to enjoy (V), the subject (S), the "barred subject" (barred S), and the object (a). In addition to the quadripartite structure of the Oedipus Complex (mother, child, father, phallus), his "schema L" has four nodes (S [or *Es*], *objet petit a*, ego, and the Other); there are four discourses (of the master, the university, the hysteric, and the analyst); there are four fundamental concepts of psychoanalysis (the unconscious, repetition, the transference, and the drive); and the *sinthome* constitutes the fourth, virtual ring in the Borromean knot (of the three orders of real, symbolic, and imaginary) that ties the three other rings together (see Evans, 1996, pp. 158–159).

In this respect, Lacan shares a core interest with Jung. For, throughout the development of his psychological system, Jung demonstrated a remarkable passion for the detection of opposites and their resolution through the constellation of quaternities (see McLynn, 1996, pp. 474–475). Not only are there the four psychic functions of thinking, feeling, sensation, and intuition, but he pointed to Empedocles' four elements, Hippocrates' four "humours," the ascending quaternity of anima figures (Eve, Helen, Mary, Sophia), and the four figures of the Trinity together with the Virgin Mary, and he frequently quoted the lines from the "Cabiri Scene" of Goethe's *Faust II*: "Three have we brought, we could not/The fourth, for come he would not" (*Faust II*, ll. 8186–8187; Goethe, 1908, Part II, p. 164). Could this schematic interest in the quaternity mark the point where a *rapprochement* between Jungian and Lacanian psychology might take place?

Yet the heart of the major conceptual (and also clinical?) difference between Lacan and Jung might, however, be expressed by examining their attitude to a theme on which we have already touched—namely, religion; and, in particular, in their relation to the intellectual currents of the first three or four centuries of the Common Era, Gnosticism, and Neoplatonism.

Lacan, Jung, and Gnosticism?

Does, one wonders, Lacan really understand the religious? One feels obliged to ask this question despite—or perhaps because of—his flirtation in various ways with Roman Catholicism (see Pound, 2008). Consider, for instance, his (in)famous discussion of Bernini's remarkable statue, the *Ecstasy of Saint Teresa* at the end of his sixth session in Seminar XX, *Encore*:

> You need but to go to Rome and see the statue by Bernini to immediately understand that she's coming. There's no doubt about it. What is she getting off on? It is clear that the essential testimony of the mystics consists in saying that they experience it, but know nothing about it.
>
> *(Lacan, 1998, p. 76)*

To this analysis of Bernini's statue, we might reply with Jung: "The unconscious recasting of the erotic into something religious lays itself open to the reproach of a sentimental and ethically worthless pose" (Jung, 1991, para. 126). Leaving aside the question of ethics, Lacan's comments on Bernini's *Ecstasy of Saint Teresa* seem to point to an aesthetic deficit, or to a religious deficit, or possibly even to both.

Nevertheless, according to some commentators, there are significant affinities between Lacan and Gnosticism. For Daniel Burston, for instance, there are elements of Gnosticism in Lacan's characterization of the ego as an "imaginary function," as a creature of "specular identification," or as an illusory, artificial construct embedded in "the discourse of the other." The goal of Lacanian analysis—the deconstruction of the ego, not its support and strengthening—echoes "the ancient Gnostic view that all but a handful of *cognoscenti* fundamentally misrecognize themselves and their condition" (Burston, 2000, p. 122). One of the most striking characteristics of Gnosticism is its antagonism to the body.[9] We might therefore see a key affinity on the part of Gnosticism with Lacan, who is not interested in the body (except in its "symptoms"), and especially not in biological instincts.[10]

Lacan distinguishes strictly between instincts and drives, associating *Instinkte* in his early writings with biology (and, in his later writings, differentiating between demand, desire, and pre-linguistic need) and using *Triebe* as cultural and symbolic constructs. Surely we cannot get any further away from Jung than when, in *The Four Fundamental Concepts of Psycho-Analysis*, Lacan informs his listeners that his teaching invites them, if they are to "understand the unconscious," to "renounce" any "recourse" to "a reference to some ultimate given, something archaic, primal" (Lacan, 1978, p. 162)? Lacan's thought is a de-biologized thought. He is interested in *structures*, and these structures are (somehow) disembodied; so, Lacan's thought is a non-anatomical, non-physiological thought as well. This would arguably give rise to the question: can there, then, be such a thing as a Lacanian aesthetics?[11]

This absence of an interest in the body in Lacan's thought marks out its strongest affinity with Gnosticism; and it also seems to me that a further hallmark of Gnosticism is that, like Lacan, it does not really have a concept of the sublime (cf. Costelloe, 2013). For, strangely enough, the sublime as a category is missing from Lacan's thought. This point is made by Philip Shaw in his extremely useful primer on the subject of the sublime, where he points out that although in *The Ethics of Psychoanalysis* (1959–1960) Lacan notes that the "conjunction" of *the sublime* (as it is defined by Kant) and *sublimation* is "probably not simply an accident nor simply homonymic" (Lacan, 1992, p. 301), he does not actually explain what the significance of that conjunction is (Shaw, 2006, p. 132). Indeed, in an earlier session, Lacan had passed, in a masterful act of delegation, the task of talking about the beautiful and the sublime in Kant to another seminar participant, Pierre Kaufmann (Lacan, 1992, pp. 286–287). This is a point to which I shall return.

By contrast, Jung has a reputation for being *all too* gnostic, a reputation whose origins can be traced with some precision. For in the late 1950s, at around the time that he was working on his *Answer to Job* (1952), Jung became caught up in a controversy with the Jewish philosopher Martin Buber (1878–1965). Buber's accusation that Jung was a Gnostic was one that he, Jung, strongly rejected and, one might add, hotly disputed.[12] Yet one can see why Buber was suspicious. After all, Jung does use Gnostic vocabulary, not least in the text privately published as the *Septem Sermones ad Mortuos*, which opens with the notions of Pleroma and Creatura, and features the figure of a Gnostic deity, Abraxas. In the light of the publication of *The Red Book*, we can see that this deployment of Gnostic vocabulary is part and parcel of a larger engagement with world mythology; as evidenced, for instance, by the figure of Izdubar. Moreover, *The Red Book* is the text that makes my case: that Jung is interested in *beauty*, to be sure, but he is also interested in the *religious sublime*. I shall argue that it is *here* that the real dividing line between Lacan and Jung should be seen.

It is surely telling that when Lacan does try to develop an approach to art, he does so with reference to the theme of "the Thing" (*la chose* = *das Ding*)—and by invoking the notion, not of the sublime, but of sublimation. In his seminar on *The Ethics of Psychoanalysis*, Lacan tells us: "This Thing, all forms of which created by man belong to the sphere of sublimation, this Thing will always be represented by emptiness, precisely because it cannot be represented by anything else—or, more exactly, because it can only be represented by something else. But in every form of sublimation, emptiness is determinative" (Lacan, 1992, pp. 129–130).[13] While it is true that, as Michel Cazenave has suggested, the Thing can be read as the equivalent of some kind of originary maternal (Cazenave, 2012, comments at 27:00), it is striking that Lacan, in an entirely characteristic way, emphasizes its emptiness—*le vide*. Indeed, he thematizes it, declaring that "all art is characterized by a certain mode of organization around this emptiness," while adding (in a way that is highly significant for our discussion here) that "religion in all its forms consists of avoiding this emptiness" (Lacan, 1992, p. 130).

Now, it is true that an alternative view of sublimation and the sublime from a Lacanian perspective is offered by Paul Allen Miller when he discusses Lacan's presentation in his seminar on *The Ethics of Psychoanalysis* of Sophocles' *Antigone* as a pure model of desire. For Miller, Sophocles' *Antigone* "presents," "in its beauty," "what Lacan defines as a 'Sublime Object'" (Miller, 2007, p. 2), yet this term is not actually one used by Lacan but rather, by Slavoj Žižek, who defines it in *The Sublime Object of Ideology* (1989) as "an object raised to the level of the (impossible-real) Thing" (Žižek, 1989, pp. 202–203). Although the title of Žižek's book is indebted, as has been argued, to Lacan's *objet petit a*, understood as "an unconscious and unattainable fantasy that takes a distinct form for each individual" (Parker, 2004, 2011), the actual context of Žižek's discussion is Kant's third *Critique*, rather than Lacan on Sophocles.

It is true that Lacan, in his seminar on *The Ethics of Psychoanalysis*, describes the figure of Antigone in a way that associates her with the sublime—she has an "unbearable splendour," he says, "she has a quality that both attracts us and startles us, in the sense of intimidates us; this terrible, self-willed victim disturbs us" (Lacan, 1992, p. 247). Nevertheless, it is Žižek who really supplies the definition of the sublime in Lacanian terms, not Lacan himself. For Žižek, who is drawing on Kant and Hegel rather than directly on Lacan, the sublime is conceived "not […] as a transcendent 'Thing-in-itself' beyond the field of representation," but rather, as "an indicator of the traumatic emptiness, the primordial lack, residing at the heart of all forms of symbolization" (Shaw, 2006, p. 138). Thus, on Žižek's reading of Lacanian psychoanalysis, the sublime is "identified, via Hegel, as the 'reified' effect of the inconsistency of the symbolic order," and its fascination derives from "its status as an indicator of the Thing, the emptiness at the heart of the Real without which signification could not occur" (Shaw, 2006, p. 147). Nevertheless, the sublime as a concept is not so much an absence *for* Lacan as it is absent *from* him (yet supplemented by Žižek). One might say that when one looks for the sublime in Lacan, all one finds is an absence …

By contrast, the sublime is very much present in Jung—not as a concept (for we run here into Jung's reluctance to deal with aesthetic concepts or to conceptualize his own work in aesthetic terms), but through something even more important: its *enactment*. One can already detect the sublime in the soaring rhetoric that Jung, from time to time, deploys: one thinks, for example, of the opening paragraphs of *Transformations and Symbols of the Libido*:

> The impression made by [Freud's] simple reference [to the Oedipus legend] may be likened to that wholly peculiar feeling which arises in us if, for example, in the noise and tumult of a modern street we should come across an

ancient relic of the Corinthian capital of a walled-in column, or a fragment of inscription. Just a moment ago we were given over to the noisy ephemeral life of the present, when something very far away and strange appears to us, which turns our attention to things of another order; a glimpse away from the incoherent multiplicity of the present to a higher coherence in history.

(Jung, 1991, para. 1)

Or, then again, in the conclusion to *Answer to Job*, in a passage which in its own way exemplifies the sublime:

Even the enlightened person remains who he is, and is never more than his own limited ego before the One who dwells within him, whose form has no knowable boundaries, who encompasses him on all sides, fathomless as the abysms of the earth and vast as the sky.

(Jung, 1969, para. 758)

Yet the sublime is most unmistakably, patently, and self-evidently present in its most tangible form in the case of Jung's *Red Book* (Jung, 2009). For, while *The Red Book* is, as I have argued elsewhere, above all a quest for beauty (Bishop, 2014), this beauty is, as I have also tried to suggest, a special kind of beauty: it is a beauty beyond beauty, and from *a certain point of view* this quest for beauty also involves the sublime. And if we rightly understand the relation between the beauty and sublimity, we can understand the role that both beauty and sublimity alike play in the psychoanalytic outlook expounded by Jung. To understand this, however, we must not confuse the sublime as a *discourse* with the sublime as an *affect*.

Schiller on the sublime

Within the long and complicated history of the discourse on the sublime, from Longinus via Burke, Kant, and Hegel to Lacan and Žižek, we should not overlook the contribution of a leading poet, playwright, and aesthetician in the classical period of German culture, Friedrich Schiller (1759–1805). On the topic of the sublime, Schiller contributed two important essays, "On the Sublime" (*Vom Erhabenen*) (1793) and "Concerning the Sublime" (*Über das Erhabene*) (pub. 1801, but composed between 1794 and 1796) (Schiller, 2005, pp. 22–44, 70–85).[14] In both these essays, Schiller makes insightful remarks on beauty as well as the sublime, and it is clear that, for Schiller, beauty and the sublime are *separate*, albeit *clearly related*, concepts.

In his second essay, Schiller explains the relation of the sublime to the beautiful as follows:

Nature gives us two genii to accompany us through life. The one, sociable and comely, shortens our trouble-filled journey with its cheerful games; it eases the bonds of necessity for us, and in the midst of joy and levity it guides us to those dangerous places where we must act as pure spirits and lay aside everything corporeal, in other words, it leads us to the knowledge of truth and to the exercise of duty. Here it abandons us, since its realm is only the world of the senses and its earthly wings cannot carry it beyond this world. But then another genius steps forward, a strong-armed genius, serious and silent, that carries us across the dizzying depth.

(Schiller, 2005, p. 73)

Of course, the first of these genii is "the feeling of the beautiful"; the second is "the feeling of the sublime." What exactly *is* the sublime for Schiller? He defines it as "a mixed feeling"—"a combination of *being in anguish* (at its peak this expresses itself as a shudder) and *being happy* (something that can escalate to a kind of ecstasy)"—which, "although it is not actually pleasure, is still preferred by noble souls over all pleasure" (italics in original). He distinguishes between two kinds of "sublime object," those that relate to "our powers of comprehension" and those that relate to "our powers of living" (Schiller, 2005, p. 74). Elsewhere in this essay, Schiller distinguishes the beautiful from the sublime as follows: "Reason and sensuality harmonize in the case of what is beautiful, and only on account of this harmony does it hold any charms for us." By contrast, "in the sublime [...] there is *no* harmony of reason and sensuousness and the spell that captivates our minds lies precisely in this contradiction" (ibid., p. 75).

So these statements might prompt one to ask: why do we need the sublime at all? As Schiller explains,

In this way nature has wielded a sensuous means to teach us that *we are more than simply sensuous*. It has known how to employ even sensations to lead us to the realization that we have been subjected to their brute force in nothing less than the manner of a slave. This is a completely different effect than can be accomplished by beauty, namely, by the beauty of the actual world, since *even the sublime must lose itself in something ideally beautiful*.

(Schiller, 2005, p. 75)

In other words, the sublime is related (as is beauty, albeit in a different way) to the great Schillerian theme of *freedom*:

The sublime thus fashions for us a beautiful point of departure from the sensuous world in which the beautiful would gladly detain us forever. Not gradually (since there is no transition from dependency to freedom), but only suddenly and through a kind of shock, does something sublime tear the independent spirit loose from the net a sophisticated sensuousness uses to ensnare it.

(Schiller, 2005, p. 77)

In order to explain how this works, Schiller has recourse—as he so often does—to the classical realm, and specifically to Homer:

> Beauty in the shape of the goddess Calypso had enchanted the courageous son of Ulysses, and by the power of her charms she long held him captive on her island. Although he was simply lying in the arms of lust, he long believed he was paying homage to an immortal divinity. But suddenly, in the shape of Mentor, a sublime impression took hold of him; he recalled his higher calling, dove into the waves, and was free.
>
> *(Schiller, 2005, p. 77)*

Schiller makes use of a further classical image to convey his message in a way that would surely have been congenial to Jung—"as long as the human being was merely a slave of physical necessity" and "as long as he found no way out of the narrow circle of needs," the human being does not have a clue about "the lofty *daimonic* freedom lurking in his heart": that is, "something enduring in his own being" or "the absolute grandeur within him" (Schiller, 2005, p. 78; translation modified), what Schiller earlier calls "this discovery of an absolute, moral capability" (ibid., pp. 75–76). Indeed, on Schiller's account, the discovery of this capacity *is* the sublime: "the melancholy feeling [...] that completely distinctive, unspeakable charm, that *sublimity* that no pleasure of the sense, however noble it be, can ever compete with" (ibid., p. 77).

Hence, for Schiller, the sublime appeals to the *daimon* within each of us: indeed, on his account, there is something about the sublime that lies beyond the purely human:

> The capacity to feel the sublime is thus one of the most glorious dispositions in human nature, deserving our *respect* due to its origin in a self-sufficient capacity to think and will; because of its influence on moral human beings, it deserves as well to be developed in the most complete possible manner. The beautiful renders itself deserving on the account of the *humaneness* in a human being, the sublime on account of the *purely daimonic* in him.
>
> *(Schiller, 2005, p. 83; translation modified; italics in original)*

Thus, the sublime completes the "aesthetic education" which, in his major treatise of 1795, *On the Aesthetic Education of Humankind in a Series of Letters*, Schiller had so closely related to the beautiful:

> Because it is our calling to orient ourselves, in the face of all sensuous limitations, according to the lawbook of pure spirits, the sublime must come to the assistance of the beautiful in order to make the *aesthetic education* a complete whole and expand the human heart's sensitivity to the entire scope of our calling, extending even beyond the world of the senses.
>
> *(Schiller, 2005, pp. 83–84)*

Seen in these Schillerian terms, how do Lacan and Jung contribute to our "aesthetic education"? Lacan, it would seem, has little to contribute, whereas Jung, by contrast, has an enormous amount to contribute. For it would be impossible to understate the importance of beauty to Jung. In *The Psychology of the Unconscious*, for instance, he argues:

> It is rather the *incapacity to love which robs mankind of his possibilities*. This world is empty to him alone who does not understand how to direct his libido towards objects, and to render them alive and beautiful for himself, for Beauty does not indeed lie in things, but in the feeling that we give to them.
>
> *(Jung, 1991, para. 284, italics in original)*

Because of this investment in "objects" and the "feeling" we give them, Jung does not share Lacan's antagonism toward the body. After all, the archetypes are not simply structures; they are structures that must be embodied. As Jung puts it in one of his early Nietzsche seminars, archetypes are "images that represent typical situations of great and vital practical importance, which have repeated themselves in the course of history innumerable times" (Jung, 1989, p. 21). "All archetypes," he states, "were originally situations" (Ibid., p. 23).

Over recent years, a number of commentators have begun reading Jung in the light of Neoplatonism.[15] From the point of view of our discussion here, the important thing about the Neoplatonic tradition is that it takes a very sophisticated approach to the body and to the soul (or psyche). Its belief in order, teleology, and hierarchy, coupled with its interest in the problem of the One and the Many, is a hallmark of Jungian analytical psychology. Furthermore, the emphasis on the divine in Platonic thought is entirely compatible with Jung's notion of individuation as the path to salvation. And this leads me to a concluding point: Jung can have a notion of religion, because Jung is open to the experience of the sublime. Hence, the sublime is *the* key to the decisive difference between Lacan and Jung.

Conclusion

"And the Word became flesh, and dwelt among us": ultimately Jung is the inheritor of this tradition, not Lacan. This difference is reflected in their attitude toward the sublime: in Lacan, the sublime is neither theorized nor practiced; for Jung, it is not theorized, but it is nevertheless practiced.

For Lacan, human subjectivity is based on a split or organized around an absence. Just as entry into the Imaginary involves a moment of joy in a moment of self-(mis) recognition, followed by the devastating realization that the "ideal I" is unattainable, so the entry into the Symbolic is marked by another structuralization of loss. The *objet petit a* is (always already) missed or missing, and at the heart of the Symbolic lies a void or "the Thing," something that can never be represented yet must nevertheless be presupposed in order for reality to cohere (cf. Shaw, 2006, p. 134). As Lacan puts it in his seminar on *The Ethics of Psychoanalysis*, "the fashioning of the signifier and the introduction of a gap or a hole in the real is identical," and correspondingly "the Thing is characterized by the fact that it is impossible for us to imagine it" (Lacan, 1992, pp. 121, 125). Or, as Philip Shaw has argued, "the Thing for Lacan is a kind of non-thing; we become aware of it as a kind of void or absence residing at the heart of signification" (Shaw, 2006, p. 135).

By contrast, what Jung discovers in *The Red Book*—and what he actually *shows* us in *The Red Book*, both in its various details and in the sheer fact of its existence—is the exact opposite. Within the overall economy of *The Red Book*, a crucial turning-point comes in the moment when Jung comes to identify the tower which the Cabiri have constructed for him: "I set foot on new land [...] I serve myself and I myself serve. Therefore I have what I need" (Jung, 2009, p. 321). This tower is remarkable, not least because of how it has been constructed: "It has not arisen from a patchwork of human thoughts, but has been forged from the glowing heat of the innards; the Cabiri themselves carried the matter to the mountain and consecrated the building with their own blood," after which Jung himself "built it out of the lower and upper beyond"—recall the etymological origin of "the sublime" from the Latin *sublimis* = *sub* ("up to") and *limen* ("lintel," or top piece of a door)—"and not from the surface of the world" (Jung, 2009, pp. 321–322). Yet the tower in *The Red Book* is equally remarkable for what it represents, namely, "the happiness of [him] who surveys things [...] and who lives from himself" (Jung, 2009, p. 321). Jung tells us how, with the construction of the tower, he has acquired a kind of Goethean "permanence in change," or *Dauer im Wechsel* (Goethe, 1998, pp. 84–87), which he defines in terms of solidity:

> Thus I built a firm structure. Through this I myself gained stability and duration and could withstand the fluctuations of the personal. Therefore the immortal in me is saved [*Dadurch ist das Unsterbliche an mir gerettet*].
>
> *(Jung, 2009, p. 323)*

Now, by speaking of how he has saved what is immortal about him, Jung touches on an extremely important theme in the work of earlier thinkers, including Spinoza and Schelling, that can be traced back to Plato and finds its classic statement in a dialogue attributed to him, *Alcibiades I*.[16] For reasons of space, let me concentrate here on Spinoza, Schelling, and Schiller.

In a famous passage in the fifth and final part of his *Ethics* (pub. 1677), Baruch Spinoza (1632–1677) tells us that we know—indeed, that we *experience*—that we are "eternal":

> We feel and know by experience that we are eternal. [...] Although, therefore, we do not recollect that we existed before the body, we feel that our mind, insofar as it involves the essence of the body under the form of eternity, is eternal, and that this existence of the mind cannot be limited by time nor manifested through duration.
>
> *(Ethics, part 5, proposition 22, scholium;*
> *Spinoza, 1928, p. 385)*

When we read the question posed in Jung's *Memories, Dreams, Reflections*, "Are you related to something infinite or not?" (Jaffé, 1963, p. 356), we might well hear in it not just an echo, but a reformulation of Spinoza's invitation in this fifth part of his *Ethics* to regard the world (as he repeatedly puts it) *sub specie aeternitatis*, "under the form of eternity" (*Ethics*, part 2, proposition 44, corollary 2, and part 5, propositions 22, 23, 29 and 30; Spinoza, 1928, pp. 191, 384–385, 387–389).[17]

Spinoza's argument about the experience of our eternity recurs in a work by F. W. J. Schelling. In his *System of Transcendental Idealism* (1800), we find Schelling, in the context of a discussion of the categorical imperative (or the moral law), writing about what he calls "the eternal in me" as follows:

> [In transcendental philosophy] even the moral law is merely deduced as a condition of self-consciousness. This law originally applies to me, not insofar as I am this particular intelligence, for indeed it strikes down everything that belongs to individuality and completely destroys; it applies to me, rather, as an intelligence in general, to that which has as its immediate object the purely objective, the eternal in me [*das Ewige … in mir*].
>
> *(Schelling, 1978, p. 188)*

In other words, the moral law applies not to the individual *qua* individual, but rather, to the individual as a vehicle for, or as a bearer of, immortality; and thereby it makes us aware of what is "eternal" within us.

As we have seen, this is an important notion for Schiller as well, when he speaks of "the lofty *daimonic* freedom lurking in [our] heart," "something enduring in [our] own being," or "the absolute grandeur within us." Elsewhere, Schiller strikingly depicts this idea, writing in his poem entitled *The Ideal and Life* (*Das Ideal und das Leben*):

> When humanity's suffering surrounds you
> When Priam's son wards off the snakes
> In a pain that cannot be named, then may
> The human being become incensed! His cry
> Knock at the overarching vault of Heav'n,
> And your compassionate heart be torn!
> Let nature's terrible voice win out,
> And let the cheek of joy turn pale,
> And to sacred sympathy succumb
> What within you is immortal!
>
> *(Schiller, 2004, pp. 119–120)*[18]

If we trace this tradition even further back to its Platonic and Neoplatonic sources, its affinity with Jung's thinking becomes even clearer. In the section of the second speech of Socrates in the *Phaedrus* devoted to the soul, Socrates offers an account of "that place beyond the heavens [of which] none of our earthly poets has yet sung, and [of which] none shall sing worthily" (*Phaedrus*, 247c; Plato, 1997, p. 494). On this mythical account, the moral forms are to be found in this "place beyond the heavens," and it is here that the soul may behold them:

> It is there that true being dwells, without color or shape, that cannot be touched; reason alone, the soul's pilot, can behold it, and all true knowledge is knowledge thereof. [...] And while [the soul] is borne round she discerns justice, its very self, and likewise temperance, and knowledge [...], the veritable knowledge of being that veritably is. And when she has contemplated likewise and feasted upon all else that has true being, she descends again within the heavens and comes back home.
>
> *(Phaedrus, 247c–e; Plato, 1997, p. 494)*

In the philosophy of Plotinus, however, this account undergoes a remarkable transformation. For here, the moral forms are to be found not in "that place above the heavens," but within the soul itself, and what, in Plato, the soul sees as transcendent realities are, in Plotinus, introjected within and made part of the soul's self-vision (see editorial footnote in Plotinus, 1984, pp. 384–385):

> For it is not by running hither and thither outside of itself that the Soul understands morality and right conduct: it learns them of its own nature, in its contact with itself, in its intellectual grasp of itself, seeing deeply impressed upon it the images of its primal state.
>
> *(Ennead IV.7, §10; Plotinus, 1956, p. 354)*

It is precisely this move that Jung makes in his *Red Book*: turning from the world without to the world within, letting himself "drop" (as he puts it in *Memories, Dreams, Reflections*), and discovering an entire world of visions, images, forms, and principles *within himself*: a vision that may, stylistically speaking, be properly described as *sublime*.

Moreover, what we find time and again in this remarkable work are expressions of a *religious sublime*. In the very first chapter of *Liber primus*, "The Way of What Is to Come," we are told: "The way is within us, but not in Gods, nor in teachings, nor in laws. Within us is the way, the truth, and the life" (Jung, 2009, p. 231). In the third chapter, "Soul and God," Jung cries out to his own soul:

> I am weary, my soul, my wandering has lasted too long, my search for myself outside of myself. Now I have gone through events and find you behind all of them. For I made discoveries on my erring through events, humanity, and the world. I found men. And you, my soul, I found again, first in images within men and then you yourself I found you where I least expected you. You climbed out of a dark shaft. You announced yourself to me in advance in dreams. They burned in my heart and drove me to all the boldest acts of

daring, and forced me to rise above myself. You let me see truths of which I had no previous inkling. You let me undertake journeys, whose endless length would have scared me, if the knowledge of them had not been secure in you.

(Jung, 2009, p. 233)

Further on in *Liber primus*, in the chapter entitled "Descent into Hell in the Future," Jung comments on his vision of a blond hero, a black scarab, and a stream of thick red blood that he had had on the night of December 12th, 1913:

Depths and surface should mix so that new life can develop. Yet the new life does not develop outside of us, but within us. What happens outside us in these days is the image that the peoples live in events, to bequeath this image immemorially to far-off times so that they might learn from it for their own way; just as we learned from the images that the ancients had lived before us in events.

Life does not come from events, but from us. Everything that happens outside has already been.

(Jung, 2009, p. 239)

In the final chapter of *Liber primus*, "Resolution," we read: "Man doesn't only grow from within himself, for he is also creative from within himself. The God becomes revealed in him" (Jung, 2009, p. 253), and shortly later in this chapter Jung declares:

In the end I found that I wanted myself in everything, but without looking for myself. Therefore I no longer wanted to seek myself outside of myself, but within. Then I wanted to grasp myself, and then I wanted to go on again, without knowing what I wanted, and thus I fell into the mystery.

(Jung, 2009, p. 254)

In the conclusion to the fourth chapter of *Liber secundus*, "One of the Lowly," we find one of the most sublime moments of this most sublime of works:

The moon is dead. Your soul went to the moon, to the preserver of souls. Thus the soul moved toward death. I went into the inner death and saw that outer dying is better than inner death. And I decided to die outside and to live within. For that reason I turned away and sought the place of the inner life.

(Jung, 2009, p. 267)

And the sublimity of Jung's writing becomes more sublime still when in the central chapter of *Liber secundus*, "The Remains of Earlier Temples," he himself undergoes a transformation into a Green Man:

But I was no longer the man I had been, for a strange being grew through me. This was a laughing being of the forest, a leaf green daimon, a forest goblin and prankster, who lived alone in the forest and was itself a greening tree being, who loved nothing but greening and growing, who was neither disposed nor indisposed toward men, full of mood and chance, obeying an invisible law and greening and wilting with the trees, neither beautiful nor ugly, neither good nor bad, merely living, primordially old and yet completely young, naked and yet naturally clothed, not man but nature, frightened, laughable, powerful, childish, weak, deceiving and deceived, utterly inconstant and superficial, and yet reaching deep down, down to the kernel of the world.

[…]

Within myself I had become one as a natural being, but I was a hobgoblin who frightened the solitary wanderer, and who avoided the places of men. But I greened and bloomed from within myself. I had still not become a man again who carried within himself the conflict between a longing for the world and a longing for the spirit. I did not live either of these longings, but I lived myself and was a merrily greening tree in a remote spring forest. And thus I learned to live without the world and spirit; and I was amazed how well I could live like this.

(Jung, 2009, pp. 276–277)

This is to say nothing of the further transformations that Jung undergoes in the remainder of this work. What Jung "sees," paints, describes, and transcribes in *The Red Book*—in all senses, its "vision"—is captured well in the quotation from Coleridge that Hull felt prompted, after reading *The Red Book*, to propose as the motto that now prefaces Jaffé's introduction to *Memories, Dreams, Reflections*—"He looked into his own soul with a telescope. What seemed all irregular, he saw and shewed to be constellations: and he added to the consciousness hidden worlds within worlds" (Bair, 2003, p. 617; cf. Coleridge, 1957, no. 1798).[19]

To summarize the conclusions of this chapter: *if* there is a Lacanian sublime (and it is by no means clear that there necessarily is one), then it is a sublimity of absence: a dizzying void, a gnawing absence, or a "primordial lack." By contrast, there certainly *is* a Jungian sublime, and it is a sublimity of a profoundly religious kind. For *The Red Book* is many things—such as a "quest for beauty," or a "cathedral" for "the silent spaces of your spirit where you will find renewal" (cf. Jung's remark to Christiana Morgan; Jung, 2009, p. 216), or even something utterly mad (cf. Richard Hull's comment to William McGuire; Jung, 2009, p. 221)—and yet it is also an exercise in sublimity; albeit one that, from time to time, risks slipping from the sublime to the ridiculous. Perhaps this is what we should also see *The Red Book* as being: as an exercise in taking risks.

Notes

1   An earlier version of this chapter was given at the Joint Jung/Lacan Conference, "The Notion of the Sublime in Creativity and Destruction," co-convened by Lionel Bailly,

Bernard Burgoyne, Ann Casement, and Phil Goss, and held in St John's College, Cambridge, September 12–14, 2014. I am grateful to participants at this conference for their comments and feedback.

2 Steinthal was a pupil of Wilhelm von Humboldt, whose writings on linguistics he edited. Himself a Jew, and one of the directors of the Deutsch-Israelitische Gemeindebund, in 1860 he founded, together with the German philosopher and psychologist (and his brother-in-law) Moritz Lazarus (1824–1903), the *Zeitschrift für Völkerpsychologie und Sprachwissenschaft*, a journal dedicated to the "science" of racial psychology. In *Transformations and Symbols of the Libido*, Jung cites two papers by Steinthal: see Steinthal (1862a, 1862b).

3 On Lacan's fascination with Spinoza, see Homer (2005, pp. 3–4, 72).

4 For a fuller discussion, see the entry on "desire" in Evans (1996, pp. 35–39) as well as Lacan (2002).

5 Cf. Jung's remark: "This conception [of a continuous life impulse, the will-to-live] coincides with the idea of the Will in Schopenhauer, for we can conceive the Will objectively, only as a manifestation of an internal desire" (Jung, 1991, para. 223).

6 To be precise, Jung refers to Cicero's *Tusculan Disputations*, book 4, chapter 6 (with reference to Pythagoras, Plato, and the Stoics, especially Zeno), where a distinction is made between delight with a present and with a future good; to Sallust's observation that "rage is part of a desire," a definition developed in *The War with Catiline*, chapter 7, and his *Letter to Caesar*, chapter 13 (for further discussion of this aspect of desire, see Harris, 2001, esp. 207); and St Augustine's *The City of God*, book 14, chapter 15 (Jung, 1991, paras. 212–217).

7 For further discussion, see Cardew (2012, p. 131).

8 See Drews (1907, p. 127); cf. Plotinus (1956), *Enneads*, II.4.3–5 and 16.

9 In this respect, it is useful to compare Plotinus' attack on the Gnostics in his *Enneads*, II.9, "Against the Gnostics; or Against Those that Affirm the Creator of the Cosmos and the Cosmos Itself to be Evil."

10 For further discussion, and a defense of the view that for Lacan the body is "a reality," see Soler (1995).

11 Compare with Ruth Ronen's observation regarding Lacan's seminar on anxiety: "Lacan's aesthetics is in this sense derivative and cannot be straightforwardly applied to the aesthetic dilemma. The fact that Lacan's thought on art does not constitute an aesthetic theory yet somewhat paradoxically points at its affinity rather than distance from Kant" (Ronen, 2009, p. 26).

12 For further discussion of the Jung/Buber debate and the issues involved, see Sborowitz (1956), Progoff (1966), Erlenwein (1987), and Dourley (1994).

13 For the context of these remarks, see Lacan's earlier comments: "As far as the signifier is concerned, the difficulty is to avoid leaping on the fact that man is the artisan of his support system. For many years now I have habituated you to the notion, the primary and dominant notion, that the signifier as such is constituted of oppositional structures whose emergence profoundly modifies the human world. It is furthermore the case that those signifiers in their individuality are fashioned by man, and probably more by his hands than by his spirit. And here we encounter the linguistic usage that, at least in connection with sublimation in the sphere of art, never hesitates to speak of creation. We must now, therefore, consider the notion of creation with all it implies, a knowledge of the creature and of the creator, because it is central, not only for our theme of the motive of sublimation, but also that of ethics in its broadest sense. I posit the following: an object, insofar as it is created object, may fill the function that enables it not to avoid the Thing as signifier, but to represent it" (Lacan, 1992, p. 119).

14 For further critical discussion of these works, see Barnouw (1980) and Hinnant (2002).

15 For further discussion of Jung's interest in Neoplatonism in general and in Plotinus in particular, see Barnes (1945), Schwyzer (1975a, 1975b), Robertson (2002), and MacLennan (2006). In *Revisioning Psychology*, James Hillman drew links between Renaissance Neoplatonism and archetypal psychology (Hillman, 1975, pp. 193–211).

For the most recent discussion, see Henderson (2014) and Shaw (2016).

16 In the crucial passage in this dialogue attributed to Plato, Socrates discusses with his eponymous interlocutor the question of how the soul can know itself. In the immediately following passage, subsequently added by a later Neoplatonist, this argument is linked to a preceding discussion about the injunction of the Delphic Oracle, "know thyself," and the role of vision as a model of knowledge (*Alcibiades I*, 133c; in Plato, 1997, p. 592).

17 For further reflections on Jung's part on the eternal, see Jaffé (1963, p. 327).

18 This poem, written in 1795 and originally entitled *The Realm of the Shadows* (*Das Reich der Schatten*), was subsequently retitled *The Realm of Forms* (*Das Reich der Formen*) and given its present title. In his analysis of this poem, one commentator has emphasized that "it is absolutely vital to realise that in this poem—as elsewhere—Schiller does not advocate an ivory-tower escapism or a permanent withdrawal from the unpleasant realities of life," but rather that, "although we are seldom if ever capable of achieving absolute perfection, we should not underestimate the value of our ability to entertain in our minds the notion of perfection; and he shows how in the midst of our struggles and conflicts this thought may strengthen and sustain us," so that "thus fortified we should be better able to deal with the problems of our everyday lives" (Fowler, 1969, p. 158). In other words, the function of Schiller's poem is intended to be *therapeutic*. For further discussion of this poem, see Carus (1991) and Packer (2006); and, most recently, Bishop (2017, pp. 143–165)..

19 For further discussion of the affinities between Coleridge and Jung, see Toor (2012).

References

Bailly, L. (2009). *Lacan: A beginner's guide*. London: Oneworld.

Bair, D. (2003). *Jung: A biography*. Boston, New York and London: Little, Brown and company.

Barnes, H. E. (1945). Neo-Platonism and analytical psychology. *The Philosophical Review*, *54*(6), 558–577.

Barnouw, J. (1980). The morality of the sublime: Kant and Schiller. *Studies in Romanticism*, *19*(4), 497–514.

Bishop, P. (2014). Jung and the quest for beauty: *The red book* in relation to German Classicism. In T. Kirsch and G. Hogenson (Eds), *The red book: Reflections on C.G. Jung's "Liber novus"* (pp. 11–35). London and New York: Routledge.

Bishop, P. (2017). *On the blissful islands: With Nietzsche & Jung in the shadow of the Superman*. London and New York: Routledge.

Bodlander, R. C. (1990). Heraklit und Jung. *Analytische Psychologie*, *21*(2), 142–149.

Burston, D. (2000). *The crucible of experience: R.D. Laing and the crisis of psychotherapy*. Cambridge: Harvard University Press.

Cardew, A. (2012). The archaic and the sublimity of origins. In P. Bishop (Ed.), *The archaic: The past in the present* (pp. 93–146). London and New York: Routledge.

Carus, P. (1911). The ideal and the life: By Friedrich Schiller. *The Monist*, *21*(2), 278–284.

Cazenave, M. (2012). *Continents intérieurs*: La beauté, reflet du divin. Retrieved from www.continents-interieurs.info/Michel-Cazenave/La-beaute-reflet-du-divin (accessed 31 January 2017).

Coleridge, S. T. (1957). *The notebooks of Samuel Taylor Coleridge, 1794–1804, vol. 1*, ed. K. Coburn. London: Routledge & Kegan Paul.

Costelloe, T. M. (Ed.) (2013). *The sublime: From antiquity to the present*. Cambridge: Cambridge University Press.

Dourley, J. P. (1994). In the shadow of the monotheisms: Jung's conversations with Buber and White. In J. Ryce-Menuhin (Ed.), *Jung and the monotheisms: Judaism, Christianity and Islam* (pp. 125–145). London and New York: Routledge.

Drews, A. (1907). *Plotin und der Untergang der antiken Weltanschauung*. Jena: Diederichs.

Erlenwein, P. (1987). Individuation und Begegnung: Überlegungen zum Verhältnis von Tiefenpsychologie und Religion an Hand der Werke C. G. Jungs und M. Bubers. *Zeitschrift für Religions- und Geistesgeschichte, 39*, 69–83.

Evans, D. (1996). *An introductory dictionary of Lacanian psychoanalysis*. London and New York: Routledge.

Fowler, F. M. (Ed.) (1969). Notes, in Schiller. *Selected poems* (pp. 111–169). London: Macmillan; New York: St Martin's Press.

Goethe, J. W. (1908), *Faust: Parts I and II*, trans. Albert G. Latham. London: Dent.

Goethe, J. W. (1998). *Selected poems*, trans. J. Whaley. London: Dent.

Harris, W. V. (2001). *Restraining rage: The ideology of anger control in classical antiquity*. Cambridge: Harvard University Press.

Henderson, D. (2014). *Apophatic elements in the theory and practice of psychoanalysis: Pseudo-Dionysius and C.G. Jung*. Hove: Routledge.

Hillman, J. (1975). *Revisioning psychology*. New York: Harper & Row.

Hinnant, C. H. (2002). Schiller and the political sublime: Two perspectives. *Criticism, 44*(2), 121–138.

Homer, S. (2005). *Jacques Lacan*. London: Routledge.

Jaffé, A. (Ed.). (1963). *Memories, dreams, reflections of C.G. Jung*, trans. R. and C. Winston. London: Collins.

Jung, C. G. (1907). *Psychology of dementia præcox* [Collected works of C.G. Jung, vol. 3, pp. 1–152], trans. R. F. C. Hull. London: Routledge and Kegan Paul.

Jung, C. G. (1952). *Answer to Job* [Collected works of C.G. Jung, vol. 11, pp. 355–470], trans. R. F. C. Hull. Hove and New York: Brunner-Routledge.

Jung, C. G. (1968a). *The archetypes and the collective unconscious* [Collected works of C. G. Jung, vol. 9/i], trans. R. F. C. Hull. Princeton: Princeton University Press.

Jung, C. G. (1968b). *Psychology and alchemy* [Collected works of C.G. Jung, vol. 12], trans. R. F. C. Hull. London: Routledge and Kegan Paul.

Jung, C. G. (1969). *Psychology and religion: West and east* [Collected works of C.G. Jung, vol. 11], trans. R. F. C. Hull. Princeton, Princeton University Press.

Jung, C. G. (1989). *Nietzsche's "Zarathustra": Notes of the seminar given in 1934–1939*, ed. J. L. Jarrett, vol. 1. London: Routledge.

Jung, C. G. (1991). *Psychology of the unconscious: A study of the transformations and symbolisms of the libido: A contribution to the history of the evolution of thought*, trans. B. M. Hinkle, intr. W. McGuire. London: Routledge.

Jung, C. G. (2009). *The Red book: Liber novus*, ed. S. Shamdasani, trans. M. Kyburz, J. Peck, and S. Shamdasani. New York: Norton.

Lacan, J. (1963). Kant avec Sade. In *Écrits* (pp. 765–790). Paris: Seuil.

Lacan, J. (1966). *Ecrits: A selection*, trans. A. Sheridan. New York: Norton.

Lacan, J. (1978). *Four fundamental concepts of psycho-analysis*, ed. J.-A. Miller, trans. A. Sheridan. New York: Norton.

Lacan, J. (1991a). *Le séminaire de Jacques Lacan. Livre VIII: Le transfert, 1960–1961*, ed. J.-A. Miller. Paris: Seuil.

Lacan, J. (1991b). *The seminar The ego in Freud's theory and the technique of psychoanalysis, 1954–1955*, ed. J.-A. Miller, trans. S. Tomaselli. New York: Norton.

Lacan, J. (1992). *The seminar. Book 7: The ethics of psychoanalysis, 1959–1960*, ed. J.-A. Miller, trans. D. Porter. New York: Norton.

Lacan, J. (1998). *The seminar. Book 20: Encore 1972–1973: On feminine sexuality; the limits of love and knowledge*, trans. B. Fink. New York: Norton.

Lacan, J. (2002). *The seminar. Book VI: Desire and its interpretation, 1958–1959*, trans. C. Gallagher. London: Karnac.

MacLennan, B. J. (2006). Individual soul and world soul: The process of individuation in Neoplatonism and C. G. Jung. In T. Arzt and A. Holm (Eds). *Wegmarken der Individuation* [Studienreihe zur Analytischen Psychologie, 1] (pp. 83–116). Würzburg: Königshausen & Neumann.

McLynn, F. (1996). *Carl Gustav Jung: A Biography*. London: Bantam.

Miller, P. A. (2007). Lacan's *Antigone*: The sublime object and the ethics of interpretation. *Phoenix, 61*(1–2), 1–14.

Packer, J. M. (2006). "Zwischen Sinnenglück und Seelenfrieden": Chiasmus and symmetry in Schiller's "Das Ideal und das Leben." *Colloquia Germanica, 39*, 257–273.

Parker, I. (2004). *Slavoj Žižek: A critical introduction*. London: Pluto Press.

Parker, I. (2011). Slavoj Žižek. In *Encyclopædia Britannica*. Retrieved from https://www.britannica.com/biography/Slavoj-Zizek#toc301049 (accessed 1 June 2017).

Plato (1989). *Collected dialogues*, ed. E. Hamilton and H. Cairns. Princeton: Princeton University Press.

Plato (1997). *Complete works*, ed. J.M. Cooper. Indianapolis: Hackett.

Plotinus (1956). *The Enneads*, trans. S. MacKenna, revised B. S. Page. London: Faber and Faber.

Plotinus (1984). *Ennead IV*, trans. A. H. Armstrong. Cambridge: Harvard University Press.

Pound, M. (2008). *Žižek: A (very) critical introduction*. Michigan: Eerdmans.

Progoff, I. (1966). The man who transforms consciousness: The inner myth of Martin Buber, Paul Tillich, and C.G. Jung. *Eranos-Jahrbuch, 35*, 99–144.

Robertson, R. (2002). Stairway to Heaven: Jung and Neoplatonism. *Psychological Perspectives: A Quarterly Journal of Jungian Thought, 44*(1), 80–95.

Ronen, R. (2009). *Aesthetics of anxiety*. Albany: State University of New York Press.

Sborowitz, A. (1956). *Beziehung und Bestimmung: Die Lehren von Martin Buber und C.G. Jung in ihrem Verhältnis zueinander*. Darmstadt: Gentner.

Schelling, F. W. J. (1978). *System of transcendental idealism*, trans. P. Heath. Charlottesville: University Press of Virginia.

Schiller, F. (2004). *Sämtliche Gedichte und Balladen*, ed. G. Kurscheidt. Frankfurt am Main and Leipzig: Insel.

Schiller, F. (2005). On the sublime, concerning the sublime. In *Essays*, ed. W. Hinderer & D. O. Dahlstrom (pp. 22–44, 70–85). New York: Continuum.

Schwyzer, H.-R. (1975a). Archetyp und absoluter Geist: C.G. Jung und Plotin. *Neue Zürcher Zeitung*, July 25–26, 1975, "Literatur und Kunst", *38*.

Schwyzer, H.-R. (1975b). The intellect in Plotinus and the archetypes of C.G. Jung. In J. Mansfeld and L.M. de Rijk (eds), *Kephalaion: Studies in Greek philosophy and its continuation offered to Professor C.J. de Vogel* (pp. 214–222). Assen: Van Gorcum.

Shaw, G. (2016). Archetypal psychology, dreamwork, and Neoplatonism. In H.T. Hakl (Ed.), *Octagon: The Quest for Wholeness: Mirrored in a Library Dedicated to Religious Studies, Philosophy and Esotericism in Particular*, Vol. 2 (pp. 327–358). Gaggenau: Scientia Nova.

Shaw, P. (2006). *The sublime*. London: Routledge.

Soler, C. (1995). The body in the teaching of Jacques Lacan. *Journal of the Centre for Freudian Analysis and Research, 6*, 6–38.

Spinoza, B. (1928). *Selections*, ed. J. Wild. London: Scribner.

Steinthal, H. (1862a). Die ursprüngliche Form der Sage von Prometheus. *Zeitschrift für Völkerpsychologie und Sprachwissenschaft, 2*, 1–29.

Steinthal, H. (1862b). Die Sage von Simson. *Zeitschrift für Völkerpsychologie und Sprachwissenschaft, 2*, 129–178.

Toor, K. (2012). Dream weaver: Samuel Taylor Coleridge and the prefiguring of Jungian dream theory. Retrieved from www.friendsofcoleridge.com (accessed 31 January 2017).

Tourney, G. (1956). Empedocles and Freud, Heraclitus and Jung. *Bulletin of the History of Medicine, 30*, 109–123.

Žižek, S. (1989). *The sublime object of ideology*. London and New York: Verso.

INDEX